The Story of
Big Bend
National Park

THE STORY OF BIG

BEND

NATIONAL PARK

JOHN JAMESON

 University of Texas Press, Austin

First edition, 1996

Requests for permission to reproduce material from this work should be sent to
Permissions, University of Texas Press, Box 7819, Austin, TX 78713-7819.

⊗The paper used in this publication meets the minimum requirements of
American National Standard for Information Sciences—Permanence of Paper
for Printed Library Materials, ANSI Z39.48-1984.

LIBRARY OF CONGRESS CATALOGING-IN-PUBLICATION DATA

Jameson, John R., 1945–
    The story of Big Bend National Park / John Jameson. —1st ed.
        p.   cm.
    Includes bibliographical references and index.
    ISBN 0-292-74043-3 (alk. paper)—ISBN 0-292-74042-5 (pbk. : alk. paper)
        1. Big Bend National Park (Tex.)—History.   I. Title.
    F392.B53J37   1996
    976.4'932—dc20   96–1212

For Ernest and Marie,
Dorothy and Jim,
and my parents, who
first introduced me to
Big Bend National Park

CONTENTS

List of Illustrations ix

Preface xiii

Prologue. A "Fabulous Corner of the World": An Introduction
to Big Bend 3

1. The Campaign for Texas' First National Park 17

2. Texas Politics and the Park Movement, 1935–1944 31

3. A Park for the People from the People: Land Acquisition at
Big Bend 45

4. Promoting a Park to "Excel Yellowstone": Publicity and
Public Relations 53

5. From Dude Ranches to Haciendas: A Half-Century
of Planning 70

6. The "Predator Incubator" and Other Controversies:
Managing Natural Resources 85

7. "The Ultimate 'Tex-Mex Project'": Companion Parks
on the Rio Grande   102

8. Life and Work in a Desert Wilderness: Visitor and
Employee Experiences   121

Epilogue. Big Bend at Fifty: Into the Twenty-first Century   141

Notes   147

Bibliography   175

Index   187

ILLUSTRATIONS

Map of Big Bend National Park   6

PHOTOS

The Basin and the "Window" in the Chisos Mountains from the
   summit of Lost Mine Peak in the late 1940s   xii

Stewart L. Udall, secretary of the interior, and Lady Bird Johnson in
   the Chisos Mountains, April 1966   2

The First Lady's raft entering Mariscal Canyon   4

Lady Bird Johnson, Mr. and Mrs. Stewart Udall, and party in rubber
   raft on Rio Grande above Mariscal Canyon   5

Everett E. Townsend, the "father of Big Bend National Park"   8

An agave, or "Century Plant," high in the Chisos Mountains   9

Old building near Castolon Store before restoration   10

Old steam engine at Castolon Store   10

Oyster fossil found near Hot Springs and San Vicente   11

Mule Ear Peaks   12

Tilted blocks of limestone in Santa Elena Canyon create the illusion that the river flows uphill   13

Fishing in the Rio Grande at lower Hot Springs looking southwest into Mexico   14

Mariscal Canyon   16

The Chisos Mountains engulfed in a cloud   21

Boquillas Canyon; Sierra del Carmen range in Mexico   22

Ben Ordoney telling J. Frank Dobie's fortune with a "rifa"   24

Initial National Park Service inspection of Big Bend site in January 1934   26

Civilian Conservation Corps (CCC) tent camp in the Chisos Basin, 1934   28

Horace Morelock, chair of the Local Park Committee of the Alpine Chamber of Commerce and president of Sul Ross State Teachers College   37

A sign erected by the Texas State Parks Board to deter vandalism   41

University of Texas historian Walter Prescott Webb prepares to launch *Big Bend* and *Cinco de Mayo*, May 1937   56

Embedded in the "desert pavement" are ocotillo bushes and creosote bushes; the Chisos Mountains on the horizon   59

Quicksilver mine, Terlingua, Texas, west of the park   59

Giant Dagger from Dagger Flats   67

Judge Roy Bean's Jersey Lilly saloon before restoration   73

"Dallas Huts" in the Basin beneath Casa Grande   77

Motel units at the Lodge in the Basin   80

White-tail deer browsing   97

The Big Bend Museum building, destroyed by fire in December 1941   98

Aftermath of the fire   99

The village of Boquillas, Mexico   107

Saddle party at South Rim of the Chisos Mountains   108

Roger Toll and Daniel Galicia stand in front of two U.S. government bi-planes before their flight over the Big Bend Country   109

"The roads in Mexico at present are not the best in the world": the Boquillas–San Isidro "highway"   110

Truck and car carrying International Park Commission members stuck in the Rio Grande   110

Members of the International Commission examine grass cover and timber growth on the summit of Picacho de las Vacas in Mexico   112

International Commission members in Boquillas, Coahuila, Mexico, February 19, 1936   114

Tiled-roof cottages in the Basin two thousand feet below Casa Grande   115

The Sierra del Carmen near Jaleaucillas, Coahuila, Mexico   119

Ross A. Maxwell near Boot Spring, Chisos Mountains, January 1940   124

Superintendent Maxwell in his office   125

The Chisos Mountains from the southeast with the road between Marathon and Boquillas in the foreground, 1936   129

An arroyo near Boquillas, Mexico   131

The Tornillo Creek Bridge, a Mission 66 project   132

Another Mission 66 project, Park Headquarters at Panther Junction   132

"Dallas Huts" in the Basin   133

The view from Rio Grande Village: Sierra del Carmen range and pond   134

Camping in the Basin before improvements: A family with trailer at the foot of Casa Grande, 1945   135

Mission 66 provided the Chisos Basin campground ramadas with tables and charcoal broilers, restrooms, and campsites for tents and trailers   135

The Glenn Springs Store, site of border violence in 1916   136

Upstream view of the Rio Grande from Boquillas, Mexico   140

A family visits a "hermit's hut" in June 1959   144

The Basin and the "Window" in the Chisos Mountains from the summit of Lost Mine Peak in the late 1940s. The Basin, a popular destination for visitors, is in the center of the photograph. Photo by W. Ray Scott, National Park Concessions, Inc., National Park Service, Harpers Ferry, West Virginia.

PREFACE

In 1923 historian Walter Prescott Webb visited the Big Bend Country for the first time when he accompanied a party of Texas Rangers into the arid region. Over the years, the University of Texas professor returned to listen to reminiscences of old-timers and once even assisted with the arrest of a border desperado as he gathered material firsthand for a book on the Texas Rangers. Webb and his good friend Roy Bedichek, a faculty colleague in biology, spent one memorable Christmas holiday camped at the mouth of Santa Elena Canyon with a one-armed silk-stocking salesman for a guide. The two enjoyed themselves so much that they promised "to do at least one foolish thing each year," a vow which brought Webb back several times to the Big Bend, including a brief stint as a contract historian for the National Park Service (see Chapter 4).

Years after Webb's first visit, my parents loaded a future historian and his three brothers into the family car in Dallas for our initial trek to Big Bend National Park in the mid-1950s. Four decades and three generations later the lure of the rugged and mysterious landscape continues to draw the Jamesons back from as far away as Pullman, Washington, and Kent, Ohio. A further incentive for me to return to Big Bend was provided by Roderick Nash, a cultural and environmental historian. In 1968 Nash observed that scholars had neglected to tell the stories of many of America's national parks, including Big Bend, which gave me all the rationale I needed to combine avocation and vocation. Spurred on by Nash and inspired by Webb's example, I return as often as possible to the park, allowing equal time for the library as for field research (hiking the trails, driving the roads, watching sunsets through the Window of the Chisos Basin).

This narrative, then, is a response to Roderick Nash's charge to provide individual case studies of the units that comprise America's national parks, a system dedicated to the difficult task of preserving selected natural and cultural resources for the enjoyment of present and future generations. The story of America's twenty-seventh national park, and the first in the Lone Star State, began in the 1880s, when an El Paso editor proposed an expedition to the "Great Bend" in the Rio Grande. He was convinced that the "sublime and majestic scenery" of the border would "eclipse anything" in North America, surpassing Yellowstone and the Grand Canyon as a prospective site for a national park. Despite the editor's conviction, over five decades would pass before Congress authorized the park, and it would take another nine years before the site was open to the public.

The Story of Big Bend National Park discusses the politics, intrigues, and controversies of the park movement. Not all Texans favored the project. Some ranchers even regarded it as a "predator incubator" that provided a refuge for mountain lions to hide out in after preying on livestock outside the park. The difficult task of acquiring title to over 700,000 acres also caused friction. A few absentee landowners were upset when they found that unscrupulous developers had sold them the largely vertical Dead Horse Mountains, which appraised at one dollar an acre. Other topics include the campaign for an international (or companion) park with Mexico; publicity and public relations; managing natural resources; life and work in a remote desert wilderness; and an evaluation of the effectiveness of a half-century of planning at a park.

Although a case study of the National Park Service's management of natural, cultural, and recreational resources, *The Story of Big Bend* does not neglect the people in the story. The Big Benders include former Texas Ranger Everett E. Townsend, one of the first to suggest setting aside the Chisos Mountains as a park; Maggie Smith, proprietor of the Hot Springs store and godmother to *los pobres*, the poor ones on the border; and Albert Dorgan, World War I aviator and unemployed landscape architect, who drew up plans for a "Friendly Nations Park." It was not a faceless federal bureaucracy that administered the park, either. Ross Maxwell, the first superintendent, was considered "just as plain as an old shoe . . . the salt of the earth," who got along so well with local residents that for years one opponent of the park sent Christmas cards to the Maxwell family. Roger Toll, Yellowstone's superintendent and chief investigator of proposed sites, kept a journal of his trips to the Big Bend, including visits on both sides of the border. He regarded the area as "one of the noted scenic spectacles of the United States." *The Story of Big Bend* also describes expeditions through the canyons of the Rio Grande by geologist/explorer Robert T. Hill (1899), historian Walter Prescott Webb (1937), and Lady Bird Johnson (1966) that publicized the region and the park.

Finally, it is the story of a unique landscape and its effect on people as well as the impact of human beings on a fragile desert environment, a land of contrasts where cool mountain forests of ponderosa pine and Douglas fir look down on arid lowlands of mesquite and cactus. High overhead, a golden eagle soars above a ribbon of silver as the sun reflects off the Rio Grande far below. In the 1990s air pollution threatens the panoramic vistas of eagles and humans alike as Big Bend enters its sixth decade. The challenges of the twenty-first century will sorely test the capability of the Park Service to preserve Lady Bird Johnson's "fabulous corner of the world" for future generations.

The image of the solitary author at work is misleading, for research and writing is a team effort. I am indebted to the following, who generously contributed their time and expertise: W. Eugene Hollon, professor emeritus, University of Toledo, who first encouraged me to write about the park; Robert Kvasnicka, National Archives; Claudia Anderson, Lyndon Baines Johnson Library; Andrew Sansom, executive director, and Bill M. Collins and Jess Caldwell, Texas Parks and Wildlife Department; Jim Steely, Texas Historical Commission; Ronnie C. Tyler, director, Texas State Historical Association; Karen Andrews, cartographer; Mary Moody, photographer, Denison, Texas; and Nancy Myers, word processor and departmental secretary, who coordinated the project. National Park Service people in Washington, D.C.; Harpers Ferry, West Virginia; Santa Fe, New Mexico; and Big Bend also have been most helpful, especially Tom Alex, Frosty Bennett, Tom DuRant, Mike Fleming, Arthur Gomez, Mark Herberger, and Ramón

Olivas. The staff and editors at the University of Texas Press made the process of preparing a manuscript for publication, which can be a grueling process indeed, downright pleasant. In particular, I want to thank Shannon Davies, acquisitions editor, Lois Rankin, manuscript editor, and Nancy Warrington, copy editor. Travel and research grants from Washington State University and Kent State University helped underwrite trips to Washington, D.C.; Austin, Texas; and Big Bend National Park.

The editors of *The Public Historian, Forest and Conservation History, West Texas Historical Association Year Book,* the Texas Western Press, and the University of Toledo Press graciously gave me permission to use ideas or portions of the manuscript previously published in their journals, series, or anthology. Full citations are in the bibliography.

Three generations of Jamesons and other family and friends have contributed to *The Story of Big Bend* in many ways. Over the years, my "correspondents" have clipped and sent newspaper and magazine articles on the park that have filled a filing-cabinet drawer. Ernest and Marie Dickinson, my wife's parents, have accompanied me on expeditions to the park and conducted research in the Federal Records Center in Fort Worth. Bob and Molly Jameson, my parents, not only introduced me to the Big Bend Country, but have also assisted with research, most recently at Harpers Ferry. Perhaps most enjoyable has been the "field research," or visits to the park, where my wife Suzy, sons John, Jr., and Andrew, and yours truly, along with family and friends, have shared Big Bend experiences. Of course, any errors of fact or interpretation are my own responsibility.

The Story of
Big Bend
National Park

Stewart L. Udall, secretary of the interior, and Lady Bird Johnson in the Chisos Mountains, April 1966. Photo by Robert L. Knudsen, Lyndon Baines Johnson Library.

PROLOGUE

A "Fabulous Corner of the World": An Introduction to Big Bend

According to local folklore, an old forgotten cowboy at the turn of the century gave directions to the Big Bend by telling travelers to "go south from Fort Davis until you come to the place where rainbows wait for rain, and the big river is kept in a stone box, and water runs uphill. And the mountains float in the air, except at night when they go away to play with other mountains." Decades later, Secretary of the Interior Stewart L. Udall described the "awesome, silent splendor of Big Bend" with its "spectacular mountain and desert scenery, the myriad of wildly improbable geological structures, all enclosed in the great bend of the Rio Grande," all of which "combine to provide an unearthly sense of visiting another world." [1]

Secretary Udall had visited Big Bend National Park in April 1966 with First Lady Mrs. Lyndon Johnson. The purpose of the trip was to promote the See America First campaign and to call attention to the fiftieth anniversary of the National Park Service, an agency in the Department of the Interior. Liz Carpenter, Mrs. Johnson's press secretary, was in charge of planning the itinerary and travel arrangements for over seventy press and White House staff. Big Bend's remote and arid location created a few problems and anxieties for such a large group. To reassure her traveling companions, Carpenter wrote on the itinerary handout, "You are headed for wide open spaces. It is two hours to ev-

The First Lady's raft entering Mariscal Canyon. National Park Service, Harpers Ferry, West Virginia.

erything! Relax, take a tranquilizer, enjoy the landscape. It's bigger than all outdoors. It is all outdoors! Get with the wilderness spirit!" Only half-jokingly she had written a warning to the pilot of the chartered American Airlines Electra to "please watch for cattle and antelope on runway" at the Presidio County Airport. Sure enough, as the plane landed a herd of antelope scampered out of the way. Carpenter arranged for a modern-day "Pony Express"—the code name for National Park Service ranger Bill Newbold—to pick up the journalists' stories and photographs at stops along the two-hour bus drive from the airport to Big Bend. Newbold delivered them to the airline captain at Presidio, who then flew to Love Field in Dallas where representatives of the various newspapers, magazines, and wire services met the plane.[2]

Activities for the First Lady and the secretary of the interior (Mrs. Udall also accompanied her husband) included a barbecue and a hike up Lost Mine Trail with a ranger on horseback for security. As Mrs. Johnson stood on the ridge between Juniper Canyon and Green

Lady Bird Johnson, Mr. and Mrs. Stewart Udall, and party in rubber raft on Rio Grande above Mariscal Canyon. Photo by Robert L. Knudsen, Lyndon Baines Johnson Library.

BIG BEND NATIONAL PARK

SANTIAGO MOUNTAINS

385

Persimmon Gap

Persimmon Gap
Ranger Station

TEXAS

Alpine   Marathon

20

90

385

118

90

10

Big Bend
National Park

Harte
Ranch

Dagger
Mountain

Pitcock
Rosillos
Mountains
Ranch

Tornillo Flat

SIERRA DEL CARMEN MTNS.

DEAD HORSE MTNS

UNITED STATES

MEXICO

to Big Bend Ranch
State Natural Area

Study
Butte

Terlingua

118

Terlingua Creek

Park Headqtrs.

Banta
Shut-in

Tornillo Creek

The Window

Lost Mine
Peak

Maverick
Ranger
Station

Ross Maxwell
Scenic Drive

The
Basin

Green Gulch

Pine Canyon

Nugent
Mtn.

Juniper Canyon

Mesa de Anguila

Blue Creek

South Rim
MOUNTAINS

Rio Grande
Village

Boquillas C.

Santa Elena Canyon

SIERRA PONCE

CHISOS

SIERRA
QUEMADA

Glenn
Springs

Hot Springs

Boquillas

Mule Ear
Peaks

Castolon

Santa
Elena

Johnson's
Ranch

Rio Grande

UNITED
STATES

MEXICO

Mariscal Canyon

CHIHUAHUA
COAHUILA

N

——— Road

- - - Primitive Road

· · · · · Trail

0 1   5   10 miles

0 1   5   10 kilometers

Gulch in the Chisos Basin, she commented that "This looks like the very edge of the world." At the end of the first day, she concluded that the Big Bend was indeed "wild country, completely untamed by man, but a good place to come to get your troubles in perspective." In the evening the entourage returned to the cabins in the Chisos Basin.[3]

The highlight of the Big Bend visit was a six-hour, eleven-mile float trip through Mariscal Canyon on the Rio Grande. William Blair, special correspondent to the *New York Times*, wrote that it was a "wonder" that the First Lady "survived" the adventure. After getting his readers' attention, he explained that there never was any danger, just "traffic jams" which "resembled Times Square at rush hour" as the twenty-four rubber rafts drifted through the shallow (12″–20″ deep) and narrow river at a speed of two m.p.h. Mrs. Johnson and Mrs. Udall even paddled for twenty-five minutes to give the secretary and the accompanying park ranger a rest. Along the route Mrs. Johnson admired the wildflowers clinging to the canyon walls. Other than occasional Canyon Wrens, White-throated Swifts, and Turkey Buzzards circling above the canyon walls, and feral burros on the Coahuila side, she saw little wildlife. Adding an international touch, four Mexican nationals standing in the shade of riverbank trees shouted greetings to the First Lady. Unknown to Mrs. Johnson, the foursome concealed a stack of candelilla bundles to smuggle across the river. The wax of the plant was used in a variety of products such as chewing gum and shoe polish. At the conclusion of the float trip, Liz Carpenter summed it up as "a wild experience."[4]

The First Lady really did seem to enjoy herself and appreciated the beauty of the park and its environs, an area she had long wanted to visit. Back at the White House later that month, Mrs. Johnson wrote Conrad Wirth, a good friend and former director of the Park Service, about "that fabulous corner of the world." She recalled "watching the Sierra del Carmen mountains about sunset as we had barbecued steaks under the cottonwood trees . . . There was every hue of blue, lavender and mist color and the changing light made them look quite magical."[5]

Big Bend had impressed earlier travelers as well. In 1872, over ninety years before the First Lady's visit, Englishman Frank Collinson came to the United States and worked as a cowboy across the Southwest. In September 1882, he climbed onto the rim of Santa Elena Canyon and "drank in the magnificent view, the finest I had seen during my sojourn in the Southwest. There were the mountain ranges of the Big Bend, the Santiago, the Chisos. It was a breath-taking view." Later Collinson would return to ranch in the Big Bend Country from 1888 to 1895 when he left, calling the harsh arid environment "another Pharaoh's Dream—a few good years are followed by more lean years, which eats up all that the good years have made, and then some."[6]

Former Texas Ranger Everett Townsend remembered vividly the first time he saw the Chisos Mountains on August 31, 1894. For Townsend the scenery "was so awe inspiring" that it "touch[ed] the soul of a hardened human bloodhound trained in the relentless service of the Texas Rangers." In fact, he claimed to have seen "God as [I] had never seen Him before." He wrote down the experience in his scout book and vowed "that upon the arrival of my ship I would buy the whole Chisos Mountains as a hunting and playground for myself and friends and that when no longer wanted I would give it to the State."[7]

In 1899 geologist-explorer Robert T. Hill offered a different perspective, this time from the depths of one of the canyons. Here he spent three days blocked by the rock slide within Santa Elena Canyon. "The scene within this cañón is of unusual beauty," he wrote. "The austerity of the cliffs is softened by colors which camera or pen cannot reproduce. These rich tints are like the yellow marble of Portugal and Algiers, warmed by reddening tones which become golden in the sunlight."

Hill could not always find fitting similes for what he saw. "Every other aspect of the Big Bend Country—landscape configuration, rocks, and vegetation—is weird and strange," he wrote, "and of a type unfamiliar to the inhabitants of civilized lands." The Terlingua Desert, according to Hill, was "one of the most bizarre pieces of landscape that can be imagined," and the Chisos Mountains (*los Chisos,* the ghosts) were "weird forms . . . appropriately named." From

Everett E. Townsend, left, with unidentified man. Townsend, the "father of Big Bend National Park," earned the title from a lifetime devoted to the park movement. Photo by George A. Grant, National Park Service, Harpers Ferry, West Virginia.

painful firsthand experience he described the "spiteful vegetation" which "wounded, caught, held, or anchored . . . at every step away from the beaten trails." Climbing out of a canyon's depths, he observed the contrast between "the green ribbon of river" and the "stony, soilless hills," noting that the "sight of this aridity almost within reach of the torrent of life-giving waters below . . . was shocking and repulsive."[8] Nevertheless, Hill's fascination with the beautiful, the "weird and strange," overshadowed his aversion to the harsh desert. The article Hill published in *Century Magazine* in 1901 on the expedition through the canyons of the Big Bend would influence legislators decades later to set aside the unique area as a park.

Authorized on June 20, 1935, an Act of Congress established Big Bend as the twenty-seventh national park on June 12, 1944. Located on the 108-mile boundary[9] along the "elbow" the Rio Grande makes on the United States–Mexico border south of El Paso, the park contains over 800,000 acres (about the size of Rhode Island) in southern Brew-

An agave, or "Century Plant," high in the Chisos Mountains. Contrary to its name, after 25 years or so, the plant blooms in a prolific growth spurt, then dies. Photo by M. Woodbridge Williams, National Park Service, Harpers Ferry, West Virginia.

(*Left*) Old building near Castolon Store before restoration. (*Right*) Old steam engine at Castolon Store. Photos by Fred Mang, Jr., National Park Service, Harpers Ferry, West Virginia.

ster County, Texas in the Trans-Pecos region. Arid to semi-arid (5″– 20″ annual precipitation) in climate, it lies in the northern portion of the Chihuahuan Desert. The topographical and climatic extremes of mountain, desert, and river provide habitats for a variety of plants and animals, including cottontail rabbits, jackrabbits, collared peccaries (or javelinas), pocket mice, kangaroo rats, gray and kit foxes, coyotes, badgers, mountain lions (locally called panthers), beavers, bobcats, pocket gophers, raccoons, Golden Eagles, Cliff Swallows, Roadrunners, copperheads and four species of rattlesnakes, leopard frogs, eleven species of stinging scorpions, tarantulas, Green-winged Teals, blue catfish, long-nosed gars, claret cup cactus, bluebonnets, lechuguilla plants, tamarisks (or salt cedar, an exotic tree), thistles, prickly poppies, and rock-nettle—to give a representative sample. Several species in the United States can only be found at Big Bend: the Del Carmen whitetail deer, the Colima Warbler, and the drooping juniper. One plant species, the Chisos agave, grows nowhere else in the world. Relict flora surviving from the late Pleistocene era in the Chisos Mountains are Ponderosa pine, Arizona cypress, and Douglas fir, living fossils from the Ice Age.[10] All told, Big Bend is home to over 1,000 species of plants, 3,368 insects, 78 mammals, 71 reptiles and amphibians, about 36 fish, and 434 birds (more than any other U.S. park and over one-half the species of birds in North America). No other national park has as many cacti; more than 70 kinds grow in Big Bend, and within an hour's drive there are another dozen varieties. Endangered species found at Big Bend are the Peregrine Falcon, Black-capped Vireo, Mexican long-nose bat, and Big Bend gambusia (a tiny fish discovered only in the ponds of the park).[11]

Humans came relatively late (over ten thousand years ago), and often just passed through on their way to less hostile environments, leaving campsites in caves and rock shelters. Nevertheless, the park archaeologist estimates there are over ten thousand sites at Big Bend from the Late Paleo-Indian (8000–6500 B.C.), Archaic (6500 B.C.–A.D. 1000), Late Prehistoric (A.D. 1000–1535), and Historic eras (A.D. 1535–present) representing the Jornado Mogollon, Chisos, Jumano, Mescalero Apache, and Comanche Indians, among others. Nine National Register archaeological and historic sites or districts document the Indian and Anglo-Mexican presence: Castolon Historic District (trading post), Hot Springs Historic District (recreational and therapeutic springs), Mariscal Mining District, Homer Wilson Ranch Site, Rancho Estelle, Luna's Jacal (a Mexican goatherd's abode) and three archaeological sites. The prehistoric and historic activities occurred over ten millennia during which the Big Bend emerged from the end of the Ice Age, passed through a brief wet period when woodlands covered much of the area, and gradually evolved into its present form and climate, the best example in the United States of the Chihuahuan Desert.[12]

The climate changes during human occupation are but the blink of an eye in geological time. The National Park Service considers Big Bend "one of

Oyster fossil found near Hot Springs and San Vicente. National Park Service, Harpers Ferry, West Virginia.

the outstanding geological laboratories and classrooms of the world."
According to Apache legend, after creating the universe, the Great
Spirit tossed a large pile of leftover boulders and debris on the Big
Bend. In fact, over 300 million years of the earth's history are visible to
visitors. There are limestone mountains and marine fossils deposited
by seas which covered the area during the Paleozoic ("ancient life") and
Mesozoic ("middle life") eras 350 to 135 million years ago. During the
late Cretaceous period (75 million years ago) the seas receded, giving
way to marshes and forests. Fossils of ferns, petrified trees, dinosaurs,
and flying reptiles were left, including a specimen of a pterodactyl with
a wingspan of thirty-five to thirty-eight feet, the largest flying creature
ever. Other recovered fossils of note are a large bivalve (an early oyster)
three feet by four feet, the skulls of two crocodile-like dinosaurs (each
six feet long), and the intact skull of a chamosaurus (a horned dinosaur).
During the late Cretaceous and early Tertiary periods of the Cenozoic
era (100 to 40 million years ago), tectonic forces (earthquakes, folds,
faults) in the earth's crust created the Rocky Mountains and the Sierra
Madre, which includes the Sierra del Carmen and Mariscal and San
Vicente anticlines in the Big Bend Country. Block faulting caused the

Mule Ear Peaks. Photo by George A. Grant, National Park Service, Harpers
Ferry, West Virginia.

Sunken, tilted blocks of limestone in Santa Elena Canyon create the optical illusion that the river flows uphill. Photo by M. Woodbridge Williams, National Park Service, Harpers Ferry, West Virginia.

Fishing in the Rio Grande at lower Hot Springs looking southwest into Mexico. Photo by Matt Dodge, National Park Service, Harpers Ferry, West Virginia.

central portion of the park, between the Santiago Mountains to the east and the Mesa de Anguila-Sierra Ponce to the southwest, to drop (Sunken Block), which forced up the Chisos Mountains. The topography of the Big Bend is so barren and jagged that America's astronauts in the 1960s took field trips to the park to prepare them for landing on the moon.[13]

The first mammals in Texas appeared 40 to 100 million years ago in the Big Bend, including ancestors of the panther, hippopotamus, and horse. The fossil bones of some of these extinct animals can be viewed at the exhibit near the Tornillo Creek bridge. About 30 million years ago during the late Eocene period, volcanic activity began and continued for over 15 million years. Big Bend had two volcanoes, one at Sierra Quemada, the other in the vicinity of Pine Canyon, both of which poured out ash and lava visible in the park today as dikes, laccoliths, plugs, and volcanic rocks. Well-known landmarks on the Ross Maxwell

Scenic Drive, for example, are Mule Ear Peaks, two dikes left standing when weaker surrounding rock eroded away. The geological forces of volcanism and tectonics mostly ceased eons ago, but erosion caused by wind, sheet flow from flash flooding, and the relentless flow of the Rio Grande continues to shape the topography of the Big Bend. As the river carves deep canyons through Cretaceous limestone, it exposes sunken, tilted blocks, creating an optical illusion of a stream flowing uphill.[14]

Fascination with this strange, ghostly, even magical corner of the world lures an average of 230,000 people each year to Big Bend, a figure well below other national parks. Activities include viewing exhibits in the visitor centers, hiking, river rafting, fishing, horseback riding, birding, camping, and desert exploration; Park Service staff schedule interpretive programs year-round. Many visitors also enjoy panoramic vistas, a sunset from the Basin high in the Chisos, or the chance to escape to the solitude they find in a remote desert wilderness. A recent poll of over two thousand readers of *Texas Highways* magazine rated the park as one of the Lone Star State's "top tourist attractions" (6th), "favorite vacation destinations" (2d), "top camping areas" (1st), and "scenic drives to remember" (2d).[15] Yet despite its current popularity, the scenic and recreational attractions of the Big Bend Country were not always well known, even to Texans.

Mariscal Canyon. Photo by Jean Speiser, National Park Service, Harpers Ferry, West Virginia.

ONE

The Campaign for Texas' First National Park

In 1916 on the eve of America's entry into the First World War, Sergeant Jodie P. Harris of Mineral Wells was stationed with Company I, 4th Texas Infantry, at Stillwell Crossing on the Rio Grande guarding the border during the Mexican Revolution. To boost morale, he published a four-page, hand-lettered service newspaper, *The Big Bend*. The versatile Harris served as reporter, artist, and editor. He also drew cartoon postcards about a soldier's life on the border, which were put on his hometown drugstore bulletin board. On one postcard he portrayed two officers discussing the Big Bend. A Major Coulter of the 10th Pennsylvania Infantry calls it "a wonderful country—molded by nature for a park." A Captain Davis in Harris's Company I agrees: "Sure! It's great! When we get back home let's start a move to make it a NATIONAL PARK." When the soldiers returned home, they publicized the Big Bend, which in turn encouraged others to visit throughout the 1920s. Nevertheless, as the decade drew to a close, the Lone Star State still did not have a national park almost sixty years after the establishment in 1872 of Yellowstone, the nation's first. But it was not because Texans hadn't tried.[1]

One of the earliest documented attempts to establish a park at Big Bend occurred in 1883 when the editor of the *El Paso Daily Times* asked other West Texas newspaper executives to finance an expedition to explore the "Great Bend" in the Rio Grande. He was convinced that the "sublime and majestic scenery" of the border region would "eclipse anything that has heretofore been produced within the limits of North America," even surpassing Yellowstone and the Grand Canyon. After sixteen years of delays geologist-explorer Robert T. Hill finally led an expedition in 1899 through the canyons of the Big Bend. Although Hill published an article on his trip in 1901, a national park for Texas was still decades away.[2]

Texas politicians also had tried for years to accomplish this objective, but to no avail. One of the first was United States Congressman John H. Stephens from Wichita Falls, who had sponsored bills in 1908, 1911, and 1915 to create Palo Duro Canyon National Forest Reserve and Park near Amarillo. He considered the area "the finest natural park in the entire Southwest." When none of his bills passed, Stephens complained that the largest state in the union still had neither a national park nor a forest reserve.

The local press and chambers of commerce throughout the Texas Panhandle and the Red River regions of Texas, Oklahoma, and Louisiana endorsed Stephens's Palo Duro project. Two of the most influential groups were the Texas Federation of Women's Clubs and the Red River Improvement Association. The latter included in its membership congressmen whose districts bordered the Red River. Its president was U.S. Representative Morris Sheppard of Texarkana, later elected to the United States Senate, and an unwavering champion for a national park in Texas.

Yet even with such strong support, Stephens's proposal had little chance of success, for it required the cooperation of two federal rivals— the Departments of Agriculture and Interior—to administer a combined national forest watershed and a national park. The rift between the ideologically opposed agencies had widened in the years following the Hetch Hetchy controversy in 1913 when the Forest Service's Gifford Pinchot in the Department of Agriculture had defended the construction of a water reservoir in Yosemite National Park for the city of San Francisco. Perhaps if Stephens had presented separate bills, one for a national park at Palo Duro Canyon and the other for a national forest along the Red River, he might have had more success. Regrettably, the Congressman never got the chance before he retired from politics in 1918.[3]

The 1920s and early 1930s produced a flurry of activity in Texas directed toward the creation of national and state parks. In 1923 at Governor Pat Neff's urging, the 33d Legislature established a State Parks Board, but neglected to appropriate funds for land acquisition or maintenance. Seven years later, with the Great Depression in its early months, the State Democratic Convention meeting in Galveston called for an expanded system of state parks and asked the Texas congressional delegation to acquire at least one national park for the Lone Star State, sentiments likewise echoed by Governor Ross Sterling in his inaugural address in 1931.[4]

The worsening depression and the creation of the Civilian Conservation Corps (CCC) by Congress on March 31, 1933, finally encouraged the Texas legislature to establish over the next eight years more than three dozen state parks, including one in the Big Bend Country. The CCC set up camps in most national and a few selected state parks, providing funds for their operation and development and jobs for thousands of unemployed young men.[5]

The Texas legislature also continued its efforts to gain a national park. In 1931, it adopted Senate Concurrent Resolution 9, which demanded "an immediate survey" of Texas' scenic areas to determine if they measured up to national park standards. Two years later Senate Concurrent Resolution 73 noted that the state still did not have a national park or forest and called for its creation "to assist the unemployment situation in Texas." Senator Morris Sheppard obtained a copy of S.C.R. 9, which he published verbatim in the *Congressional Record,* and sent a copy to Secretary of the Interior Ray Lyman Wilbur requesting that the survey "be made at an early date." Wilbur gave Sheppard's letter to Horace M. Albright, director of the National Park Service, who wrote the senator that the Park Service had six projects under consideration in Texas: Davis Mountains in Jeff Davis County, Guadalupe in Culberson and Hudspeth Counties, McKittrick Canyon in Culberson County, Palo Duro in Randall County, Alto Frio Canyon in Uvalde County, and Texas within Jeff Davis, Brewster, Presidio, Pecos, Culberson, and Hudspeth Counties. Albright indicated that in due time the NPS would examine each of the proposals, but there were "almost one hundred other proposed projects on record for investigation, some with very decided priority rights."[6]

Albright's terse response reflected the director's frustrations over what he regarded as major threats to the quality and integrity of the national park system with the addition of substandard sites. To a private correspondent, Albright admitted his disapproval of S.C.R. 9 and a similar request from the state of Florida. "The underlying idea," he wrote, "is the selection of a National Park within a State, thereby perhaps stressing the idea of location for a park rather than the idea of scenic grandeur irrespective of state lines." According to Albright, if a state's scenery were not already well known, "there was no use to hunt for it" as a site for a national park. Albright feared that such a policy, dictated as it was by local and state politics, would eventually result in a system of mediocre parks national in name only.[7]

The director's high standards prescribed that a prospective national park site must have "scenery of quality so unusual and impressive, or natural features so extraordinary as to possess national interest and importance as contradistinguished from merely local interest." Worthy criteria indeed, but Albright had mistakenly assumed that no remote areas of outstanding natural beauty or national worth existed that remained unknown both to local citizens and to the Park Service. Obviously at this time Albright was ignorant of the Everglades in Florida or Big Bend in Texas. He was not alone. A local resident of isolated Brewster County estimated that ninety-nine percent of his fellow Texans were not aware of Big Bend's striking scenic and natural attractions.[8]

The Park Service concentrated instead on other areas in West Texas. The first to receive serious consideration as a national park site was the Guadalupe Mountains. The NPS viewed the Guadalupes as a possible extension to Carlsbad Caverns or as a separate national park. In September 1934, the Park Service recommended the latter choice to the secretary of the interior, but nothing was done about it until Congress finally authorized Guadalupe Mountains National Park in 1966, the second national park created in Texas. Of the remaining five sites, prior to 1934 none specifically included the geographical landmarks in southern Brewster County that today comprise Big Bend National Park: the Chisos Mountains and Boquillas, Mariscal, and Santa Elena Canyons on the Rio Grande.[9]

Nevertheless, Park Service officials maintained that their inventory of potential sites in Texas did include Big Bend, which had been filed under "Texas National Park." Yet no Big Bend documents were in the file. Instead, the Texas National Park folder contained proposals for national parks in Jeff Davis and Presidio Counties. United States Congressman C. B. Hudspeth of El Paso introduced a bill in 1924 and again in 1929 to create a national park in Jeff Davis County. His bills died in

The Chisos Mountains engulfed in a cloud. Photo by M. Woodbridge Williams, National Park Service, Harpers Ferry, West Virginia.

the House Committee on Public Lands. In 1933 the Texas National Park idea emerged again when the owner of 23,000 acres in Presidio County offered to donate the land for a state park if legislators would cancel a $10,000 debt he owed the state. They refused, and D. E. Colp, chairman of the Texas State Parks Board (TSPB), suggested to the National Park Service that the federal government purchase the land for a park. Colp inadvertently doomed any chance of this happening when he informed Conrad Wirth, the Park Service official in charge of acquisitions, that the TSPB had only planned to develop the land for recreation rather than for its scenic qualities. "Apparently," Wirth concluded, "this area is not of national park standards." In January 1933 it was removed from the list of proposed parks.[10]

Clearly, the 23,000 acres in Presidio County and Hudspeth's proposal in Jeff Davis County did not include southern Brewster County, the location of today's Big Bend National Park. The Texas National Park proposal embraced a huge area of 25,460 square miles in six of the Lone Star State's largest counties. Furthermore, it contained three of

Boquillas Canyon, left center; Sierra del Carmen range in Mexico to right.
National Park Service, Harpers Ferry, West Virginia.

the other sites under investigation by the NPS: Davis Mountains, Guadalupe, and McKittrick Canyon. Apparently, as of January 1933, the
Park Service still had not discovered the Big Bend Country. Meanwhile, local boosters had already taken steps that would bring the region
to the attention of Texans and others, including NPS officials and
President Franklin Roosevelt.

The first step was taken when Abilene's Representative R. M. Wagstaff read a copy of the December 1930 *Nature Magazine*, an issue devoted entirely to Texas. An article by J. Frank Dobie, a folklorist on the
English faculty at the University of Texas, caught Wagstaff's attention.
Dobie pointed out that the Lone Star State had not set aside any of its
millions of acres of public lands for parks. He recommended several
ideal sites: the Hill Country around Austin, the Gulf Coast, and the
"wild Big Bend." Another article focused on the Big Bend Country
itself, and featured throughout the magazine were photographs of the

Rio Grande's magnificent canyons. Wagstaff consequently decided to introduce a bill to establish a state park at Big Bend during the second session of the 42d Texas Legislature. After talking with T. H. Walker, the land commissioner, Wagstaff changed his mind. Walker pointed out that although the state owned several thousand acres in the Big Bend vicinity, private individuals had acquired options to purchase a few parcels of land but had neglected to make interest payments to the state. Since the policy of the General Land Office was to notify delinquent landholders when condemnation proceedings began, they would have the opportunity to pay the interest and exercise their purchase options. But if Wagstaff delayed until the next session of the legislature, the options would have expired. Wagstaff, himself a lawyer, followed Walker's advice.[11]

While he waited, Wagstaff, who had not seen Big Bend firsthand, obtained a copy of Robert Hill's *Century Magazine* article on his expedition through the canyons of the Rio Grande. The pictures and descriptions so impressed Wagstaff that he asked retired Texas Ranger E. E. Townsend about their accuracy. Townsend was the representative for the Eighty-seventh District, which included Brewster County. When Townsend confirmed that the scenery was truly outstanding, Wagstaff purportedly said, "Then why don't you do something about it?" The Abilene representative now considered that Big Bend had the potential to become "one of the grandest parks in the nation." Townsend, as we know, was already a convert and had been saying the same thing since the summer of 1894. Discouraged that he would never be able to purchase the area, he likewise had despaired "of ever seeing it [a park] put through as a State or Governmental development." Wagstaff's interest revived the project.[12]

On March 2, 1933, Texas Independence Day, Wagstaff, with Townsend's encouragement, introduced House Bill 771 to create Texas Canyons State Park on fifteen sections of land in the vicinity of Santa Elena, Mariscal, and Boquillas Canyons. The bill was referred to the appropriations committee, where testimony was heard from Townsend, who had polled his constituents and reported their enthusiastic support for the project. He also showed his fellow legislators a portfolio of scenic photographs, many taken by W. D. Smithers, who had been photographing the Big Bend Country since his arrival there in 1916. Another effective lobbyist was J. Frank Dobie, author of the article that first caught Wagstaff's attention and a former professor at Sul Ross

Ben Ordoney, left, telling J. Frank Dobie's fortune with a "rifa," a custom-made fortune-telling device, April 1938. Big Bend National Park, National Park Service.

State College in Alpine before joining the University of Texas faculty. Speaker Coke Stevenson laid the bill before the House on May 19, where with minor revisions it passed 90–27. Senator Ken Regan of Pecos sponsored the bill in the state senate, and with the legislative session drawing to a close, he deftly guided the bill through to a 26–3 victory on May 24. Back in the House for concurrence, it passed by an even larger margin than the first time, 109–3. After several more procedural steps, it reached the desk of Governor Miriam "Ma" Ferguson on May 27, where she signed it.[13]

Three months later in August 1933, President Franklin D. Roosevelt approved four CCC camps for Texas, one "near Big Bend Park in Brewster County." Wagstaff and Townsend subsequently introduced separate bills in the House that added over 150,000 acres to the park, including the Chisos Mountains. Both were reported favorably out of the Committee on Public Lands and Buildings. Since Townsend's bill was first on the calendar, Wagstaff tacked his on as an amendment. Its main provision was to change the park's name to Big Bend. The amended bill easily passed on both sides of the legislature, and on October 27, the last day of the session, Governor Ferguson signed it into law. Big Bend's 225,000 acres ranked it as Texas' largest state park.[14]

Townsend meanwhile continued to campaign for a national park at Big Bend. Throughout the summer and fall of 1933 he sent a barrage of letters and photographs to the Park Service, which included several of Smithers's panoramic aerial prints that captured the vastness and contrasting beauty of the area's desert, canyon, river, and mountain landscapes.[15] Because of the tenacity of Townsend, the effective lobbying of the Brewster County Chamber of Commerce for a CCC camp, and the efforts of other boosters in Alpine, Marfa, Fort Stockton, San Angelo, El Paso, and elsewhere, the still relatively unknown Big Bend Country finally attracted the attention of the NPS.

The agency was responsible for designating and supervising CCC camps in national and state parks. Roger Toll, superintendent of Yellowstone and, in the off season, chief investigator of proposed national park and national monument sites, inspected the Big Bend for four days in January 1934, accompanied by Townsend, historian J. Evetts Haley, and a half-dozen others. Superintendent Toll's subsequent report endorsed the Big Bend area for a national park, calling it "decidedly the outstanding scenic area of Texas" with the "promise of becoming one of the noted scenic spectacles of the United States." He also recommended construction of a CCC camp at Santa Elena Canyon, since the prospect of finding water in the Chisos Basin seemed remote.[16]

Toll, born and raised in Denver, Colorado, began his Park Service career in 1919 after he had a chance encounter in Hawaii with Stephen Mather, the first director of the Park Service. Mather had had his eyes on the young man ever since first meeting him when Toll was employed by the Coast and Geodetic Survey in Washington, D.C. Unknown to each other, Mather and Toll were both vacationing in Hawaii in 1919. Mather, in a chauffeur-driven automobile, immediately recognized Toll and ordered his driver, "Stop! There's a man I want for my National Parks." Toll accepted Mather's offer to join the NPS and shortly thereafter served stints as superintendent of Mount Rainier (1919), Rocky Mountain (1921), and Yellowstone (1929) National Parks. An avid mountaineer (in the Hawaiian Islands, Toll had scaled Mauna Loa and Mauna Kea on Hawaii, and Haleakala on Maui), he climbed all fifty peaks in Rocky Mountain National Park and published an article de-

Initial National Park Service inspection of Big Bend site in January 1934. Left to right, J. Evetts Haley, University of Texas historian; Everett E. Townsend; Roger Toll, Yellowstone superintendent and chief investigator of proposed national park sites. Photo by Roger Toll, National Park Service, Harpers Ferry, West Virginia.

scribing his ascent of Mount Rainier. His appreciation of natural beauty, however, was not confined to the Rocky Mountain West, the Pacific Northwest, or the Hawaiian Islands. Indeed, Toll had an unusual talent, a keenly developed aesthetic sense that allowed him to see beyond the seeming prerequisite for many of the early parks; namely, a preoccupation with nature's exotic creations. For some, Big Bend was the epitome of harsh mediocrity containing neither the highest peak in Texas nor gorges as deep as the Grand Canyon in Arizona. Yet Toll immediately had sensed that there was more to the mysterious and compelling landscape, something the locals had long felt. His favorable report, completed in February 1934, would be the deciding catalyst for the official NPS action toward the creation of Big Bend National Park.[17]

Despite Toll's endorsement, Arno B. Cammerer, who succeeded Albright as director of the Park Service in 1933, held reservations about the Big Bend project. "If we could be assured," he wrote in early April 1934, "that there was enough federal land in the Big Bend country to establish such a park, and it were further investigated for facts as to wildlife, and how to take care of visitors (water supply, camping space, etc.), I would feel there is a better prospect there than in the Guadalupes." [18]

By the end of the month, Cammerer's doubts had been laid to rest. On April 16, a party led by E. E. Townsend discovered water in the Chisos Basin, enabling the CCC camp to be established there the following month. The Park Service completed its preliminary wildlife survey on April 18, which recommended that "from the wildlife point of view" the Big Bend "is of national parks caliber." Toll's report had partially allayed Cammerer's concern about land acquisition when it estimated that private holdings could be purchased for one to five dollars an acre. The director, influenced by these recent developments, approved the proposed Big Bend National Park on May 1, 1934. Before the Park Service could begin drafting congressional legislation, it next had to secure Secretary of the Interior Harold Ickes's endorsement. [19]

In the summer of 1934, Cammerer authorized an agency investigation of Big Bend to gather information for the secretary of the interior so he could determine if the project should be presented to Congress. It had two other objectives as well: (1) to begin preliminary planning for roads, camp sites, trails, and other park projects and (2) to provide guidelines for future work performed by the CCC. Herbert Maier, an NPS regional officer headquartered in Oklahoma City, headed up the study team. [20]

The Maier report, completed in January 1935, underscored several unique opportunities and problems at Big Bend, but overall it revealed the Park Service's commitment to the project. The report for the first time officially proposed the concept of an international park on both sides of the Rio Grande, a "vast playground" that "would create ties of kindly sentiment that would multiply and become stronger between the Mexican and American peoples, now almost unknown to each other." Significantly, the author of the section on the "Adjoining Area in Mexico" was E. E. Townsend. [21]

The Maier report also thoroughly examined the crucial issue of land ownership and acquisition. Of the 1,500,000 acres proposed for the park, the Texas State Parks Board only owned 1,640 acres in fee simple title, but had acquired another 90,000 acres through tax forfeitures. The Texas Permanent School Fund held the mineral rights to the

Civilian Conservation Corps (CCC) tent camp in the Chisos Basin, 1934. Big Bend National Park, National Park Service.

90,000 acres and owned outright an additional 150,000 acres. Private individuals owned 1,125,000 acres, the bulk of the projected park lands. An additional 6,000 acres, regarded as unpurchasable, belonged to quicksilver mining companies.[22]

The report considered the resolution of the mineral rights controversy especially crucial. To permit mining within the boundaries of a national park would nullify the intent of the 1916 mandating legislation; namely, "to conserve the scenery and the natural and historic objects and the wildlife therein and to provide for the enjoyment of the same in such manner and by such means as will leave them unimpaired for the enjoyment of future generations." While Texas insisted on retaining the mineral rights, Maier optimistically predicted that these "might be contributed to a national park project by the State Legislature." The 150,000 acres controlled by the Texas Permanent School Fund likewise complicated matters. The state legislature in 1933 had granted the surface rights to the Texas State Parks Board for one cent per acre, but the state attorney general later determined that it was a gift rather than a purchase and the land consequently still belonged to the School Fund. The Maier report estimated that a price of twenty-five cents per acre would make the transaction constitutional and thus acceptable by the attorney general's office. The privately owned lands posed less of a problem, despite their quantity (1,125,000 acres). Predominantly low-grade grazing lands, forty to fifty acres of which were required to sustain a single steer, the submarginal holdings were only worth from three to five dollars an acre. Overall, the Maier report supported the contention previously made by Toll that land acquisition was not a serious obstacle to the early development of Big Bend National Park.[23]

Late in January 1935, U.S. Representative Ewing Thomason of El Paso received a copy of Maier's report. A convert to the Big Bend movement ever since he toured the area in November 1933, Thomason was anxious to introduce in the House of Representatives a bill to create the park. Conrad Wirth of the Park Service advised Thomason to wait until Secretary of the Interior Harold Ickes had approved the project, which he did on February 5, 1935. Wirth and Thomason now could begin drafting a bill.[24]

President Franklin Roosevelt first learned of a proposed national and international park at Big Bend in a letter he received from Senator Morris Sheppard dated February 16, 1935. Three days later the president asked Ickes to investigate Sheppard's proposal. Ickes sent a copy of Maier's report to Roosevelt and suggested that the State Department extend an invitation to the Mexican government to begin deliberations on the project on the U.S.-Mexico border.[25]

On March 4, 1935, Congressman Thomason introduced House Resolution 6373 and Senators Sheppard and Tom Connally submitted Senate Bill 2131 to establish Big Bend National Park. Sheppard had the clerk print several letters into the *Congressional Record* on the international features of the project. Big Bend received an additional boost when the attorney general of Texas reversed his position and determined that one cent per acre was sufficient payment by the Texas State Parks Board to the Texas Permanent School Fund for its 150,000 acres. The attorney general concluded that it was a fair exchange because the School Fund had obtained the mineral rights to lands acquired through tax forfeitures, which the Fund had not held before the passage of the Big Bend State Park Act in 1933. Although this later became the basis of controversy over mineral rights, the Parks Board now held title to almost 250,000 acres, or one-quarter of the revised size of Big Bend.[26]

Popular support in Texas for the Big Bend Park measure remained high throughout the spring and early summer of 1935. The citizens of Alpine, Marfa, Fort Stockton, and other nearby communities eagerly awaited passage of the act that they hoped would eventually produce a bonanza of tourist revenues for their depressed region. In fact, the economic promise was so alluring that of the three major park projects proposed in 1935—Olympic in Washington, Kings Canyon in California, and Big Bend—only the Texas project would pass without serious local and congressional opposition. On June 20, 1935, President Roosevelt signed into law the enabling act for Big Bend. The Lone Star State finally had its first national park, at least on paper. A provision in the act stipulated that before the park could actually be established, Texas had to present to the federal government the title to all of the acres included in the park boundaries.[27]

 Texas Politics and
the Park Movement,
1935–1944

The passage of the Big Bend Act in June 1935 occurred shortly after the adjournment of the 44th State Legislature, awkward timing indeed. The lawmakers convened biannually in January of each odd-numbered year, which meant an appropriation for land acquisition might have to wait until winter 1937 unless Governor James V. Allred called a special session in fall 1935. Counting on this, the National Park Service completed the boundary survey, and Secretary of the Interior Harold Ickes sent the governor a map with a description of the acreage to be included in the park. The Park Service also provided legislators the same information to help them determine the amount of the appropriation needed to purchase the Big Bend lands. Regrettably, the governor failed to call a special session that fall or throughout 1936.[1]

Governor Allred, however, did publicly support Big Bend, visiting the area with his wife in November 1935. E. E. Townsend and J. E. Casner of Alpine led the governor's party on horseback through the park. A near tragedy was averted when Mrs. Allred's horse fell down an incline and lodged against a tree, enabling her to dismount. The accident didn't dampen the governor's interest, as Townsend reported that Allred "frankly expressed his approval for the project and said he would do everything he could for it." He even encouraged state legislators to visit Big Bend to help "sell" them on Texas' first national park.

Despite the governor's rhetoric, neither the executive nor legislative branches of state government took any further steps that fall or the following year.[2]

Meanwhile, Park Service and local boosters prepared to tackle what they considered the major obstacle blocking the establishment of Big Bend: the mineral rights which Texas statutes guaranteed to the Public School Fund. Their position clashed with Department of the Interior policy that lands within national parks must have fee simple title; that is, the federal government alone must own the mineral rights. Herbert Maier of the Park Service met with School Fund supporters to discuss a compromise alternative, one which reserved the mineral rights for the Fund but left the authority to extract resources in the park solely in the hands of the secretary of the interior. Not surprisingly, school officials opposed the option on the unlikelihood that the secretary would release the mineral rights as long as Big Bend was a park.[3]

The Park Service strategy to overcome the objections of School Fund backers was twofold: first, to convince Texans that few mineral resources remained in the Big Bend; and second, to argue that tourist dollars from travel to a national park would generate substantially more revenues for the state's schools than minimal or nonexistent ores or petroleum. The chief geologist for Humble Oil and Refining Company helped the cause when he informed an NPS scientist that Big Bend contained "possible" but not "probable" crude oil deposits. Unfortunately, when the 45th Legislature convened in January 1937, the Park Service had not had enough time to complete a thorough investigation. The case for the economic advantages of a national park fared better. In October 1936, the Executive Committee of the State Teachers Association endorsed Big Bend as both economically and educationally beneficial to the schoolchildren of Texas. A favorable economic factor cited by the group was the projected increased revenues from the gasoline tax. Nevertheless, Ben F. Tisinger, president of the State Board of Education, told Maier that his organization still supported retention of Big Bend's mineral rights by the School Fund.[4]

By fall 1936 the establishment of Big Bend through acquisition of its private- and state-owned lands had become a top priority of the National Park Service. In early November, Director Arno B. Cammerer met in Austin with Lieutenant Governor Walter Woodul (Allred was out of state) to discuss an appropriation bill for the Big Bend lands. Also present at the meeting were Assistant NPS Director George Moskey, Herbert Maier, E. E. Townsend, a couple of other Park Service staff, and Major Wood from the State Planning Commission, along with two assistants from the State Attorney General's Office. Cammerer and Woodul agreed that the amount requested at the session in January should be increased from $1.25 to $1.4 million to provide adequate funding for a special Land Acquisition Commission. Woodul also wanted to subsidize an inspection trip to the Big Bend during the upcoming legislative session for all state senators and representatives. Cammerer reiterated his agency's willingness to accept certain mineral reservations subject to approval by the secretary of the interior. By now both sides knew that as long as Big Bend was maintained as a park no mining or resource exploitation could take place, hence no revenues for the School Fund. Despite the impasse, Maier concluded that the overall "tenor of the meeting was good and there is every reason to believe that the State will undertake to carry out its commitment" to purchase the park lands.[5]

Governor Allred was in a difficult position indeed. Texas had a $15 million deficit, and the governor had publicly pledged to oppose any measures requiring additional taxes. Yet he had also repeatedly endorsed the Big Bend project. The best way to determine Allred's priorities—balance the budget or support an appropriation for the park— was to present him with a Big Bend bill to see if he would sign or veto it. To that end the Park Service began working with two old allies, Senator H. L. Winfield and Speaker Coke R. Stevenson in the House.[6]

The bill, drafted in the State Attorney General's Office, was put on the calendar for introduction in both houses late in February 1937. It consisted of two significant provisions: first, the School Fund would relinquish its mineral rights to the federal government in exchange for fair compensation; and second, a special commission would be in charge of land acquisition and serve as mediator between the demands of the School Fund and the secretary of the interior. Commission members would include representatives from the State Board of Education as well as other state officials.[7]

Coke Stevenson, with the aid of Park Service staff, prepared a press release on the economic benefits national parks brought to their regions. Travel agencies in 1936 estimated, for example, that the average tourist spent five dollars a day. If only 50,000 tourists visited Big Bend annually and stayed an average of five days in Texas, the state would receive over a million dollars. Stevenson's figures were not extravagant;

if anything, they were conservative. In 1936, nearby Carlsbad Caverns in New Mexico had over 150,000 annual visitors, and over 500,000 chose Rocky Mountain National Park in Colorado. Texas could also count on additional revenues from federal maintenance, development, and payrolls. Finally, Stevenson pointed to the success of the Texas centennial celebrations held in Dallas and Fort Worth in 1936 that had attracted thousands to the Lone Star State. Big Bend had an advantage over temporary attractions such as the centennial, for the park was a "permanent exposition." The speaker's persuasive arguments were carried by newspapers across the state, including the influential *Fort Worth Star-Telegram*.[8]

On schedule, committees in both houses reported favorably in March on a $2 million appropriation bill to purchase roughly one million acres for a national park at Big Bend. Park backers, fearful of opposition in the Senate because of its alliance with the state's large industries—which would have to bear the burden of taxation for Big Bend—chose to have Winfield first introduce the bill in the upper house. If the Senate approved the measure, passage in the House was considered a certainty.[9]

The Senate quarreled over two of the main provisions of the bill: the $2 million appropriation and the independent commission responsible for land acquisition. Nonetheless, it passed the measure in late April, reducing the appropriation to $750,000. With the session drawing to a close and scheduled for adjournment on May 11, it appeared doubtful that a separate bill would have time for passage in the House. Representative Stevenson saved the measure by attaching it to the appropriation bill for the general revenue fund. To appease the Senate, he proposed two amendments. First, he lowered the House's appropriation to $750,000 in line with the Senate's; and second, he called for the Texas State Parks Board to take over land acquisition from the special commission. In a final conciliatory move toward the School Fund, Representative Alf Roark's amendment allowed the public schools to retain the mineral rights at Big Bend. The bill was reported favorably out of conference committee and was forwarded to Governor Allred, who had until June 11 to make up his mind. Although the governor had promised park backers he would not veto an appropriation bill that passed both houses, he had likewise continued to campaign against increased spending.[10]

While they waited, the NPS and other boosters used various means to persuade the governor, some more ethical than others. According to a rumor, Allred hoped at the end of his term to be appointed by President Roosevelt to a recently created federal judgeship in east Texas. One Park Service official suggested that U.S. Representative Sam Rayburn and U.S. Senator Morris Sheppard, both supporters of Big Bend and influential in the selection of federal judges, should telephone Allred and "mention the two things in one breath." Pro–Big Bend groups lobbied in the governor's office daily and often used data provided by the Park Service in their arguments. From his Washington office, Director Cammerer wired the governor directly about the recreational and economic benefits a national park would bring to Texas, ones which he stressed would repay the appropriation "one-hundred fold." But the governor still did not sign the bill. A veto was of particular concern because of the negative effect it might have on continuing negotiations over the international park project between Mexico and the United States. Herbert Maier asked Mexican officials to express their anxieties through U.S. Ambassador Josephus Daniels to Allred about how important the passage of the appropriation bill was to the negotiations. In fact, Mexico regarded an appropriation by the Texas legislature as proof of earnest intent and a necessary step before work on a park south of the border could even begin. Despite these efforts, the governor vetoed the Big Bend bill.[11]

Allred justified his veto on several grounds. He considered the $750,000 appropriation insufficient to complete the purchases, which in turn could cause the value of unsold acres to skyrocket far beyond their actual worth, yet taxpayers would have to pick up the difference. Furthermore, the governor disapproved of tacking such a large appropriation onto the general revenue fund, which would unduly burden an already strained treasury. There was also the issue of mineral rights. Allred believed that the federal government probably would not accept the acres with mineral rights still possessed by the School Fund. He was also concerned that park enthusiasts would lobby legislators for an additional appropriation and subsequently pressure School Fund board members to relinquish title to mineral rights because the state had such a stake in the project.[12]

Governor Allred's reasons for the veto, while understandable, were nevertheless contradictory and illogical. On one hand he opposed the appropriation because it was not enough to purchase all the Big Bend acres, yet on the other hand he resisted increased taxation for new projects that would inflate the state's deficit. Allred's demand for a separate park bill was out of touch with political reality. As noted, with the legislative session close to adjournment, the only way to salvage the Big Bend measure was to attach it to the general revenue fund appropriation. If Allred had had his way, there would not even have been a bill to veto. And finally, despite his public statements, the governor's position on the mineral rights issue did not indicate wholehearted support for the park by the executive branch.

The governor's inertia motivated West Texans to take over the leadership of the campaign. A *Fort Worth Star-Telegram* editorial on June 11, 1937, appealed to one million Texans to contribute one dollar each, an idea inspired by Virginians, who had given approximately one million dollars toward the purchase of Shenandoah National Park. The Park Service's Herbert Maier asked James Record, managing editor of the *Star-Telegram*, if his paper would sponsor the fund drive. Horace Morelock, on behalf of the Local Park Committee of the Alpine Chamber of Commerce, likewise backed the newspaper, the daily with the largest circulation in West Texas.[13]

The *Star-Telegram* and other Texas newspapers joined in a cooperative effort to promote Big Bend. The Fort Worth paper regularly featured a list of donor names with amounts given, often accompanied by a feature story about the park's attractions. One article and photograph showed Governor Allred kicking off the campaign with a one-dollar contribution. Schoolchildren were encouraged to give their nickels and dimes, and a fifth grade class from Marfa, Texas, sent in a dollar, the prize the grade-schoolers received for their parents' perfect attendance at a PTA meeting.[14]

The most active organizations in the subscription campaign were the Brewster County and Alpine Chambers of Commerce under the leadership of Dom Adams, Jim Casner, and Horace Morelock. They organized a statewide fund-raising drive that began in mid-July 1937 when they asked citizens in each of the Lone Star State's 254 counties to set up Local Park Committees comprised of prominent business leaders, educators, and public officials. Morelock, chair of the Local Park Committee of the Alpine Chamber of Commerce and president of Sul Ross State Teachers College, spent almost half his time promoting Big Bend through speeches and personal correspondence. He estimated that he wrote two to three dozen letters per day and traveled thousands of miles each year to talk with anyone interested in the park, including potential large donors in railroad and oil corporations. Morelock had ulterior motives, which also justified him working during college time, for he considered Big Bend National Park as an extension campus for Sul Ross and an economic stimulus for the town of Alpine. Regrettably, Morelock's unflagging zeal and the efforts of the Brewster County and Alpine Chambers of Commerce, the Local Park Committees, and the newspapers fell short. After four months only $50,000 of the $1 million had been collected.[15]

Park Service officials had been encouraged by the initial results of the drive, but as donations fell off, they expressed concern. When a special session of the 45th Legislature in fall 1937 appropriated no funds for Big Bend land purchase, the agency took steps to close the CCC camp in the Chisos Mountains, where the largely Hispanic enrollees had built twenty miles of roads, trails, and other projects. All in all, the federal government had spent $323,680 on improvements, yet with no guarantee that title to the park acres would be transferred to the Department of the Interior the NPS could not develop the site further. The CCC camp was subsequently abandoned on December 15, 1937, despite vigorous protests by Big Bend's sup-

Horace Morelock, chair of the Local Park Committee of the Alpine Chamber of Commerce and president of Sul Ross State Teachers College, estimated he wrote two to three dozen letters a day promoting Big Bend National Park. Archives of the Big Bend, Sul Ross State University, Alpine, Texas.

porters. As the year drew to a close, they found some consolation in Conrad Wirth's confidence that the project would eventually succeed, at which time a CCC camp would be reinstated in the area. Also encouraging were the activities of the Texas legislature.[16]

In fall 1937 at the special session of the 45th Legislature, both houses passed legislation that officially recognized the national park, approved the boundaries proposed by the secretary of the interior, and authorized the Texas State Parks Board to receive donations of land and money. The legislature also granted the Board the power of eminent domain. Governor Allred signed the bill. Finally, after more than two years of consistent effort, the legal and governmental machinery to establish Big Bend National Park was in place.[17]

The next step was to find a way to raise $1 million, a large sum indeed during the depression. Since one fund drive had fared poorly and the legislature would not meet again until winter 1939, Big Bend boosters considered several other options but eventually agreed to try another popular subscription campaign. They reorganized the Local Park Committees and the State Parks Board. To give the drive more visibility as well as clout, Allred appointed a temporary Executive Committee of fifteen of the state's wealthiest and most powerful citizens. Amon Carter was unanimously chosen chairman, partly because of his organizational skills but also for the extensive coverage the *Fort Worth Star-Telegram* had given Big Bend. Other Executive Committee members were Wendell Mayes, Brownwood; J. E. Josey, Houston; W. B. Tuttle, San Antonio; John W. Carpenter, Dallas; Jesse H. Jones, Houston; C. H. Bassett, El Paso; Gus Taylor, Tyler; W. L. Moody III, Galveston; Mrs. Richard J. Turrentine, Denton; Mrs. M. A. Taylor, Bonham; James R. Record, Fort Worth; John E. King, Dallas; Luther Stark, Beaumont; H. W. Morelock, Alpine.[18]

In May 1938 Governor Allred invited the interim Executive Committee and 150 other prominent Texans to meet in Austin. From this number, Allred appointed twenty-six to the permanent Executive Committee of a new organization, the Texas Big Bend Park Association (TBBPA). Its purpose was twofold: publicize the national park, and raise funds for land acquisition. Officers of the TBBPA were Amon Carter, chairman, and H. W. Morelock, vice-chairman; the governor was the honorary president. At the meeting Carter emphasized how tourism would benefit the Lone Star State and predicted a fruitful popular subscription campaign. The participants agreed that the major obstacle to a successful project was the old nemesis, mineral rights. Almost three years had elapsed since passage of Big Bend's enabling legislation, and the School Fund still held one-sixteenth royalty on 343,354 privately owned acres and full royalty on 139,168 acres of state land. After acknowledging the problem, however, the Executive Committee focused on generating enthusiasm for the fund drive.[19]

To get things off to a good start, Carter donated $5,000 and other committee members pledged an additional $20,000 to a working fund to cover rent for a headquarters office and related campaign expenses. The professional fund-raising firm Adrian Wychgel and Associates, which had raised almost $2 million total for Mammoth Cave and Shenandoah National Parks in Kentucky and Virginia, was asked to assist with the drive. Adrian Wychgel, the firm's founder, assured Governor Allred that "very little, if any, money would have to be appropriated by the State." His company had reached its goal at both Mammoth Cave and Shenandoah in less than six months. Wychgel offered to begin the drive immediately and, based on past performance, estimated a successful conclusion by November 1938, six months later.[20]

Yet despite Wychgel's optimism and desire to begin a large-scale drive, very little occurred throughout the summer and fall of 1938. True, the Texas press continued its publicity efforts, and contributions trickled in, but the Texas Big Bend Park Association's major campaign needed a "jump start." According to Carter, it could not begin until the working fund was paid in full by the directors, who had only contributed $15,500 of the necessary $25,000 (and, as noted previously, Carter had donated $5,000 of the amount).[21]

Meanwhile, the Park Service, despairing of the lethargic efforts of the Association, prepared for the upcoming regular session of the legislature. In July U.S. Representative Ewing Thomason met with NPS officials in Washington, D.C., to discuss solutions to the school lands impasse and another appropriation bill for Big Bend. Thomason was confident that a new governor and a large number of new faces in the 46th Legislature would work in favor of the national park.[22]

The Big Bend Park movement had a real friend in Governor-elect W. Lee "Pappy" O'Daniel. A flamboyant flour salesman and radio entertainer before entering politics, he had won a decisive victory over twelve rivals. In the spring Democratic primary, O'Daniel had stumped the state with his daughter Molly, sons Mike and Pat, and his Hillbilly Band. The contributions and votes poured in. Not surprisingly, his campaign remains one of the most colorful in Texas political history, a state noted for memorable campaigns and elections. Park backers in Brewster County suggested that the governor-elect employ his successful tactics to raise money for Big Bend. Although unable to do this, O'Daniel did visit the site and came away even more impressed with its beauty and tourism potential. Later, the governor-elect expressed his unqualified support for Big Bend to Arthur Demaray, acting director of the NPS, and promised to "do everything possible for the project."[23]

The lieutenant governor in the new administration was Coke Stevenson, who had introduced the unsuccessful appropriation bill in 1937. In the 1939 session he and State Senator H. L. Winfield, a member of the Banking and Finance Committee, would team up to draft legislation for Big Bend. The strategy was to ask only for a nominal appropriation of one thousand dollars, which would give the bill priority status in committee hearings and an early calendar date in the House and Senate. Amon Carter had specifically requested that no substantial appropriation be attached to any Big Bend legislation. Explanations for Carter's unusual request ranged from his having lined up a major donor to speculation that the publisher did not want to obligate himself to the new governor. The most likely reason was that Carter believed an appropriation was unnecessary, since the Texas Big Bend Park Association hoped to complete its drive by May 1939 when the 46th legislative session would adjourn.[24]

Winfield's Senate Bill Number 123 expanded on several provisions contained in the earlier act passed in fall 1937; namely, it granted the Texas State Parks Board the right of public domain and the power to acquire land through purchase, condemnation, and donation. It also set the maximum price for privately held land (exclusive of improvements) at two dollars an acre. The bill did have two significant additions: Sections III and IV. Section III provided for the transfer of unsold School Fund lands to the state in fee simple title at a price of one dollar an acre to be paid from the general fund. Section IV dealt with the mineral rights the School Fund held on privately owned lands, transferring these to the state for a consideration of fifty cents an acre.[25]

Governor O'Daniel supported Winfield's bill, calling it "an investment which would pay good returns." He warned the Texas Senate that an emergency existed at Big Bend. For almost two years publicity about the area's unique features had attracted the curious, some of whom engaged in acts of vandalism, including unauthorized collecting of botanical, archaeological, and geological specimens. The governor was concerned that if the 46th Legislature did not act immediately, only the picked-clean skeleton of a once-great national park might remain.

Although O'Daniel was somewhat prone to hyperbole, the governor's exuberance and concern could not be ignored. He referred to Big Bend as "this great 'GIFT OF GOD' to Texas and our nation." The Chisos, "the most rugged mountains in the world," were the most prominent geological feature in a landscape that he regarded as "the most gorgeous on the continent." The governor persuasively discussed the revenues the project would produce. He also included in his message to the legislature a personal letter from Franklin D. Roosevelt, in which the president advised "that this large and very interesting area could be bought for a comparatively small sum—a sum that would be insignificant in comparison with the economic returns that would flow to the State of Texas after the creation of the Park." Furthermore, Roosevelt wrote that "it would be very gratifying to me personally" if Big Bend "could be dedicated during my Administration." Governor

A sign erected by the Texas State Parks Board to deter vandalism. Big Bend National Park, National Park Service.

O'Daniel then concluded his own remarks demanding that the legislature give the park bill "IMMEDIATE ATTENTION" (the capitals are O'Daniel's in both quotations).[26]

The Senate responded by unanimously passing the Winfield bill. In the House, Representative Jeff Stinson was concerned that Big Bend might still hold undiscovered quicksilver deposits and oil reserves. He argued that future royalties from these mineral rights belonged to the School Fund. Representative Albert R. Cauthorn, who had introduced Winfield's bill in the House, assured School Fund supporters that if the park were not established, the federal government would return the acres to the state. Cauthorn demonstrated that Big Bend National Park would produce annual tourist revenues of $3.5 million, considerably more than mineral rights royalty projections. The House then passed the bill by a 109–20 margin. O'Daniel signed it on May 12, 1939, the only real victory of his first administration. The Park Service, encouraged by the provision for the transfer of Big Bend lands in fee simple title to the federal government, reestablished the CCC camp in the Chisos Basin.[27]

As predicted, the delay forced the value of the park acres to rise one-half million dollars to $1.5 million. Unfortunately, the Texas Big Bend Park Association still had not begun fund-raising, because Amon Carter refused to proceed until the working fund reached $25,000. Two years later it was still one thousand dollars short. Furthermore, Carter doubted that the business climate in Texas was stable enough to sustain a major drive. He hoped to raise the funds mainly from substantial donations from large corporations and philanthropies, but Humble Oil, the wealthiest Texas corporation, only pledged a thousand dollars, indicative of the hard times. Meanwhile, the deteriorating political and military situation in Europe and Asia erupted in world war, further dampening prospects for a successful campaign. By fall 1940, after three years of the campaign, the TBBPA Committee had raised only $9,582.93. That, along with direct contributions to the Texas State Parks Board by Texas cities and assorted organizations brought the total to an estimated $50,000–$100,000, far short of the $1.5 million goal.[28]

The failure of the private popular subscription campaign left only one alternative: a state appropriation. Accordingly, Governor O'Daniel asked the 47th Legislature in January 1941 to honor its commitment to the federal government to acquire the Big Bend acres. The Park Service assisted in several ways. Its lobbyist, E. E. Townsend, remained in Austin at his own expense, offering firsthand testimony on the attractions of the area and helping draft a bill. Southwest Regional Director Minor Tillotson testified before the state House Appropriations Committee on the increased tourism revenues Big Bend would generate. Tillotson also provided economic data on other national parks for Governor O'Daniel to use in his weekly radio program. The combination of the above, along with new members in the legislature and a new governor, produced the desired results. On March 19, the House Committee reported favorably on the Big Bend appropriation bill by an 11–3 vote; the Senate Finance Committee unanimously approved it.[29]

During the discussion of the bill before the House, Representative G. C. Morris of Greenville introduced an amendment to reserve the mineral rights to the state. Morris, an East Texan and a School Fund supporter, noted that Big Bend had the potential to equal the productivity of his own region's oil fields. With no scientific evidence to back him up, a joint committee of the House and Senate deleted the Morris amendment. The revised draft of the bill passed both chambers, and on July 3, 1941, the governor signed the $1.5 million appropriation measure into law. The appraised value of Big Bend's unacquired acres was $1,486,000 (including improvements).[30]

At long last the land acquisition could begin in earnest (see Chapter 3). It proceeded so smoothly that by November 1942 only 13,316 acres remained in private ownership. Newton B. Drury, Cammerer's successor as director of the National Park Service, fully expected the state to acquire these acres and transfer them to the federal government. But Drury also did not want to hold up the project over such a small percentage of the total acreage (less than 2 percent). Consequently, in June 1943 he recommended to Harold Ickes, secretary of the interior, that the federal government accept title to the acquired acres on the condition that the Texas State Parks Board transfer the outstanding land as soon as possible. Ickes concurred.[31]

On September 5, 1943, Governor Coke Stevenson, long a champion for Big Bend, presented the land deeds to the Park Service's Minor Tillotson. When U.S. Senator Morris Sheppard died in 1941, Governor O'Daniel had appointed himself to fill the vacancy, thus elevating Lieutenant Governor Stevenson into the Governor's Mansion. Before Governor Stevenson could sign over the deed of cession of jurisdiction to the Interior Department, several preliminary steps had to be completed, such as a final check on the land titles. On December 30, 1943, Stevenson signed the deed of cession and asked Amon Carter personally to deliver it to Secretary Ickes. Carter wanted the formal transfer to occur at the White House with the president participating, which delayed it considerably, since Roosevelt was in and out of the capital during these critical months of the war. The ceremony finally took place on June 6, 1944, when the Allies under General Dwight Eisenhower invaded France. Ironically, news of the landings at Normandy Beach and elsewhere relegated Big Bend to the back pages of the nation's newspapers. In July 1944, Big Bend—America's 27th national park—officially opened to the public.[32]

A Park for the People from the People: Land Acquisition at Big Bend

The purchase or condemnation of privately owned acres for a national park, especially during wartime, can cause friction between the federal government and local citizens. President Franklin D. Roosevelt received several letters during World War II from owners upset that they would have to leave their properties during the global crisis. A woman whose family had ranched in Brewster County for forty years wrote, "How are we going to feed our sons and fellow men if they take our farms and ranches away from us?" She continued, "What good is parks? No rubber, no tourist to visit it and the country won't be any good if we don't win this war." [1]

A mother whose oldest son was fighting in Europe implored the president to save the family's ranch for her son's sake. She wrote, "I wish that you might read some of his letters in which he writes about the hills, canyons, and trails that he longs for at home. The park project has passed since he entered the service, in fact his home was given away on D-Day [June 6, 1944] when he was fighting for freedom and liberty." She concluded by asking Roosevelt if her family could remain at their ranch until the end of the war. "The park cannot be developed until the war is won so why should all of those honest, patriotic ranchmen have to move or give up their business of production while our boys are fighting?" [2]

Another problem concerned several people who bought property from dishonest real estate developers. An angry woman from Washington, D.C., found out that she had paid $225 for fifteen acres whose appraised value was only fifteen dollars, or a dollar an acre. An Ohio resident traveled to West Texas to see her land and was not pleased at all to learn that she had purchased ten acres on the largely vertical Dead Horse Mountains. Most poignant of all was the experience of three schoolteachers. The lifelong friends planned to retire to the Big Bend Country. They invested their savings in fifteen acres for which they paid $1,500 only to discover that their property likewise was on a mountain top and worth only a dollar an acre.[3]

Despite the criticisms and tensions suggested by the preceding, the enormous undertaking to survey, acquire (through purchase, forfeiture, condemnation, or donation), and transfer title to over 785,000 acres overall was a model of efficient administration and cooperation among local, state, and federal officials. Also essential for the program's success were planning and organization, which began late in 1934, over half a year before the passage of Big Bend's Enabling Act, when the National Park Service appointed E. E. Townsend project manager to coordinate the classification of the then-proposed 1,500,000 acres. Townsend, working closely with the Texas State Parks Board and the NPS, helped lay the foundation for an efficient land acquisition program.[4]

Since Texas had been a republic for nine years before it entered the Union, the Lone Star State originally contained no federal public lands. Consequently, the Park Service followed the precedents set at its eastern parks in two significant areas: first, it was the responsibility of the state to acquire title to the land to present to the federal government; and second, at Big Bend, as earlier at Isle Royale and Everglades National Parks, the enabling acts were passed before the exact area was determined. This was done because much of the acreage was privately owned. The Park Service had learned that as owners and the government negotiated during the acquisition process, a park's boundaries went through several adjustments.[5]

The Park Service first recommended boundaries for Big Bend in September 1935 and over subsequent years revised them several times to conform to surveys and to guarantee that only essential properties were included in the park. None of the boundary revisions affected the four main geological and scenic features of Big Bend—the Chisos Mountains and Boquillas, Mariscal, and Santa Elena Canyons.[6]

By fall 1936 Townsend completed the classification of the lands for the park, most of which were only suitable for submarginal grazing worth an estimated one to five dollars an acre. After several boundary adjustments, the area proposed for the park in 1941 contained 788,682 acres, of which the state held title to 112,907 acres, or almost one-seventh of the total. Private corporations and individuals owned the remaining 675,775 acres. As noted in Chapter 2, the private subscription campaign begun in 1937 had raised only a few thousand dollars toward land purchase by 1941 when the 47th Legislature came through with a $1.5 million appropriation to acquire land appraised at $1,486,000. That same year the Texas State Parks Board set up the Big Bend Land Department, headquartered in Alpine, and appointed Eugene "Shorty" Thompson administrator and E. E. Townsend as his assistant. They faced a formidable task indeed, one made even more difficult by the legislature's stipulation that they only had twelve months to complete the job. Otherwise, any unexpended funds would revert to the state's general fund. In September 1941 Thompson, Townsend, and their staff went to work in their race against the calendar.[7]

Before the Big Bend Land Department could really get started, two major hurdles blocked the way: a court injunction, which delayed the start of land acquisition by five months, and the entry of the United States into World War II in December 1941. Park boosters worried that patriotic Texans would demand that the $1.5 million for Big Bend be forfeited to projects essential to winning the war. State Senator George Moffett (Chillicothe) and State Representative G. C. Morris (Greenville), both from East Texas, voiced these sentiments and suggested that there was no time for frivolous play in parks anyway. They proposed to stop land purchases and to let any options lapse. Horace Morelock, however, expressed the viewpoint of many park supporters when he said, "After World War II is only a tragic memory, the American people will be greatly in need of such relief scenes as an International Peace Park will provide." Also coming to the defense of the park was Amon Carter, chairman of the Texas Big Bend Park Association, who strongly endorsed continuing the land acquisition program. Carter's stand was significant because earlier he had postponed his organization's fund-raising drive because of the outbreak of war in Europe.[8]

J. H. King, state representative from Throckmorton in East Texas and an opponent of Big Bend, initiated the court injunction when he sued State Comptroller George H. Sheppard to block him from paying out any of the $1.5 million appropriation for park acres in Brewster County. King's suit contended that the appropriation was unconstitutional, since the state had a substantial deficit and did not have the money to spend. In December 1941 the Texas Court of Civil Appeals in Austin ruled against King. When the Texas Supreme Court refused to review the case two months later, land acquisition finally could get under way with only seven months remaining.[9]

The Texas State Parks Board and the Big Bend Land Department had taken advantage of the hiatus imposed during the King litigation. Although the injunction forbade land purchase, it did not enjoin against preliminary steps. Consequently, the Board had legally sent out option-to-purchase contracts to over three thousand property owners. The overwhelming response foreshadowed a successful campaign even in the short time remaining. According to Thompson, the King injunction actually had been a "blessing in disguise," for it had provided adequate time for the Big Bend Land Department staff to get to know the owners, which helped remove the onus of impersonal government bureaucrats seizing private property at unfair prices. W. B. Hunter of San Angelo willingly accepted the option price of $1.50 per acre for his first thousand acres, then donated the last seventy-nine to the park. Thompson considered Hunter's generosity a "good omen." In fact, in February 1942 when the injunction was lifted, the Board was able to purchase almost 300,000 acres, make offers on another 300,000, and initiate condemnation proceedings against an additional 45,000 acres.[10]

The Big Bend Land Department staff maintained a relentless pace over the remaining half year, obtaining clear title to an average of two hundred sections of land each month. An adjustment down from 788,682 to just under 708,000 acres was made so that the appropriated amount could cover the cost and administration of land acquisition and the percentage fee paid to the Permanent School Fund for its mineral rights. By the end of 1942, all of the $1.5 million was spent or encumbered, and Thompson and Townsend had accomplished what many considered impossible. Park Service Director Newton B. Drury had privately confided, "I doubt if the money can be expended within a year." He was wrong. The Big Bend Land Department had acquired 98 percent of the park lands at an average cost of two dollars an acre; administrative expenses were approximately 3.5 percent of the total, a record in efficient management for land acquisition in a national park.[11]

Federal officials congratulated the Texans on their successful efforts. Nevertheless, 2 percent of the acres, or twenty-five sections, still remained in private hands. Director Drury cautioned that nonfederal ownership of key holdings, in particular several thousand acres at Castolon on the Rio Grande, would hinder the park's development. The director advised that until the Castolon acres were acquired, he could not recommend the establishment of Big Bend to the secretary of the interior.[12]

Through fall 1942 and winter 1943 the acquisition program was stagnant due to a paucity of money in both public and private sectors. Drury and Southwest Regional Director Minor R. Tillotson encouraged the Texas State Parks Board to seek out funds wherever possible, but to no avail. Governor Coke Stevenson's administration had engaged in budget "belt tightening," so another appropriation in the near future seemed unlikely. Drury tried to persuade Amon Carter either to release the Texas Big Bend Park Association's Working Fund and apply it to land purchase or to undertake another popular subscription campaign. Carter refused both suggestions. He felt that the organization might need the money for future activities, yet he adamantly opposed another drive for a familiar reason. "The public," Carter said, "is too concerned with war causes, defense bond sales and similar patriotic movements to participate in any fund raising for parks." [13]

Other unsuccessful money-raising schemes included a proposal by U.S. Representative Ewing Thomason to use a $25,000 surplus left over from a federal grant for the Texas centennial and a suggestion that the state legislature consider a deficiency appropriation. Director Drury was anxious that Texas fulfill its charge to obtain all of Big Bend's acres. "If this is not done," he wrote, "I am afraid that the State will not feel obligated thereafter to acquire the remaining lands and it is apt to be a long time before the Federal Government will appropriate land acquisition funds for our use." On June 7, 1943, Drury reluctantly forwarded his recommendation to the secretary of the interior that the acres acquired be accepted "with the understanding that the State Parks Board will continue to exert every effort to acquire the remaining privately owned lands within the project boundaries." The secretary approved the request on June 24, 1943.[14]

Over the next twelve months, federal and state officials completed the myriad tasks remaining: preparation of title insurance, checking title abstracts for accuracy, and the transfer of deeds and exclusive jurisdiction from Texas to the United States. On June 6, 1944, the president and the secretary of the interior accepted the deed, and six days later Big Bend National Park was officially established, over nine years after the passage of the enabling legislation.[15]

The TSPB actively pursued acquisition of the remaining twenty-five sections of land with a sense of urgency. Estimated at a value of $75,000 in 1945, the acres had risen to nearly $100,000 two years later. In 1947 State Senator H. L. Winfield, the sponsor of the original $1.5 million appropriation bill, reluctantly was persuaded to back a request for another $125,000 from the state. His reluctance stemmed from an earlier promise to the legislature not to ask for more money for Big Bend. Despite Winfield's support, the 50th Legislature appropriated a stingy $12,000. The Parks Board combined this with $5,000 from other sources and by April 1949 acquired another 7,680 acres. Still almost 9,000 acres remained in private ownership, including the Castolon property and several other sections along the Rio Grande.[16]

The private holdings posed a dilemma for the National Park Service. During 1948 and 1949 the agency had spent $450,000 on improvements for Big Bend, mostly for roads, which increased the value of the private acres by making them more accessible. The owners of the Castolon tract, for example, had considered $39,006 a fair price in 1942, but demanded $125,000 in 1949 (the assessed value was only $60,000, however). Obviously if the Park Service continued to implement its $10,600,000 master plan, there was a strong likelihood that prices for the private land inside the park would continue to escalate. As if that were not enough, the private acres on the Rio Grande blocked access to the stream, including the mouth of Boquillas Canyon. On April 13, 1949, Ross A. Maxwell, the park superintendent, testified before the Appropriations Committee of the Texas legislature, and asked for $100,000 to purchase the outstanding acres. Although he reminded the legislators of their obligation and the problems caused by the private lands, he failed to persuade them.[17]

Precedent for the legislature's hope that Washington would take over acquisition had been set throughout the latter 1940s when Congress made appropriations to purchase acres at Persimmon Gap, the northern entrance to the park. However, these funds were restricted to road construction and right-of-ways and did not affect Castolon and the other river properties. The 3,756 acres at Castolon, for instance, were the source of much international friction when Mexican laborers crossed illegally to work on ranches and farms in the Big Bend Country. Other Mexican nationals processed wax from candelilla plants and rubber from guayule plants in the park and smuggled their products to sell on both sides of the border.[18]

The longer the private lands remained out of federal control, the more the environmental conditions deteriorated. In addition to the manufacturing of wax and rubber, which could legally occur on privately owned acres, cattle and sheep grazing further depleted the already sparse vegetation. Another problem pertained to property improvements on the private holdings. When owners added a fence or a barn, they expected additional compensation. The Park Service was concerned about improvements made solely to inflate property values. One individual, for example, had plans to construct a hunting lodge. Park Service fears were not imagined—land worth $55,000 in 1942 had increased in value to $257,000 by 1954.[19]

By August 1953, Congress, fully aware that the state did not intend to acquire the acres, authorized the secretary of the interior "to procure, in such manner as he may consider to be in the public interest, the remaining non-federal land." By 1972 the Park Service had purchased, condemned, and accepted donation of the remaining 8,561.75 acres at a cost of $300,375. Although consisting of only 1 percent of the park acreage, these acquisitions had averaged slightly over thirty-five dollars an acre, or 16 percent of the $1,822,120 expended for Big Bend's land acquisition program. It had taken almost four decades, but Big Bend National Park finally belonged to the American people. Although there still were, and are, mineral interests inside the boundaries of the park, they constituted only 0.5 percent of the park acreage. Furthermore, the secretary of the interior has to authorize any mineral exploitation in the national parks, which is improbable.[20]

Since 1972, additional acquisitions have increased the total acreage from 708,118.40 to 801,163.02. The two largest additions were the Pitcock Rosillos Mountains Ranch (24,737.90 acres, 1980) and the Harte Ranch in the North Rosillos Mountains (56,719.65 acres, 1987). The Park Service's main reason for the acquisitions was to provide buffers against speculators and developers whose projects threatened to intrude on the aesthetic, natural, and cultural setting of the park and its environs. One entrepreneur, for example, has divided up land adjacent to the northwest boundary into twenty- to forty-acre "ranchettes" where owners can park mobile homes in the middle of their estates. Budget constraints since the 1970s throughout the park system have hampered expansion at individual sites. At Big Bend, substantial donations have helped considerably; nevertheless, over 35,000 acres enclosed in the park boundaries remain in private ownership, with the consequence that occasionally one can view hunters stalking game, or livestock grazing in a national park. The Pitcock property contains a private airstrip, which the Park Service uses "for emergency purposes." Unfortunately, all of these examples send the wrong message to the visiting public about what activities are permitted in a national park.[21]

 Promoting a Park to "Excel
Yellowstone": Publicity and
Public Relations

In spring 1937 the National Park Service contracted Walter Prescott
Webb to serve as a historical consultant on the Big Bend. Webb, a professor of history at the University of Texas, ranked as one of the fore-
most historians on the American West, having already published *The
Great Plains* (1931) and *The Texas Rangers* (1935). On a leave of absence
for the 1936–1937 academic year, he agreed to write a narrative history
of the Trans-Pecos area from Spanish exploration to the 1930s, empha-
sizing the Big Bend Country and its peculiar effect on people. For his
efforts the Park Service would pay him twenty dollars each day of the
two-month assignment.[1]

Webb enthusiastically began the task and by the middle of April 1937
had written two pieces, which were released on consecutive Sundays in
newspapers from coast to coast. The historian, not a stereotypical academic, preferred to write for popular audiences, which occasionally upset his peers and critics. One anonymous reviewer of Webb's first article
had harsh words for his description of the area's geology. "Webb shows
a vivid imagination with little regard for the facts," he wrote. Furthermore, the reader noted that "it was not a 'blast' [interior quotations are
from Webb's unedited draft] that wrecked the mountain. 'Explosive
gas' did not explode. There was no 'supernatural fury.' Waters did not
go down 'to the internal heat to return as steam bringing up molten

lava.' " And finally, the reviewer concluded, "All this may be 'fine writing' but his geology is all haywire." Despite such censures, Webb's style was left intact, even though he irritated a few scientists.[2]

The second article mostly concerned expeditions of river explorers down the Rio Grande, especially through Santa Elena Canyon. The idea of personally making a float trip through the canyon appealed to Webb's love of adventure. In the spirit of the nineteenth-century frontier, Webb had a desire "to do at least one foolish thing each year." While researching his book on the Texas Rangers, he had ridden with the lawmen as they patrolled the border. The river trip likewise provided the element of danger for the Big Bend project.[3]

Webb had asked E. E. Townsend to research earlier canyon expeditions, and he uncovered a wealth of material. The earliest expedition occurred before the Civil War when a Swede, pursued by Apaches, escaped by descending the Rio Grande from El Paso to Brownsville. Other trips down the river followed, including ones by Texas Rangers, geologist Robert Hill, and army and Border Patrol personnel. While most of the passages were uneventful, several people had drowned in Santa Elena Canyon, which was feared for its massive 250-foot rock slide and fierce undertow.[4]

In April 1937 Webb hired Thomas Skaggs of McCamey, Texas, to lead an expedition through Santa Elena Canyon. Skaggs, an experienced "river rat," was a good choice, as he had successfully completed the canyon run several times. The Park Service supported Webb's project because it would help round out his knowledge of the area while generating publicity for the Big Bend Park movement. It also helped that Webb paid for the expedition out of his own pocket.[5]

Locals took delight in giving advice and odds about the dangers faced by the Webb party. Uncle Jimmie Shipman, an old cowboy, warned about the cascading water, which "goes this way against one side of the cliff and plunges back against the other side, and I'm telling you boys, YOU KAINT MAKE IT." Joe Lane, the expedition's cook, was jokingly told that the treacherous river would surely cause his death by drowning. Consequently, any catfish caught would be a part of "old Joe." Lane further reported that "half the people he talks to about the trip offer him sympathy and are afraid he will not come back; the other half hopes he gets drowned and are afraid he will come back." Rumors circulated that when the local undertaker heard about the float trip, he purchased a new suit.[6]

Skaggs, however, confided to Webb that the river passage was considerably safer than driving on the highway. Dams along the upper river and tributaries had more or less tamed the once wild stream. Although flash flooding could occur, the rampaging waters echoed so loudly against the canyon walls that one had ample time to climb to safety. In light of this, Skaggs needled Webb "to pour on the publicity about the dangers of the canyon," that "turbulent, terrorizing, tragedy-marked Canyon of the Santa Helena." Skaggs felt that the trip would be "rather tame but picturesque," and offered, along with Joe Lane, to "run any rapids, capsize our boats, or perform any stunts" to give exciting film footage to the Paramount employee scheduled to accompany the expedition. The antics were unnecessary, however, because the film man had to cancel. In addition to Webb, Skaggs, and Lane, James A. Metcalf, acting chief inspector of the U.S. Immigration Service Border Patrol, also made the trip. Metcalf was a substitute for NPS historian William R. Hagan, a former Webb student, who had conflicting agency business.[7]

Despite assurances about the lack of danger, Webb took no chances. He ordered the construction of two steel, flat-bottomed boats with air chambers and christened them the *Big Bend* and the *Cinco de Mayo*. Sixteen and thirteen feet long, respectively, each boat could be dismantled for portaging over the rock slide. For safety, the four men wore life preservers, and a speed boat was positioned at the mouth of the canyon for quick emergency support. A Coast Guard plane patrolled overhead to warn of rising waters and other hazards. The plane crew devised a simple system using red and white flags to communicate with the boaters. And finally, because of the border's propensity for smugglers and bandits, Webb carried a .45 caliber Colt "for general use and signalling if necessary."[8]

When Webb's wife still expressed concern about her husband's safety, Thomas Skaggs sent a letter to the professor downplaying the river's dangers. "I note what Mrs. Webb says about the trip, and that the *Titanic* also had air chambers. Yes, but we have no icebergs on the Rio Grande in May." Skaggs further offered assurance that there was "absolutely no danger" as the party portaged over the rock slide. On Sunday morning, May 15, her husband stepped into his boat. By the next day, any peace of mind Skaggs's letter might have given her had disappeared.[9]

On Monday evening, thirty-six hours into the expedition, no news

University of Texas historian Walter Prescott Webb, left, prepares to launch *Big Bend* and *Cinco de Mayo*, May 1937. Big Bend National Park, National Park Service.

had been received about the men's whereabouts, and the press assumed the worst. One headline read, "No Word From Four Explorers: Boatmen Still Unreported After Rowing Into Danger Zone Of The Rio Grande." Another dramatically said, "Four Scientists Missing On Dangerous River Trip." The headline in the professor's hometown newspaper reported "Webb Defying Canyon Perils." In truth, the communication system with the Coast Guard had broken down, which explained the lack of news. For the most part, however, the men had experienced a routine float trip including the usual hazards of the swift river, portaging over the rock slide or dodging boulders plummeting "like comets" from the canyon walls. Much more indicative of the "perils" encountered by the so-called scientists and explorers was the following passage recorded by Webb: "A bottle of champagne had been brought, with which to christen the boats when they were put into the water, but after some discussion, it was decided that it would be a shame to waste the champagne and so it was used to toast the success of the venture." Webb did not indicate whether the toast was made at the beginning or the end of the journey. Nevertheless, they completed the trip by Tuesday noon, May 17, and if possible, Webb's enthusiasm for the park waxed even stronger. He wrote that the isolated area possessed "a peculiar romantic quality" and observed that the most beautiful country he had ever seen was in the depths of Santa Elena Canyon.[10]

The scenic attractions of Big Bend gave Texans much to brag about. President Horace Morelock of Sul Ross College at Alpine regarded the view from the South Rim in the Chisos as "the most beautiful panorama on the American continent." Several Texas newspapers condescendingly rated Santa Elena Canyon equal to Arizona's Grand Canyon. When compared to natural beauty, some Texans maintained that the Big Bend was unsurpassed in scenic splendor. Coke Stevenson told his fellow legislators in 1937 that an appropriation for Big Bend would establish a park that would "excel Yellowstone." E. O. Thompson, a member of the State Railroad Commission, bragged that the Big Bend Country was an area "that Europe, even with its Alps, cannot match." The *Woodville* (Texas) *Booster* editorialized, "Why go to Europe anytime?" The *Booster* considered Big Bend "far ahead of either Europe or Asia in beauty and sublimity."[11]

Some Park Service officials got so caught up in the park movement that their rhetoric even surpassed the bragging Texans. One syndicated NPS article that appeared in over two hundred Texas newspapers declared that the Big Bend "is noted for scenic grandeur. Nowhere in America are more picturesque peaks, gorges and valleys." Carroll Wegemann noted that the region was one of the "few areas in the United States" that remained "unchanged by the advance of modern civilization." Roger Toll, Yellowstone's superintendent and chief investigator of proposed sites, corroborated Wegemann's observation by calling the Big Bend "unspoiled." Minor Tillotson, Southwest regional director, often referred to the park as the "last frontier of America."[12]

The Texas press, the Park Service, and others stretched the truth in their efforts to promote the park. A more objective observer was Ross Maxwell, Big Bend's first superintendent from 1944 to 1952. He admitted that the park "can't boast of awe-inspiring beauty, which is found in some of the national parks, but it has scientific phenomena and scenic beauty mingled with historic incidents along the Texas-Mexico frontier that give it a charm and color that is not known in any other park." In addition, Maxwell had personally observed several canyons in the United States that had "greater splendor" than Santa Elena. Furthermore, Big Bend was hardly "unspoiled" or "unchanged by the advance of modern civilization." Decades of overgrazing by sheep and cattle had reduced to "desert pavement" land once covered with grass so profuse that an early settler estimated there was enough "to fatten every horse and cow in the United States." And corporations, chopping down trees to shore up the mines and to stoke the furnaces, exhausted timber resources. Finally, calling Big Bend America's last frontier had a romantic appeal, but was inaccurate because it ignored the vast wilderness of Alaska.[13]

For the most part, news stories on the proposed national park concentrated on its unique biological, geological, international, and scenic features. The Chisos Mountains and surrounding plains were popular subjects because they constituted the only "biological island" in the national park system, which contained species of animals, birds, and plants found nowhere else in the United States, such as the drooping juniper. The Colima Warbler's northern range in the Western Hemisphere, for example, extends into the Chisos. The Big Bend Country offers a natural classroom of earth history, with glaciation the only geological process that did not occur. Another popular subject was paleontology. Numerous photographs and stories featured fossil remains of dinosaur skeletons and giant oyster shells, the latter measuring over twelve square feet. The idea of an international "peace" park especially appealed to Americans during World War II, as it symbolized the future after an Allied victory. Furthermore, an international park on the southern border would complement Waterton-Glacier International Peace Park, the Canadian-U.S. park established in 1932.[14]

An effective publicity campaign should emphasize the positive and whenever possible avoid the controversial or unpleasant. Occasionally, however, an adverse incident surfaced at Big Bend. In 1937, newspapers carried a story describing an incident in which a black bear stampeded nineteen goats over a three-thousand-foot precipice in the park. The "goat tragedy" could not have come at a worse time, for the Park Service had finally convinced the Texas Parks and Wildlife Department to add the black bear to the protected game animal list. Ironically, it was an NPS press release that had first called attention to the incident. An agency official regretted issuing the story to the press since

Embedded in the "desert pavement" are ocotillo bushes in the foreground, creosote bushes beyond, and the Chisos Mountains on the horizon. Photo by George A. Grant, National Park Service, Harpers Ferry, West Virginia.

Quicksilver mine, Terlingua, Texas, west of the park. Photo by George A. Grant, National Park Service, Harpers Ferry, West Virginia.

it "will not be appreciated by local ranchmen." (For additional negative publicity concerning livestock and predators, see Chapter 6.)[15]

The efforts to make Big Bend appeal to the traveling public sometimes distorted reality. When the NPS commissioned a movie of the park in 1935, an agency official instructed the filmmakers to shoot most of the footage in "the very interesting forest color" of the Chisos Mountains. He apparently felt that tourists would not care to vacation in the Chihuahuan Desert, which comprised the majority of the park acres. Yet when foggy weather delayed a *Life* magazine crew doing a photographic essay on Big Bend, a Park Service critic took issue with a related newspaper story since it clashed with the publicists' image of Big Bend as a year-round park basking in the sun.[16]

Despite efforts by the Park Service to control it, adverse publicity has continued over the decades. In 1937 opponents of the park spread rumors that new veins of gold and cinnabar had been discovered, which caused a rush of speculators to the Big Bend Country and convinced some that the government's claim that the park contained only submarginal grazing lands was false. To compound the problem, the State Land Commission permitted speculators to file on the park acres.[17]

America's entry into World War II was the catalyst for negative publicity from Drew Pearson's column "The Washington Merry-Go-Round." In a piece titled "Gas Masks or Parks?" Pearson singled out Big Bend and the Park Service, accusing the agency of withholding essential resources from the military. At Big Bend the candelilla plant yields a wax used as a sealing compound in gas masks. According to Pearson's sources, a patriotic New York millionaire had invested in a factory to extract the wax, only to have the NPS close down his operation. He was informed that he had violated Service policy, which forbids the destruction of a park's natural resources. Pearson, ordinarily a staunch backer of the national parks, concluded, "So now the deer and the antelope, instead of gas mask wearers, will have the benefit of the candelilla." The situation, however, was not as drastic as Pearson implied. If the journalist had checked his facts, he would have found that much more candelilla was growing outside the park boundaries in Brewster and Presidio Counties. It also turned out that the "patriotic millionaire" was not a very good businessman, having failed to pay for machinery and other processing equipment.[18]

Over subsequent decades humorous, bizarre, and tragic incidents have continued to produce publicity and public relations crises (see

Chapter 8). Overall, the Big Bend has weathered these challenges, partly because of the attraction Americans have for their national parks, but also due to the well-organized publicity activities of the Park Service at national, regional, and local levels.

The capable coordinator of the publicity campaign was Isabelle F. Story, information officer for the NPS. Director Stephen Mather had recruited her from the U.S. Geological Survey in 1917, and early on she had demonstrated a sophisticated mastery of effective advertising techniques, which she applied to the Big Bend campaign. For example, in 1938 Story and her staff provided Texas newspapers a series of twenty-eight Sunday features on the established national parks—complete with photographs—that ran for over half a year "in the hope the civic pride of Texans will be sufficiently aroused to put over the Big Bend park." Other articles, pictorial features, and "boiler plate" editorials focused specifically on Big Bend and appeared in newspapers from coast to coast. One editorial carried in several newspapers asked, "Why should anyone ever leave Florida (or California)?" The answer: "They both go to see Big Bend." [19]

The Park Service used other media as well to promote Big Bend. For the 1936 Texas Centennial Exposition in Dallas the agency constructed a scale-model relief map, which was later displayed in the State Capitol's Rotunda during the critical 1939 legislative session. According to observers, the detailed model favorably influenced legislators, who in turn passed major park bills that year (see Chapter 2). The Park Service also undertook its first film project in several years when the Texas Gulf Sulphur Company donated $4,500 to pay for the production of a color movie on Big Bend. Other organizations and individuals likewise produced films and scheduled illustrated lectures across the state, which stimulated interest in Big Bend National Park. [20]

Another publicity technique that was especially effective was the use of prominent scholars and other well-known personalities to promote Big Bend. We have already encountered Lady Bird Johnson and Walter Prescott Webb. A good friend of Webb's was southwestern writer J. Frank Dobie, who accompanied the *National Geographic* team that visited the region in 1938. Dobie returned to the Big Bend Country during the winter of 1939 to work on a book on longhorn cattle. Robert T. Hill, the geologist-explorer still active over four decades after his expedition through the canyons of the Rio Grande, offered to publicize the park in a weekly newspaper column. And when Herbert Bolton, a noted historian of the borderlands and the American West, retraced Coronado's travels through the Trans-Pecos Country, the event was widely covered by the press.[21]

Texas' eccentric governor W. Lee "Pappy" O'Daniel had a natural flair for publicity, which he effectively used to promote Big Bend. After learning that the king and queen of England planned a visit to the United States in 1939, O'Daniel sent a telegram to "King George, care of the White House" and invited him "to bring the Queen along" on a visit to Texas and the Big Bend. That same year the governor signed the legislation that authorized transfer of the Big Bend lands in fee simple title to the federal government. Photographers recorded O'Daniel signing his name with four Texas-size pens, each forty-two inches long, one of which was later given to President Roosevelt.[22]

The president likewise was an enthusiastic Big Bend booster. In 1939 he personally had encouraged the Texas legislature—through a letter to Governor O'Daniel—to appropriate funds to acquire the park's lands. He also occasionally discussed Big Bend individually with members of the Texas delegation to Congress. In a letter to Representative Ewing Thomason, he wrote, "I have heard so much of the wildness and the beauty of this still inaccessible corner of the United States and also of its important archaeological remains that I very much hope that some day I will be able to travel through it myself." Of particular interest to Roosevelt was the international feature, which "will do much to strengthen the friendship and good neighborliness of the people" on both sides of the border. In 1940 at the dedication of Great Smoky Mountains National Park in Tennessee, the president expressed the wish that Big Bend would be the next park established during his administration.[23]

Harold Ickes was another prominent politician who spoke out in favor of Big Bend. In fall 1937, the secretary of the interior came to Texas to dedicate a New Deal reservoir project at Buchanan and Inks Dams on the Brazos River, and he devoted much of his speech to Big Bend, pointing out to Texans that their state still lacked a national park. Hoping to "light a fire" under the languishing park movement, Ickes reminded them of the unique attractions of the area that could become "one of the outstanding national parks in the whole country" if Texans would only acquire the acres. While Ickes felt the purchase price (then estimated at $1 million) was justified "on aesthetic and altruistic grounds alone," he instead offered "a business proposition" to the "hard-headed business men of Texas." As the citizens of Wyoming, Montana, Colorado, and California could attest, national parks attracted tourists who spent considerable sums of money in the states they traveled through on their way to Yosemite, Yellowstone, and Rocky Mountain National Parks. "Give me the profits that would accrue to the citizens of Texas from the establishment of this park," Ickes said, "and I would undertake to buy the land necessary and turn it over to the Federal Government even if I had to raise ten million dollars for it. Conservative investors would fight each other for an opportunity to put their money into a proposition that would pay so richly and inevitably." [24]

The Park Service itself often used economic arguments in support of Big Bend. Early in the movement, Director Arno B. Cammerer spoke in El Paso before a partisan group of representatives from West Texas chambers of commerce and city and county officials. The director told of hard times in Utah during another depression earlier in the century when Mormons had had to sell eggs for five cents a dozen, and, finding no market for surplus butter, had used it as wagon axle grease. Prosperity finally returned after the establishment of Zion National Park in 1919, when tourists flocked to the state. Minor Tillotson, the Park Service's Southwest regional director, estimated that visitors to Big Bend would annually spend at least $2,388,000 in the state. He then calculated that on the basis of a 3 percent return the figure would justify a capital investment of $79,600,000, yet Texans would only have to pay $1–$1.5 million. [25]

Texas newspapers likewise emphasized economic returns from national parks. According to the *Fort Worth Star-Telegram*, Yellowstone and Grand Teton together accounted for fully one-third of Wyoming's tourist revenues. The Fort Worth paper also carried a series of articles on the importance of the travel industry to the Lone Star State, noting that Big Bend "likely offers more surprises to the visitor than any other attraction in or out of Texas." The *San Antonio Express* pointed out that tourism in 1936 grossed $446 million making it the second largest industry in the state behind crude oil ($450 million) and ahead of agriculture ($284 million). The *Express* editor confidently predicted that Big Bend could produce $4 million during its first year, boosting tourism into a first-place tie. [26]

The Lone Star State's newspapers also backed the park in the political arena. In 1937, for example, major dailies in Fort Worth, San Antonio, Houston, and Tyler endorsed the first appropriation bill for

$750,000. When Governor James Allred vetoed it, only a few news-papers supported his action. None opposed a national park as such, but rather the wisdom of a deficit appropriation. The majority of the papers, however, criticized Allred's decision. Typical of the responses were those of the *El Paso Daily Times* and the *San Antonio Express,* which again emphasized the economic benefits of a national park. "Governor Allred says we can't afford it," the *Times* concluded. "Did you ever hear of such smallness of vision in a governor's office?" During the nine years between the passage of the enabling legislation in 1935 and the opening of the park in 1944, the Texas press continued to pro-vide coverage of political developments and fund-raising activities, as well as articles and photographs on the Big Bend's attractions. An edi-torial in the *Lufkin Daily News* expressed a common sentiment held by many Texans about the park: "It is a far cry from the piney woods of East Texas to the rugged grandeur of the Big Bend country, but the development of splendid possibilities out there for a national park of ultimate worldwide fame is an undertaking meriting the support of all sections of Texas." [27]

Individuals acting on their own also publicized the park. Cowboy artist "Las Vegas Kim" (Texon postmaster J. Edgar Kimsey) drew sketches of western scenes for anyone contributing one dollar to the popular subscription campaign. Among the recipients was Governor Allred. Brothers Roy and W. E. Swift from South Texas completed a daring passage through a dangerous twenty-one-mile stretch of Santa Elena Canyon without a boat. They swam, waded, and used inner tubes through the treacherous rapids, roping themselves over the rock slide and other impassable obstacles. Reverend and Mrs. Milton Hill from Marfa, Texas, made three float trips with friends through the major canyons in the park. Hill reported that Mariscal Canyon "has more variety and rock sculpture" than the more frequently visited Santa Elena. Rollo Walter Brown, a Boston author, wrote a book titled *I Travel by Train,* which contained several pages on Big Bend and Sul Ross College, where he had taught one summer session after arriving via the Southern Pacific Railroad. Brown commented on the spec-tacular scenery (the Chisos Mountains were "unworldly in their crag-giness"), including the natural beauty of the young women of West Texas, which he rated superior to that of women in any other region in the United States. [28]

The grandeur of the Big Bend inspired poets as well, even those who had never visited the area. Nolan Clark, self-proclaimed Texas barber poet, offered his services to promote the park when he sent the following unsolicited verses to the Park Service:

> Come all you loyal Texans,
> > I've long been one myself,
> Let's rally round this project,
> > and take it off the shelf.
> Big Bend is on the program,
> > for our Nation's greatest park,
> With Uncle Sam our Captain,
> > we need not fear embark.
>
> This program is no "ballyhoo,"
> > no "gouger," "bleeder trick."
> With government endorsement,
> > we'll truly "make her stick."
> Artistically we'll landscape
> > her nature in the "raw."
> She'll be viewed with thrilling wonder
> > and with enchanting awe.
> She'll be our Nation's playground,
> > none ere surpass we know.
> She'll be a sound investment,
> > and double pay back "dough."
>
> With scenery fascinating,
> > balmy Southwest clime,
> She'll "magnetize" vacationist
> > with delight from time to time.
> The hunter and the fisherman,
> > here is their "paradise."
> She's a sportsman's dreamland,
> > her winters have no ice.
> So loyal Texans let's all "chip in,"
> > take Big Bend "on your lap."
> And show up to the World
> > What's on our Lone Star Map.

Clark's business slogan ("'Poemize' anything about anything") was enclosed with the copy of the poem. Needless to say, his verses were not used to publicize Big Bend. While Clark's effort was sincere, his lack of understanding about activities permitted in national parks assured he would not be retained by the NPS.[29]

A verse submitted by fourteen-year-old Pete Williams from San Angelo to *Sparks,* the employees' newsletter of the Texas State Parks Board, captures the spell of the region as well as words can:

> The Big Bend's voice
>   is that of silence;
> Never a word has it spoken.
>   And its silence
> Has the power to still
>   even the memory of sound.
> The Big Bend is like a land
>   once known and then forgotten,
> Where modern machines and
>   evil ways have never come.
> A land where legend
>   is stronger than truth.[30]

Only two major magazines carried articles on Big Bend before June 1944, *Literary Digest* and *National Geographic.* Frederick Simpich, a *Geographic* associate editor, wrote an entertaining but misleading article that depicted the area as a "waste of sun and silence" in which predators roamed at will in the strange land whose human inhabitants ate cougar meat and fried Spanish daggers (a cactus) and drank burro milk. Simpich remarked that the mountain lion's flesh "looked and smelled like beef—but didn't taste like it." Incidentally, the cougar that Simpich's party feasted on was killed by a Mexican herdsman who had lost eighteen goats to the big cats. To Simpich's credit, he did discuss the proposed international park.[31]

After the park opened to the public in July 1944, articles were published in *Life, Collier's, Saturday Evening Post, Parade,* and other less well known magazines. The *Alpine Avalanche* considered the *Life* pictorial essay "probably the best piece of publicity ever given the Big Bend." NPS Director Newton B. Drury also praised the work of the magazine.[32]

Park Service officials considered the worst article one written by Kenneth Foree for the *Saturday Evening Post.* Foree sent the manuscript (originally titled "No Man's Land Becomes Park") to Superintendent Ross Maxwell for his comments. Maxwell, objecting to the article's title and content, which unduly emphasized the blood and gore of the region's past, suggested that "it should be made clear that the Big Bend National Park is not an outlaw's paradise at the present." The superintendent also corrected numerous factual errors before the manuscript went to press. Even more critical was Isabelle F. Story, editor-in-chief of the NPS. She wrote, "Why not call it 'The Hard Men of Texas'? Big Bend seems incidental. And apparently the literary standards of the *Saturday Evening Post* are deteriorating." Despite the criticisms, Foree's article did have one major strength: it gave a thorough and entertaining account of the significant contributions of E. E. Townsend to the park movement.[33]

Townsend of course had lots of help locally and across the state. Brewster County, which had the most to gain from a national park, spent over $35,000 on parades, barbecues, tours, and other promotional public relations activities. The Texas Federation of Women's Clubs,

Giant Dagger from Dagger Flats. Photo by Fred E. Mang, Jr., National Park Service, Harpers Ferry, West Virginia.

interested in a national park for the Lone Star State since early in the twentieth century, set out to educate Texans on Big Bend. Members sent scores of letters to chambers of commerce, automobile associations, and travel agencies, and set up a speakers' bureau that sent volunteers across the state. A few of the other groups who supported the park movement were the Texas Big Bend Park Association, Rotary International, Kiwanis, the Lions Club, Daughters of the American Revolution, Texas Federation of Garden Clubs, Texas Junior Chamber of Commerce, Texas Congress of Parents and Teachers, Zonta Club, Texas Real Estate Club, Cooperative Club, Texas Hotel Association, Texas Press Association, U.S. Highway 67 Association, Texas Club in New York City, International Parks Highway Association, as well as various other businesses, schools, and chambers of commerce.[34]

The well-orchestrated publicity efforts probably did not significantly shorten the time between the enabling legislation and the opening of the park in 1944, but they definitely made many Americans—Texans included—aware of the unique appeal and attractions at Big Bend. World War II made travel difficult because of rubber and gasoline rationing and the curtailment of automobile manufacturing. Consequently, from 1944 through 1945 only 4,614 people visited the park. The next two years the numbers increased to over 38,000, finally surpassing 100,000 for the first time in 1963. Since 1971, annual visitation has fluctuated between 200,000 plus and a high of 456,201 during the nation's bicentennial celebrations.[35]

After Big Bend opened to the public in 1944, publicity and public relations efforts continued along familiar directions but with new angles as well. As before, some press releases emphasized Big Bend's special attractions to draw visitors to the remote park: the best times to view the desert flowers, stories on the latest paleontological discoveries, or dates and details on international festivals. Educating the public about Park Service policies and programs likewise received plenty of print, with pieces, for example, on endangered species, recruitment of youth conservation employees, and the collection of entrance fees.[36]

Not surprisingly, a few of the policies, such as charging a users' fee for admission, are controversial or unpopular, and public relations efforts intensify to explain them. In 1987 when the fees first went into effect, Superintendent Jim Carrico assured the public that any funds collected would be spent only at 134 national park sites. Congress had appropriated $91,000 for Big Bend as an advance on anticipated revenues. The funds would permit the extension of visitor center hours, additional interpretive programs, and other projects. "Congress expects us to spend the money," Carrico said, "to protect Big Bend, to learn more about its cultural and natural history, and to expand opportunities for visitor enjoyment." [37] The public relations intent is obvious.

Unlike their counterparts of the 1930s and early 1940s, today's Park Service staff usually face negative developments head-on, which helps squelch rumors before they get started. When "killer bees" first entered the park in 1992, a news release noted their detection at the Rio Grande Village campgrounds and included instructions on how to identify the insects (by their aggressive behavior) and what to do if stung ("Don't remove the stinger by squeezing. Scrape it out with a fingernail.").[38]

A publicity and public relations strategy that has not changed over the decades stresses the substantial economic returns generated by national parks. In July 1994 Superintendent Robert Arnberger reported the results of a "Money Generation Model" used to determine Big Bend's economic effect on local communities within a hundred-mile radius of the park. The model, which analyzed visitor and park expenditures and visitation statistics, revealed that in 1993 Big Bend produced approximately $35 million in sales benefits, including $2.37 million in local and state tax revenues and the creation of over twelve hundred jobs.[39]

 From Dude Ranches to
Haciendas: A Half-Century
of Planning

In fall 1934, almost a year before Congress passed Big Bend's enabling legislation, Secretary of the Interior Harold Ickes received an unusual letter from Albert W. Dorgan, a World War I aviator and unemployed landscape architect in Castolon, Texas. Dorgan asked Ickes for a job helping with the planning and development of an international park that Dorgan proposed the federal government establish at Big Bend. Enclosed with his resume were detailed plans for a "Friendly Nations Park."

Dorgan envisioned an "International Peace Park" where each of the nations in the Western Hemisphere would offer crafts demonstrations, permanent and changing exhibits, and performances of their art, music, literature, folklore, and history. Each country would have approximately fifty acres for displays housed in structures reflecting its distinct architectural style. Dorgan's vision also included museums, living replicas of frontier towns, and health resorts in the mountains and on the shores of artificial lakes. According to Dorgan, the lakes would be created by dams "planned in such a manner that the natural beauty of the canyons would not be marred." The personnel recruited to work at the park would be of the highest caliber: clean-cut high school and college students who passed a rigorous screening test.

Dorgan also listed ideas that would help overcome Big Bend's geographical isolation. Airplane landing fields would allow affluent guests easy access to the desert park while providing them an opportunity to see Big Bend's scenery from the air. Since most visitors would arrive by automobile, Dorgan's grandest scheme involved a "Super-Scenic Highway," or "Highway Americana," winding from Alaska through the Big Bend and ending at Argentina's southernmost tip. As an added benefit, if diplomacy soured among countries along the route, Dorgan noted that the highway could be used as a "military road" by which the United States could send armies and weapons to "easily subdue Mexico."[1]

Albert Dorgan was a man ahead of his time. His plans, for example, foreshadowed Walt Disney's Epcot Center, other amusement parks (e.g., Six Flags over Texas), and the Interstate Highway System. It may be difficult to imagine one of America's scenic national parks with re-created frontier towns, dams and reservoirs, airfields, and extensive development, but Dorgan's dreams for Big Bend were prophetic.

Work began on the first master plan for Big Bend in the mid-1930s and continued for ten years as Park Service staff waited for the state of Texas to purchase the acreage (over 700,000 acres) to deed to the federal government.[2] In 1935 a Service official commented on the unique opportunity for planning at Big Bend: "After all, we are starting out with an almost untouched wilderness area, and every element of the development will have some first class prototype in some National Park." At Big Bend planners hoped development could advance by incorporating proven policies rather than the trial-and-error efforts used at some older parks, which had threatened both natural and cultural resources while diminishing the quality of visitors' experiences.[3] However, planners encountered obstacles when confronted with the reality of implementing resource use and preservation plans in a multilevel bureaucracy dependent on Congress for funding. An examination of the planning process for the park over the last fifty years sheds some light on the difficulties they faced.[4]

As part of a mandate in the agency's organic legislation, the National Park Service encouraged Americans to visit their national parks, but the Service also encouraged visits partly to convince Congress to appropriate more funds for protection and development.[5] Park Service planners estimated in the 1930s that when Big Bend opened to the public, 100,000 people would visit annually, spending $4 million in the Lone Star State. For the next decade the agency revised the number to

240,000 visitors annually, and by the park's dedication in 1955 Secretary of the Interior Douglas McKay confidently projected a half million visitors annually.[6] West Texas travel industry boosters interpreted the figures as proof of the Park Service's commitment to extensive developments at Big Bend (paved roads, bridges, a lodge, a variety of recreational activities) to lure the predicted numbers of visitors to the remote desert site. In fact, some Park Service staff proposed elaborate and expensive projects similar to Dorgan's, while other planners at the agency called for only limited improvements to preserve Big Bend as the "last frontier." The stage was set for an acrimonious debate between park boosters and those who wanted less development, a controversy that divided even Park Service staff.

Minor R. Tillotson, the National Park Service's Southwest regional director, paradoxically embraced both positions. In a 1940 speech to a local booster group, he envisioned Big Bend and its frontier atmosphere with minimal automobile roads and a vast network of horse and hiking trails. Tillotson proposed to "send the visitor on the hurricane deck of a cayuse instead of the rear seat of a limousine—give him chuck wagon instead of high hat hotel service—teach him to throw a diamond hitch and let him pack out on the trail from the [Chisos Basin] Window to Mariscal." The regional director ended his talk with a call "to make Big Bend utterly unique among the national parks" by creating unusual tourist attractions that emphasized the area's frontier heritage. Unfortunately, Tillotson's ideas would actually require more rather than less development.[7]

One attraction Tillotson considered was construction of a replica of Judge Roy Bean's Jersey Lilly saloon. (Dorgan's "frontier village" had also included a saloon.) Bean, a justice of the peace, was the self-proclaimed "Law West of the Pecos," as the hand-painted sign on the front of his establishment boasted, and from his saloon he dispensed both justice and liquor. Bean renamed both his saloon and Langtry, Texas—located on the eastern edge of the Big Bend Country—for Lily Langtry, a British actress born in the Channel Islands. Tillotson remarked that the saloon suggestion "may be well worth investigating," but the idea was ultimately discarded.[8] Two other ideas received more serious consideration: a longhorn cattle ranch and establishment of an international park.

In 1935 the Park Service began to discuss establishing a cattle operation complete with a dude ranch at Big Bend. At various times the

Judge Roy Bean's Jersey Lilly saloon before restoration. Big Bend National
Park, National Park Service.

Park Service's wildlife chief, head of recreational planning, and as-
sorted biologists and environmentalists and representatives from other
cooperating agencies endorsed the project. By the end of the decade,
a longhorn ranch seemed certain to be part of Big Bend's development plans.[9]

The Park Service justified the 200,000-acre ranch on historical, pres-
ervationist, and recreational grounds. The ranch was to serve "as a
shrine for the preservation of the true spirit of the pioneer West." The
agency maintained that buffalo and longhorn, vestiges of the open-
range cattle industry, were important symbols of the West. Both species
were endangered, but only the buffalo had begun to recover in numbers. The only effort made to preserve the longhorn had been a small
herd maintained at the Wichita Mountains Game Preserve in Oklahoma. According to the Big Bend plans, visitors would view a show
herd of thirty to forty longhorns; the Park Service would keep approximately four hundred others for breeding at Banta Shut-In, north of the
Chisos Mountains and south of Tornillo Flat. Spring and fall round-
ups, brandings, and barbecues would be part of the entertainment for
visitors.[10]

Agency officials contended that because the animals would be kept at
distant and lower elevations, they would not threaten the flora of the
Chisos Range, but local ranchers objected to the prospect of longhorns

at Big Bend. The Park Service wanted to begin moving families and their animals out of the park in June 1944, despite public clamor to let livestock remain during World War II to help feed and clothe the Allied troops. Supporters of the ranchers argued that Big Bend could not be developed until after the war anyway so ranchers should be permitted to stay until the war's conclusion.[11] The Park Service countered that the overgrazed land, incapable of supporting cattle, goats, or sheep, would take from twenty-five to one hundred years to return to its natural condition, and the war years would provide an ideal time for the recovery process to begin, since few visitors could travel to the remote park because of fuel and tire rationing. However, the agency finally responded to public pressure and allowed ranchers to remain until the end of the war, adversely affecting range recovery.[12]

Further developments in the 1940s sealed the fate of a longhorn ranch at Big Bend. As a nonessential wartime agency, the Park Service's lean appropriations meant that costly programs such as the ranch and longhorn herds were either delayed or dropped. In addition, Director Newton B. Drury opposed the plan, considering it a violation of policies against introducing exotic species into parks. Those who tried on historical grounds to justify the longhorns' presence did not have a very strong case; J. Frank Dobie, an authority on the breed, doubted if the animals had ever roamed the Big Bend Country.[13]

Minor Tillotson was among the people most disappointed about the abandonment of the longhorn project. Tillotson criticized the director's office for acting too hastily and not giving the regional office or the superintendent enough "leeway in presenting their own ideas and suggestions for the proposed park development before specific instructions were issued."[14] The conflict over development policies continued throughout the 1940s.

Of all the ideas to make Big Bend unique, the one that aroused the most interest concerned the establishment of an international park on the Rio Grande to complement Waterton-Glacier International Peace Park on the Canadian–U.S. border. The Park Service reported to President Franklin D. Roosevelt in 1935 that since the "atmosphere in the region is decidedly one of *mañana* . . . this restful spirit in architecture and daily life . . . rather than ruggedness should be the spirit of the day." Service architects drew up designs for a hacienda–style lodge and a tourist complex on the Rio Grande, which included a Mexican restaurant with waiters in native costume.[15]

Negotiations between Mexico and the United States in regard to creating the international park broke off in the late 1940s, although they have resumed sporadically in subsequent years. One hopeful development occurred in 1976 when the United Nations Educational, Scientific, and Cultural Organization (UNESCO) designated Big Bend a "Man and the Biosphere" reserve, one of twenty-eight in the United States. An important objective was to encourage international cooperation, which inspired Mexico and the United States to sign agreements concerning resource management projects and training. For example, "Project Diablos" trained twenty Mexican citizens to serve as a "hotshot" crew to assist Park Service firefighters in Big Bend. In another example, Mexican experts on adobe restorations trained park volunteers. Mexican officials also requested that the Denver Service Center, the NPS's principal planning office, help draw up plans for a companion, or "sister," park in Coahuila, Mexico. Concern about a central location in a future international park originally caused planners to consider the river site for the park headquarters and the main tourist development.[16]

When negotiations stalled in the 1940s, Park Service planners concluded that without an adjoining park on the Mexican side of the Rio Grande the location of the hacienda development would not suit Anglo visitors. Many people who traveled to Big Bend came during the hot summer months and preferred the cooler Chisos Mountains instead of the river, where temperatures often exceed 110 degrees (Fahrenheit) for several days at a time. Otherwise, the climate in this section of the park was ideal for vacationers eight months of the year.[17]

In June 1944, Texas ceded jurisdiction of Big Bend to the federal government. Shortly thereafter the Park Service completed the draft of the master plan document, which Director Newton B. Drury approved on September 18, 1944. Despite the occasional conflicts it caused between the regional and national offices of the Park Service, the plan contained sound policies for restoring and maintaining scenic, biological, geological, and historical resources while also allowing limited visitor access and use. The three principal areas designated for physical development were Panther Junction on the northeast slope of the Chisos Mountains, the old Daniels and Graham Ranch on the Rio Grande near Boquillas, Mexico, and the Chisos Mountains Basin. In addition, a concessionaire would provide visitor accommodations and services.

The Park Service selected Panther Junction as the site for park headquarters because the area had an adequate water supply, a comfortable year-round climate, and a strategic location at the center of the park's primitive road system. Opinions as to the location of the main park development vacillated between the Chisos Basin and the Rio Grande. The director's office generally favored the latter, while the regional office and the superintendent supported the former. In the first master plan, the director's office prevailed. The Park Service selected the river site at the Daniels and Graham Ranch, where it planned to construct the main lodge as visitation increased and Congress authorized increased funding.[18] Forces were already at work, however, that doomed any chance that the major development would be located on the Rio Grande.

During the brief period that Big Bend was a state park in the 1930s, a Civilian Conservation Corps (CCC) camp established its headquarters in the Chisos Basin. There the enrollees constructed crude campsites, cabins, roads, and trails. At an elevation of 5,000 feet, Chisos Basin soon became the principal summer tourist spot in the new national park. Nevertheless, as late as 1948 a Service report emphasized that "development in this area will be restrained." Concerned about the relatively small area, it further warned against extensive physical improvements, which "would seriously impair the scenic aspects . . . and depreciate [the Basin's] value as a visitor attraction." Moreover, the study doubted that sufficient water was available for a major tourist center. Despite these conclusions, Superintendent Ross A. Maxwell and Southwest Regional Director Minor Tillotson convinced Director Drury the next year temporarily to continue the development of the Basin so that there could be "good service in at least one area."[19] By the mid-1950s the temporary facilities had become permanent, and the Basin remained the park's major tourist attraction.

The Basin's main advantage was its cooler climate; most visitors came during the summer months when the lower elevations along the Rio Grande were intolerably hot. Conrad Wirth, one of a minority in the national office who backed the Basin over river development, suggested that "planners . . . spend a week down there [at the Rio Grande] during the hot summer days to determine whether it is a suitable climate for visitors." In Superintendent Maxwell's estimation, 90 percent of all visitors came to the Basin, where they would need accommodations and services. He opposed making the location a "sacred area" for "Ph.D.s to spend a vacation," which would exclude most of the park's

"Dallas Huts" in the Basin beneath Casa Grande. Purchased from the Atomic Energy Commission, the prefabricated cabins were manufactured in Dallas, Texas. Photo by George A. Grant, National Park Service, Harpers Ferry, West Virginia.

visitors. Drawing on firsthand observations as superintendent, Maxwell did not feel that "we will be able to satisfy Texans with a ballroom, shade trees and Mexican music on the banks of the Rio Grande." [20]

The company that was awarded the concession franchise at Big Bend added more fuel to the controversy of full versus limited development. National Park Concessions, Inc., a nonprofit distribution company, operated in remote parks that private businesses considered risky ventures. The concessionaire provided limited services and accommodations in a few basic government-owned buildings. Overnight facilities included forty prefabricated cabins with tar-paper roofs purchased from the Atomic Energy Commission's facility at Oak Ridge, Tennessee. After World War II, Congress failed to appropriate funds for capital improvements at Big Bend, so National Park Concessions absorbed the expense of constructing additional temporary accommodations, hoping to recover the costs from tourism revenues. Unfortunately, Americans did not travel to Big Bend in significant numbers after the war. From 1946 to 1950 the company lost $55,000 and began to explore cost-cutting measures. One idea was to close the Basin concessions from November through April, the period when overall park visitation was lowest. Superintendent Maxwell, especially sensitive to local concerns, successfully blocked the closing idea by arguing that the Park Service had promised Texans a year-round park.[21]

One of Minor Tillotson's dreams was that Big Bend "be essentially a saddle and pack horse area," a dream that went unfulfilled for five years because of insufficient funds to improve trails and establish a saddle-horse concession. In August 1949 the horse-riding concession opened and was so successful that by 1952 revenues had increased by 300 percent. Lack of funds also affected the park's interpretive programs. The first campfire program occurred in May 1947; throughout the 1940s Big Bend did not have a naturalist.[22]

Through the 1950s and early 1960s the number of tourists to Big Bend averaged 80,000 annually, a figure far below the original projections of between a quarter million and a half million visitors. Although it only handled about one-tenth the average number of visitors for other western parks, by the late 1950s the concession franchise no longer operated at a deficit and the Service no longer considered closing it for part of the year. From 1950 to 1962 the annual visitor count to Big Bend ranged from 67,000 to more than 91,000. Beginning in 1963, annual visitation counts increased rapidly. The Park Service does not offer a "precise explanation" for the increase, but Americans' growing awareness of the values of wilderness experiences may have contributed to the trend. Even relatively high gasoline prices during 1973–1974 only temporarily reduced the number of visitors to Big Bend to 191,252. By 1974 the annual count was back to more than 300,000 visitors. In 1980, however, the annual visitor count dropped to 209,650, gradually climbing back to over 300,000 by 1993.[23]

Cabins and campgrounds in the Basin and elsewhere occasionally filled to capacity, such as during the Christmas and Easter seasons. Overall, however, the limited number of visitors during the 1940s and 1950s did not adversely affect the fragile desert environment. In fact, the Service's limited budget and the temporary decline in visitors during World War II contributed more to preserving the "last frontier" and "unspoiled wilderness" of the Big Bend than any Park Service policies or planning proposals. The park's isolation and its primitive accommodations discouraged all but the most adventuresome vacationers. Big Bend supporters who had expected large economic returns were disappointed, but the natural, historic, and cultural resources remained stable. Although Park Service experts debated the extent of range recovery, all agreed that there had been noticeable improvement since the cessation of grazing in 1945. With the park's establishment and the subsequent curtailment of hunting and trapping, Big Bend's deer, panther, coyote, javelina, beaver, quail, and dove populations increased.[24]

National parks that were more visited during the 1940s and 1950s did not fare as well as Big Bend. The American public almost "loved to death" its national park system, which could adequately accommodate 21 million people, yet faced an annual onslaught of 55 million. Conrad Wirth, NPS Director from 1951 to 1964, warned that "facilities were out of date and run down, roads were in dangerous conditions, trails were washed out, employee morale was at a low level, and even scenic beauty was deteriorating." Responding to the crisis, the Park Service in 1955 presented President Dwight Eisenhower and Congress with a long-range plan called Mission 66. It estimated that the present and future needs of the parks would cost $786.5 million over a ten-year period. Physical improvements, restoration of park resources, increased staffs for protection and interpretation, and additional lands to complete the system eventually would cost American taxpayers over one billion dollars by 1966.[25]

Big Bend's share from Mission 66 was $14 million, which the Park Service used to improve roads, bridges, trails, and tourist accommodations, including a lodge, restaurant, cabins, and campsites in the Basin. A Texas newspaper editor concluded that the improvements "will neither sissify nor citify the wilderness which is the principal appeal of all national parks. It will bring the wilderness a little nearer to the average visitor, help him understand it and enjoy it without risk to his health and safety, and keep down the wear and tear on the car in which he will travel."[26] He did not, however, mention the "wear and tear" on Big Bend's ecology.

The 1960s produced a large influx of visitors to the park and healthy revenues for nearby West Texas communities. The hordes of tourists upset the balance of nature in the Chisos and elsewhere in the park, prompting the NPS Denver Service Center in 1971 to draft another master plan. It recommended a "wilderness classification" for 533,900 acres, or roughly 75 percent of Big Bend. This area would be

Motel units at the Lodge in the Basin; Casa Grande in background. Photo by Mary Moody, Denison, Texas.

without public-use roads, developed campgrounds, or picnic facilities. Later, the Service added another 25,700 acres, bringing 79 percent of the total park area under a wilderness classification.[27]

The new master plan called for limited visitor use of the Basin, which would entail eventual exclusion of overnight accommodations and the removal of the horse-riding concession. Rio Grande Village would become the park's major tourist development, with a secondary visitor-use area at Castolon near the river southeast of Santa Elena Canyon. Finally, the plan encouraged more use of desert areas and construction of tourist lodging and trailer campsites outside the park to help relieve Big Bend of the masses that flocked to the Chisos Mountains.[28]

A public hearing in Alpine, Texas, in January 1972 revealed that the Texas Highway Department, the Texas Tourist Development Agency, and Governor Preston Smith opposed the master plan and wilderness recommendation. The Texas Parks and Wildlife Department was the only state agency that supported the proposal. Johnny Newell, head of the Big Bend National Parks Development Committee, acted as principal spokesman for local sentiment. Newell accepted several parts of the master plan but rejected the wilderness classification because of its ban on public roads in much of the park. He pointed out that greater use of the desert area would be impossible without more convenient access than foot trails. Newell was also concerned that the wilderness proposal would force Mexico to abandon a sister park opposite Big Bend. "If the wilderness proposal should go through," he wrote, "we can kiss the Mexicans goodbye."[29]

Newell was not alone in these sentiments. State Representative Hilary Doran, Jr., from Del Rio and State Senator W. E. Snelson from Midland noted that Big Bend National Park was a gift of the people of the Lone Star State made to the federal government with the understanding that all the people could use it, not just a backpacking minority. Richard H. Pierce, manager of the Travel Department of the Texas Highway Department, voiced the same opinion. The wilderness recommendation would place most of Big Bend "off limits for casual family travelers . . . off limits for the station wagon family with youngsters, who are neither inclined nor equipped for crosscountry hiking and dry-camp survival . . . off limits for the senior citizens who travel so extensively, but are physically incapable of the rigors of backpacking across mountains and desert."[30]

Carter "Buck" Newsome, a former Texas Ranger and operator of the saddle-horse concession in the Basin, blamed the master plan on a "bunch of ecology nuts [who] think the horses are ruining that part of the park." He objected to moving the concession to Rio Grande Village because a "dude can't survive in the kind of temperature that we have on the desert during the summer. . . . They would faint and fall over the minute they stepped outside their air-conditioned cabins." [31]

The Park Service listened to Newsome and others. The revised master plan, published after the hearing, recommended relocating the horse concession from the Basin to Ceniza Flat, a mid-elevation site four miles below park headquarters at Panther Junction. The move to Ceniza Flat would permit access to the mountain trails and would spare horse-riding visitors the harsh summer temperatures at Rio Grande Village. Another compromise in the revised plan relegated Rio Grande Village to just one of several visitor-use developments instead of the only major development. To take pressure off the Basin, Ceniza Flat would serve as a "safety valve," with overnight facilities remaining in the Basin. [32]

Opponents of the master plan and wilderness recommendation relied on economic arguments, which pro-wilderness ecology groups characterized as "selfish, commercial interests." The charge was not entirely accurate. Newell's Big Bend Development Committee, for example, wanted what the Park Service had promised since the 1930s: a thriving tourist business for West Texas. Every city, chamber of commerce, and county near the national park disapproved of the wilderness recommendation. Many opponents of the wilderness proposal felt the Park Service had capably managed Big Bend and questioned the conversion of much of the area into undeveloped wilderness, an area "absolutely and irrevocably frozen by an act of congress." In 1978 Congress conceded to opposition pressures and eliminated the wilderness proposal for Big Bend National Park. [33]

Although the Park Service vacillated in its development policies and exaggerated visitation predictions for Big Bend, the agency never advocated large-scale physical improvements for the entire park area. In the 1990s the principal park roads and sites for visitor facilities are basically the same as those proposed in the first master plan. The furor raised at the 1972 public hearing indicated that the Park Service had successfully publicized the economic reasons for a national park, but had failed to impress upon state and local people the significance of ecological, recreational, and inspirational justifications for wilderness.

Throughout the remainder of the 1970s and 1980s and into the 1990s, as mandated by statute, the Park Service has included the public in the planning process. Every few years the park staff, assisted by the Southwest regional office in Santa Fe, prepares a comprehensive "Statement for Management" and makes it available for public review. A recent document elicited 103 letters, 88 of which were from private individuals, 14 from groups or agencies, and one from a member of Congress. Most responses (74) supported efforts to restore the Mexican wolf to Big Bend. Others dealt with a variety of concerns including management of natural and cultural resources (stopping illegal plant collecting; regulating paleontology digs), lands issues (opposition to or support for new acquisitions; support for international park project), water issues (building showers for campers in Chisos Basin), solid waste management (use of bear-proof trash cans), development (opposing widening roads; removing Chisos Basin developments), and park operations and management.

As the responses indicate, Texans and others interested in Big Bend seem to have accepted the idea of a park with only limited development as an effective way to realize the dual park purposes of use and preservation, so long as resources are not permanently locked in a wilderness classification. Since Congress disapproved the wilderness designation in 1978, the Park Service has classified most of Big Bend's acres as "natural zones," which means "natural resources and processes . . . remain largely unaltered by human activity, except for approved development essential to management, use, and appreciation." Other management zones include historic, development, and special use.[34]

In 1988, the Texas State Legislature, a fiscally conservative body that gives weight to economic arguments, appropriated $8.5 million to purchase Big Bend Ranch, an area of 300,000 acres adjacent to the national park. The acquisition doubled the size of the state park system. The Texas Parks and Wildlife Department designated the 469-square-mile site a "state natural area," one in which "development would be limited, where the land's inspiring and intimidating wilderness would be largely preserved." The ranch, one-third the size of the national park, has significant attractions that should appeal to tourists (for example, higher and cooler elevations than most of Big Bend, historical artifacts from a working ranch, and Native American pictographs in caves), and even with limited facilities, it should provide a safety valve for the fragile Chisos Basin, especially during the hot summer months. The

planning process has just begun at Big Bend Ranch, but it may benefit from lessons learned resolving conflicts at its neighboring national
park. Some potential controversies and issues echo earlier conflicts, including concern about whether the ranch's remnant longhorn herd
should be preserved and the fears of area stockmen that the ranch could
become a predator sanctuary. The Texas Parks and Wildlife Department hired Jim Carrico, former superintendent at Big Bend National
Park, as project manager, and in spring 1992 the agency issued a planning document for public review and comment.[35]

Since the 1970s, cooperative resource planning and management
that include the public in the process have become fixtures in the Big
Bend Country at state, national, and international levels. With the
emphasis on preservation of natural and cultural resources with limited development, it appears that finally, after half a century, Albert
Dorgan's dreams for Big Bend have been laid to rest.

The "Predator Incubator" and Other Controversies: Managing Natural Resources

In 1946 a rancher wrote Superintendent Ross Maxwell that he considered Big Bend National Park a "breeding ground" for predators who crept out of their sanctuary under the cover of darkness and slaughtered at will among the neighboring sheep, goats, and cattle, then snuck back over the park boundary into the protective custody of Park Service rangers. The angry rancher regarded the park as a "curse" on the livestock industry of Texas. To get even he admitted that he let his cows and horses graze illegally on the park's depleted grasses. In closing, he offered Maxwell a compromise: "You keep all your preditory (*sic*) animals within your park boundaries, and I will keep all my livestock from entering the Park."[1]

The conflict between resource managers and ranchers had begun during the Big Bend State Park years from 1933 until 1944. Understaffed and inadequately funded during the depression and World War II, state agencies had a difficult time enforcing resource policies. For example, one man, upon hearing that the Colima Warbler in the Chisos Range was near extinction, set out to collect as many bird skins as possible for his private collection. He failed, but other species were not so fortunate. Even before the area became a state park, the gray wolf and bighorn sheep had either been destroyed or driven away. Although the state enacted legislation, there were not enough game wardens to protect threatened animals. When Big Bend officially opened as a national park in July 1944, the staff of five had their hands full dealing with disgruntled livestock interests.[2]

Ranchers opposed Big Bend for various reasons, including the "predator incubator" rumor referred to earlier. As a federal project, the park removed over 700,000 acres from the county tax rolls. Criticism subsided somewhat when they found out Brewster County would only lose $4,200, an insignificant amount when compared to projected tourism revenues. Another bone of contention was that thousands of acres necessary for feeding and clothing the Allies had been closed to livestock. When federal officials permitted limited grazing for the duration of the war, it neutralized criticism, but also seriously depleted what little forage remained. The most persistent opposition continued for decades over the issue of the Park Service's policy that protects all wildlife, including large carnivores (mountain lions, coyotes, wolves, bears, Golden Eagles) and poisonous snakes.[3]

An editorial in the *Sheep and Goat Raisers Magazine*, the trade journal for West Texas, labeled Big Bend "the most perfect incubator of predatory animals in the United States today." The magazine related that a rancher whose land bordered the park had to employ a trapper full-time. After a few months on the job, the man claimed to have captured eighty cougars. Ranchers told stories about the mountain lion and other predators that further enraged livestock interests. Sam Nail, who had ranched in the Big Bend since 1909, informed a *National Geographic* writer in 1938 that panthers had killed six hundred of his horses and cattle over the three decades. Another predator horror story concerned a roundup in 1947 of one thousand mares near the Chisos Mountains. Purportedly, only one colt was left in the entire herd, a depletion the ranchers blamed on lions, who supposedly delighted in killing helpless young or infirm old animals. Related tales emphasized the cowardly nature of the lion. One cougar, adept at avoiding encounters with foes of equal strength, went on a rampage one night, slaughtering seventeen sheep, more than it could possibly consume.

In fact, the belief in "bad" versus "good" animals, according to anthropomorphic misconceptions, was widely accepted. For instance, a photograph of two dead cougars appeared in the *San Angelo Standard-Times*. The caption stated that they "had their last lamb just a short time before they were caught and slain." The accompanying article reported that the lion had long regarded lambs, the symbol of innocence and purity, as a "preferred delicacy."[4]

Golden Eagles were another favorite subject of tall tales. One witness swore that he had seen a large bird swoop down on the back of a fully grown sheep. As the desperate animal ran about, the eagle, coolly holding on with one talon, slit its victim's throat with the other. The Park Service added to the negative image in a press release that labeled the bird a "destructive outlaw," a species whose prey included domestic livestock. Nevertheless, the writer continued, the eagle's depredations were "far outweighed by the beneficial results in maintaining the balance of nature through his preying upon gophers, jackrabbits, and other rodents and parasites that are destructive to agriculture." The average West Texas rancher was not interested in "the balance of nature" and continued to regard the eagle as a wanton predator that should be destroyed. One Park Service official, realizing the adverse impact of the news release, wrote, "This is about the worst eagle story I have yet seen and I've heard of them eating babies by the dozen!"[5]

The Big Bend's first permanent cattlemen had entered the region after the Civil War. Although predators abounded, only the wolf seriously threatened the herds. Ranchers systematically trapped, poisoned, and shot wolves so effectively that they had eliminated the species early in the twentieth century. Other large predators, such as mountain lions, black bears, coyotes, bobcats, and Golden Eagles, were merely hunted for sport by ranchers since they did not pose a significant threat to cattle.[6]

Although sheep and goat raisers had come to the Big Bend at the same time as the cattlemen, they were a distinct minority until the outbreak of World War I, which created expanding markets for agricultural products. The recession after the war, drought, and poison weeds that devastated their flocks caused many ranchers to abandon the Big Bend Country. Nevertheless, in the 1920s they returned in significant numbers, and the battle began in earnest against the large carnivores that preyed on sheep and goats. From 1932 to 1945 one trapper employed by a rancher claimed to have killed 121 cougars. The first government trapper was employed in 1937.[7]

As we have seen, sheep and goat raisers especially disliked the Golden Eagle, which was difficult to trap and shoot unless surprised on the ground feeding on a carcass. Determined ranchers formed "eagle clubs" with dues of one hundred dollars a year, and they used their pooled resources to hire pilots and planes, who would surprise the big birds as they soared above the desert floor. Between 1930 and 1942 one pilot estimated he spent 1,400 hours in the air and killed 2,500 eagles. State and county governments also paid some of the costs of predator control.[8]

Another concern of the stockmen was the end of grazing throughout the park once it opened to the public. With the official establishment of Big Bend in June 1944, grazing rights legally ceased, although the Park Service did not attempt to enforce the policy until a year later. The small staff increased their efforts in 1946 and the following year reintroduced pronghorn antelope as part of a long-range plan to restock native fauna to the area. Ranchers objected to a policy that allowed wild herbivores but excluded domestic livestock. As had happened at other national parks, rumors circulated that the NPS had already brought in wolves from Arizona. When a rancher purportedly trapped a lobo, or gray wolf, the stockmen's fears seemed confirmed.[9]

As the conflict heated up, the livestock industry gathered evidence and theories to support the contention that the park was indeed a "breeding ground" for predators. The absence of domestic livestock within Big Bend, according to a popular theory, forced the large carnivores to hunt on the adjacent ranches, then to return to Big Bend under the protection of the Park Service. Predators thus experienced an unnatural increase, and consequently slaughtered a correspondingly higher number of stock. A related theory blamed the growth of the deer population outside Big Bend, which competed with domestic livestock for forage, on the ubiquitous panthers, who forced their prey to seek refuge beyond the park boundaries. When the big cats followed, they did not seem to care whether or not their meal was domestic or wild.[10]

The sheep and goat interests felt the predator controversy had reached the crisis level by late 1947, when they considered enlisting J. Frank Dobie, the internationally known author and raconteur, to persuade the federal government to employ a trapper full-time in the park. Dobie, on the faculty of the University of Texas and a good friend of Walter Prescott Webb's, had already spent time in the Big Bend writing a book on longhorns and seemed a good choice as a spokesman for livestock interests. When Dobie accepted an invitation to speak before the West Texas Historical and Scientific Society, ranchers and NPS officials were in the audience.

Dobie entertained the crowd with a typical rambling speech, only one part of which concerned Big Bend livestock interests. He compared them with Boston manufacturers since both groups expected government subsidies and protective tariffs. According to Dobie, the ranchers had already demanded federal funds to clear their acres of prickly pear plants, to build water tanks, and to dig wells, and now they wanted a government trapper inside the park itself. Dobie said the sheep and goat raisers had "criminally mined the soil" to such an extent that it was worth less than a dime an acre. Needless to say, the livestock interests dropped any plans to have him as their spokesman.[11]

The ranchers instead pursued other alternatives to resolve the crisis. At the annual convention of the Texas Sheep and Goat Raisers Association in December 1947, members passed several resolutions related to the matter. One requested additional federal funds for predator control; another proposed an alliance with a long-time antagonist, the cattlemen, to present a united front against the common foe; and a third demanded the right to follow the "hot" trail of depredating animals into the park and to kill them there. The organization furthermore reminded the Park Service of its continuing concern that Big Bend might become a "breeding ground" for large carnivores. And finally, it discouraged the NPS from importing dangerous wildlife into the park. On December 22, 1947, the Association's secretary sent copies of the resolutions to the director of the Park Service.[12]

Arthur Demaray, acting director of the NPS, replied in January 1948. He assured the Association members that his agency had never imported predators into the park and had no intention of doing so in the future. To the ranchers' fears about a "breeding ground," Demaray said that the alleged population increase was greatly exaggerated, a conclusion he based on the abundance of deer throughout the Big Bend Country. Furthermore, he added that Ross Maxwell, Big Bend's superintendent, would work out "measures for safe-guarding the interests of the ranchers" from the park's predators. Demaray emphasized that since hunting was "strictly prohibited by law" in national parks, the livestock men could not pursue the animals into Big Bend.[13]

The acting director's letter did little to ease tensions or allay fears. Demaray might have used statistical data from wildlife population studies to convince ranchers that the park was not a "predator incubator," but the information was not available because there was no park naturalist to conduct a census. Demaray's comment that the ranchers exaggerated the number of mountain lions and other predators left the

Park Service open to the charge that the agency underestimated their strength. Furthermore, he failed to mention specific ways Superintendent Maxwell intended to protect the interests of the ranchers.[14]

At an impasse with the Park Service, the stockmen launched a public relations campaign through their trade journal, the *Sheep and Goat Raisers Magazine*. In the February 1948 issue, H. M. Phillips noted that ranchers were "some of the most enthusiastic boosters of the Big Bend" as a vacation spot or wildlife refuge. Nevertheless, they strongly opposed use of the park as an "unhampered breeding ground," since it threatened their livelihood. An editorial in the same issue contradicted the notion that ranchers generally supported the park when it stated that Big Bend contained "some of the most worthless land in the country" and was hardly worth the difficult drive to view the mediocre scenery. Furthermore, the editorial ignored Demaray's letter and told its readers that NPS officials had not denied charges that Big Bend was a "predator incubator" or that the agency was restocking the park with large carnivores. The Park Service now realized that the resolution of the controversy was largely in the hands of Superintendent Maxwell, who would have to explain NPS programs to the locals and convince them to cooperate.[15]

Sensitive to the accelerating crisis, Maxwell had begun visiting neighboring ranches and towns in December 1947 to find out if local residents indeed considered the park a "predator incubator." He received several interesting reactions. A few of the most prominent ranchers believed that no increase in the predator population had occurred since the opening of the park. One even remarked that he regarded Big Bend among "the best things that ever happened to Brewster County." Another, responding to the allegations in the Association's magazine about the predator breeding ground, observed that that was hardly possible since the deer population remained stable in the park. The same individual joked that if the rumors of hundreds of panthers lurking in the shadows were true, he would be afraid to leave his house after sundown.[16]

Others Maxwell talked with felt predators had increased substantially. A personal friend of the superintendent's placed the blame squarely on the park and favored a government trapper. Another whose ranch abutted the park said he would try to remain a good neighbor but personally believed that Big Bend had caused an increase in the predator population.[17]

Maxwell's interviews with private and government trappers and game wardens, however, finally produced reliable testimony that was more than opinion or hearsay. Maxwell made a special effort to talk to the man who claimed to have trapped eighty cougars in less than a year. He told the superintendent the correct figure was "eight" and not "eighty"; the magazine reporter had misquoted him. Maxwell also learned that the lobo purportedly captured was a large, dark coyote called a "chihuahua wolf." Most importantly, the majority of those with whom the superintendent talked confirmed that the number of predators had not increased. Ray Williams, captain of the West Texas game wardens and the one credited with killing 2,500 eagles, regarded the complaints of the sheep and goat raisers as a "bunch of nonsense" and doubted if they could substantiate their charges. After his extensive investigation, Maxwell concluded that at the very most two to three cougars could be found on a single ranch, and there were several spreads that had no sign of panthers at all.[18]

Although still not convinced, the sheep and goat men finally realized that the Park Service would block any proposals that violated agency policies, such as a government trapper within the park or allowing ranchers to pursue predators into Big Bend. Consequently, in June 1948 an executive committee of the Sheep and Goat Raisers Association met in Uvalde and petitioned the NPS to provide funds for hunters and trappers to patrol the park's perimeter and to protect adjacent ranches from a "reinfestation" of cougars, wolves, coyotes, and bobcats. According to the ranchers, the predators clearly came from the national park and since the stockmen themselves had already spent considerable sums attempting to exterminate the pests, it was now the federal government's responsibility.[19]

The Park Service considered the latest resolution a positive indication that the predator crisis was subsiding. Although not willing to fund control efforts, the Park Service's Hillory Tolson wrote the Association's secretary and expressed his appreciation for the Association's willingness to limit trappers and hunters to the park's perimeter. Tolson addressed the "reinfestation" issue by referring to Superintendent Maxwell's investigation, which concluded that cougars and bobcats were rarely seen, the last wolf had been shot in the 1920s, but the coyote population had increased. Tolson pointed out that because of large quantities of small game in the park, coyotes would have little reason to leave Big Bend. He closed by assuring the Association's membership that the park's predators were no longer a serious problem for neighboring property owners.[20]

The skeptical ranchers wanted a second opinion, and in January 1949 raised the ire of Park Service officials when they asked the Fish and Wildlife Service in the Department of the Interior to look into the predator problem at Big Bend. Newton B. Drury, NPS director, wrote the head of Fish and Wildlife to emphasize that "investigations of park problems are made only on request of the National Park Service." Nevertheless, despite the breach of protocol, Drury consented to allow the sister agency to conduct the survey in February 1949.[21] The decision proved to be a wise one.

With Ross Maxwell as their guide, the Fish and Wildlife staff looked first for signs of coyotes. Surprisingly, they found little evidence of the animals, and concluded that for every coyote in Big Bend there were nine outside the park, which seemed to refute the "predator incubator" theory. If Big Bend were indeed a "breeding ground," as some ranchers contended, a corollary was that the large carnivores would return to the safety of the park after a night of predation, and not remain on the outside as 90 percent of the Big Bend Country's coyotes apparently chose to do. The investigators did find ample evidence of mountain lions, but because of a stable deer population they did not consider the cats a threat. They prophetically warned, however, that the future could be a different story. As a final recommendation, the Fish and Wildlife team suggested that Maxwell regularly attend meetings of the Sheep and Goat Raisers Association to improve relations between the Park Service and livestock interests. Maxwell followed the advice, and in 1952, his last year as superintendent, he reported that "the public relations between the park and all outside organizations has improved and I am sure that the present status is much better than it was in 1944 and 1945 when the park was first established."[22]

While Maxwell's assessment was correct as far as it went, the conflict between ranchers and the Park Service over the park's predators would continue through subsequent decades. In the 1950s a spurt of growth in the panther population alarmed NPS officials so much that they considered a policy to reduce the species. Between 1952 and 1956 ranchers and government trappers killed over seventy-five cougars on acres adjacent to the park. In Big Bend itself the cats seemed to be losing their fear of humans. On a popular hiking trail a mountain lion seized a man's trouser leg. Rangers captured the animal and disposed of it before further incidents could occur that might result in the injury or death of park visitors. Another cougar met a similar fate when a hunter tracked it into Big Bend, where a ranger killed it.[23]

Confrontations between "fearless lions" and humans have remained a serious, though infrequent, problem. In March 1990 a young cougar came within five feet of a mother and her three-year-old child on the popular Basin Loop Trail, and stood its ground until another hiker approached. The Park Service temporarily closed the trail and issued a news release warning visitors about the activities of "dispersal-age kittens," especially young males. Park officials also have enlisted university researchers in a three-phase project to place radio collars on animals in the Basin to gather data to help gain a better understanding of lion behavior and to facilitate wildlife management. Essential to the success of the research has been the cooperation of neighboring landowners who contacted the NPS when collared lions were trapped, shot, or died of natural causes on adjacent ranches.[24]

As we have seen, the Park Service since the 1950s has assisted stockmen in various ways, a couple of which compromised wildlife policies. Yet some ranchers still have expressed dissatisfaction with the agency and retaliated by spreading rumors and committing acts of vandalism. In the 1950s the black bear replaced the wolf in stories about the NPS importing predators. And one or more unidentified culprits spread poison throughout the park, killing over twenty coyotes, which further exacerbated tensions. Although the black bear rumor had no basis, the Park Service's vacillation on wildlife policies (excluding domestic livestock, but including longhorns and antelopes; opposing tracking a predator's "hot" trail into the park, then assisting in killing a marauding cougar) would create misunderstanding and friction between the NPS and ranchers that would continue the rest of the century.[25]

Ironically, black bears did begin to return to Big Bend in the 1980s, but not at the instigation of the Park Service. In June 1990 the park experienced its first "bear jam" when motorists, spotting a mother and two cubs, stopped to photograph the trio, backing up traffic on the road to Chisos Basin. Soon after the sighting the staff erected a bear crossing sign, which some regarded as premature and misleading since the permanent black bear population was estimated at only four to eight animals. The excitement was genuine, however, because bears had not been seen in the park area since the 1930s, when severe drought and predator eradication efforts had driven them out. Over fifty years later drought would again serve as a catalyst, this time forcing bears to cross over from Mexico in search of food. They gradually have begun to reestablish a resident black bear population at Big Bend, which has challenged the ingenuity of the park's resource managers.[26]

Early on, bears discovered the convenience of foraging through refuse cans at campgrounds, and at least one animal in the Basin showed no fear of humans. Experiences at other national parks revealed that bears are quick learners. Finding a garbage source, they continue to return, even teaching other bears how to get to the refuse while intimidating any humans who interfere. At Yellowstone and elsewhere, dependent, or "problem," bears are tagged and removed far from campgrounds, a practice only partially successful because persistent animals find their way back. Consequently, some parks have a policy to destroy third-time offenders, since research indicates that once bears have learned aberrant behavior they will remain problem animals throughout their lives.

Unfortunately, some of the solutions tried at other parks will not work at Big Bend. Removal to the park's far reaches was not an alternative because the only suitable bear habitat was in the Chisos Mountains, a popular area for visitors. And with a population of only four to eight, destruction of renegade bears was counterproductive to the goal of natural repatriation. The alternatives remaining were to educate the visiting public and to install bear-proof garbage cans, policies initiated by the park staff. It's too early to judge the success of the bear management program, but, significantly, it was adopted before problems could get out of hand.[27]

Whereas natural forces had brought about the return of black bears to Big Bend, the repatriation of other species would require considerably more human intervention. The Park Service earlier had had marginal success reintroducing the pronghorn antelope, but had failed in efforts to bring back the Montezuma quail. Other species under consideration in the 1990s were the Bolson tortoise, desert bighorn sheep, and the most controversial of all, the Mexican, or gray, wolf.[28]

The Sierra Club, National Audubon Society, and the Mexican Wolf Coalition of Texas supported the idea. The Coalition's vice-president promised, "I'm not going to stop until I see a wolf back out there." Another ally of the wolf was Roland Wauer, former chief naturalist at Big Bend and a retired NPS employee with thirty-two years' experience. Wauer considered the park and its environs—with ample prey, space, and "a 99 percent chance that it will work"—the best location in the Southwest for a wolf reintroduction project. In opposition were southwestern ranchers in Arizona, New Mexico, and Texas, who questioned vacillating federal policies that first had attempted to eradicate the predator and now wanted to restore it.

Big Bend's staff tried to remain neutral and to present both sides of the issue through interpretive and fireside programs, seminars, news releases, and publications, but the wolf controversy continued to heat up, even embroiling the Board members of the Big Bend Natural History Association (BBNHA), the private, nonprofit auxiliary that operated the visitor center shops, sponsored seminars, and provided funds for research and other special projects. In May 1991 the BBNHA voted down funds for a new site bulletin that suggested that species such as the wolf might be introduced in the park. Only after Superintendent Robert Arnberger promised to avoid "politically sensitive issues" in site bulletins would the Board approve the funds.

An editorial in the *Alpine Avalanche* contributed to the controversy when it erroneously stated that the BBNHA and the Park Service were united in efforts to restore the wolf to Big Bend. One reason for the newspaper's confusion was that Rick LoBello, executive director of the BBNHA and a former NPS employee, was active in the Mexican Wolf Coalition of Texas. LoBello eventually resigned from both the Coalition and the executive directorship of the BBNHA. Reflecting the sensitive nature of the issue, John E. Cook, Southwest regional director of the Park Service, assured West Texans in January 1993 that any future consideration of Big Bend National Park as a site for wolf relocation "will be based on sound science and full assessment of impacts on neighboring land owners (*sic*), including those in the Republic of Mexico." The U.S. Fish and Wildlife Department, the lead agency responsible for repatriation of endangered species, partially resolved the conflict when it selected five potential sites in Arizona and New Mexico for reintroduction of the Mexican wolf.[29]

Protection of endangered species already in the park, however, is a primary responsibility of the Park Service, although the agency seldom has adequate funds for the task. At Big Bend the endangered fauna and flora include the Mexican black bear, Black-capped Vireo, Big Bend mosquito fish, Mexican long-nosed bat, Peregrine Falcon, and three species of cacti. One problem was "cactus rustlers," who had an easy time removing the endangered hedgehog cactus, which grew along the edge of the park's paved roads. The NPS consequently dug up the plants and took them to the Chihuahuan Desert Research Institute at Sul Ross State University in Alpine to propagate them for future planting in the park far from the roads.[30] Operating with a limited annual budget of $26,705 in fiscal year 1990, the Park Service used $22,414 of the funds for fauna. The largest amount ($15,040) was divided between two Peregrine Falcon projects, the Big Bend staff's most successful protective and propagation activities.[31]

Efforts to protect the Peregrine Falcon in the park were initiated in 1973 and continue into the 1990s. In 1982 park staff and cooperating researchers began monitoring the location and number of occupied nests, or eyries. Protective measures to ensure uninterrupted nesting periods included closing trails and restricting the operation of aircraft near the park. In 1991 a record number of fifteen fledglings were counted, bringing the total to over forty hatched since 1973.[32]

Big Bend's isolation occasionally has hindered the Park Service's response to wildlife management crises. For several summers in the 1940s, for example, white-tail deer mysteriously died by the dozens, threatening the survival of the species in the region. The afflicted animals' symptoms differed from year to year, making it difficult to determine the cause of the deaths; no other fauna (including black-tail, or mule deer) were affected. Lacking a park veterinarian, the staff iced down carcasses and rushed them for autopsies two hundred miles to Sonora, the nearest state agricultural station. None arrived before putrefaction had set in, which resulted in inconclusive findings. Fortunately for the park's white-tail deer, the malady abruptly and mysteriously abated in 1948.[33]

Other so-called wildlife problems concerned domesticated stock that had escaped into the park or were abandoned by owners. An estimated five hundred to one thousand burros grazed on the park's diminished grasses, simultaneously cutting hundreds of miles of paths into the hills and mountainsides. At first, rangers merely rounded up the creatures and auctioned them off, which proved a costly procedure in time and money. They next resorted to shooting the burros and leaving them for scavengers, a practice likewise used to reduce the feral goat population. While effective, it upset animal rights groups.[34]

A much more serious threat to the park's natural resources was trespassing cattle and horses from adjacent ranches in the United States and Mexico. According to Texas laws that dated from the open-range

era, landowners had to fence their acres to keep out wandering livestock or suffer the consequences without legal recourse. Neighboring
ranchers assumed that the Park Service legally had the responsibility of
erecting barbed wire around Big Bend. Superintendent Maxwell even
cooperated with local ranchers in an unsuccessful attempt to persuade
Congress to appropriate funds to fence in the park. As Maxwell subsequently learned, federal statutes, which supersede state law, placed the
burden on the ranchers to control their animals, which went against
local custom and was not well received at all.[35]

Tensions were further aggravated when park rangers seized stray
stock and charged as much as eighteen dollars per head to return them
to their owners. An angry rancher wrote his congressman, "I cannot
understand why it should be legal for a federal bureau to do something
that in the case of an individual would be prosecuted as horse theft."
Despite the hard feelings, by the end of the 1940s Big Bend's livestock
population had dropped from forty thousand to only a few hundred
head on privately owned acres. Today, most of the adjacent ranches in
the United States are fenced.[36]

White-tail deer browsing. National Park Service, Harpers Ferry, West
Virginia.

The Big Bend Museum building, destroyed by fire in December 1941, contained geological and paleontological artifacts and other scientific specimens. Some of the objects can be seen on benches and tables in front of the museum. Big Bend National Park, National Park Service.

Occasionally, trespassing livestock wander across the Rio Grande from Mexico, a persistent problem since the 1940s that adversely affected range recovery. In 1947 a more serious crisis developed when an epidemic of hoof-and-mouth disease broke out south of the border. The Park Service, unable to enforce a quarantine along over one hundred miles of international boundary, cooperated with the Bureau of Animal Industry (BAI) in the Department of Agriculture and the Texas Livestock Sanitation Commission. The BAI maintained a special force of from nine to thirty-five River Riders, which the state agency sometimes assisted on patrol. The combined forces at first merely drove strays back across the river into Mexico. As the epidemic spread, however, the special details received orders to destroy all Mexican cattle seized in the United States and to impound horses, donkeys, burros, and mules, which did not carry the disease.[37]

To recover their property, owners had to pay the eighteen-dollar fine for each animal, which, as expected, angered Mexican ranchers just as it had their Anglo counterparts. One especially large seizure included eighty-seven horses. The owner paid the fine for one animal (apparently to confirm that they were indeed his horses), and then a few nights later purportedly returned with a few friends and rustled fifty-eight more. Incidents such as the above, along with the alleged poaching of deer in the park and dynamiting of fish in the Rio Grande by Mexican citizens, strained international relations on both sides of the border.[38]

Another threat to natural (and cultural) resources was fire. On March 11, 1989, a visitor reported smoke in the vicinity of Blue Creek in the Chisos Mountains. Because of dry conditions and valuable resources in the area, Big Bend's staff called in an interagency team from New Mexico to help fight the blaze. Although the fire burned 331 acres, the 260 firefighters (including a team of Mescalero Apaches) and a 66-member command crew contained the conflagration by March 14 before it could destroy endangered or threatened plant and animal species at the higher elevations. The only recorded wildlife casualty was a snake.[39]

Fires in the Chisos Mountains and elsewhere are a common occurrence at Big Bend. Since the park's establishment in 1944 there have been approximately three hundred human- or lightning-caused fires, with over eighty of these occurring in the Chisos. Even earlier one engulfed the park's first museum, at 3:10 A.M. on December 26, 1941. From the beginning, Park Service staff disagreed over fire protection policy. Lightning-caused fires, according to an early ecological report on Big Bend (1944), were "as natural as the rain itself and play a legitimate part in the development of plant and animal communities." The authors of the report, however, wanted to provide fire protection for the Chisos Mountains' natural resources and Park Service facilities located there, but stated that for "*all outlying* portions of the park, no fire protection is necessary." Park Service hierarchy ignored its ecolo-

Aftermath of the fire. Big Bend National Park, National Park Service.

gists when Big Bend's first "Emergency Fire Plan" (1945) called for "aggressive suppression of all fires" throughout the park, a policy that would remain in effect for over twenty years.[40]

By 1977 a revised fire management plan was adopted for Big Bend that reflected a change in Park Service policy, one that recognized the importance of burning to maintain or restore natural areas. The revised plan called for "prompt suppression" of fires in the Chisos Mountains and at elevations above 3,500 feet; below that elevation fires could burn unhindered as long as they did not threaten life or property, a policy similar to the ecologists' 1945 report.

After "Yellowstone's Red Summer" of 1988, when approximately one million acres (almost half the national park) was consumed by five major fires, critics questioned the Park Service's ability to manage such valuable resources. Thousands of firefighters (including army troops), at a cost of over a million dollars, could not contain flames up to two hundred feet high that threatened Old Faithful, the bison and elk herds, and the lodge and other visitor facilities at America's premier (and oldest) national park. Responding to criticisms of mismanagement, secretaries of the Departments of Agriculture and Interior appointed a Fire Management Policy Review Team to study federal fire policies at national parks and wilderness areas. Each targeted unit selected a Fire Policy Review Team. At Big Bend the team recommended a combined program of fire management, which would allow fires, regardless of cause, to burn so long as lives or resources were not threatened. Park Service staff could also ignite fires to remove hazardous fuel from developed areas or to reintroduce fire into areas of the park where suppression had upset the natural order. Assistant Superintendent Kevin Cheri summed up his agency's position: "We are always mindful of our obligation to preserve park resources and natural processes, as well as to provide for visitor and employee safety." In July 1994 the fourteen-hundred-acre Estufa Fire, ignited by lightning, burned two and one-half miles east of Panther Junction headquarters in a natural zone. Firefighters, including the crew from Boquillas, Mexico, employed a passive confinement strategy, relying on creek beds and roadways to confine the flames, while they monitored the fire's progress to ensure that it did not threaten resources, property, or lives.[41]

Although the current fire management policy at Big Bend is ecologically sound, it unfortunately represents an unfulfilled ideal and reflects a major problem affecting overall natural resource management at Big

Bend and other national parks. Until Big Bend has the budget and staff to fully implement resource management plans, stopgap measures will continue to erode sound policies and adversely affect resources. For example, as we have seen, frequent fires in the Chisos Mountains have been a natural phenomena for eons. Yet with inadequate staff and funds, the prudent Park Service response to fire in the Chisos is full suppression to avoid an out-of-control conflagration.

 "The Ultimate 'Tex-Mex Project'": Companion Parks on the Rio Grande

In fall 1973 Michael Frome, conservation editor of *Field and Stream* magazine and a vocal supporter of the national park system, visited Big Bend, where he received a briefing from Superintendent Joe Carithers on the new master plan, the expanded wilderness proposal, and an idea already several decades old, an international park on the Rio Grande. After returning to his office, Frome wrote Ronald H. Walker, director of the Park Service, that he considered the "most pressing issue at Big Bend" the establishment of "a great new international peace park" that would include "a substantial portion of the Sierra del Carmen Mountains on the Mexican side." Frome felt the time was right to approach Mexican officials, since Mexico had begun construction of "a high-standard road" that would link Boquillas on the park border with the interior.[1]

Fifteen years later in 1988, Frome's "most pressing issue" still had not materialized, although it was far from dormant. In June of that year John E. Cook, Southwest regional director of the National Park Service, had written a brief memo to the director of his agency about positive developments between Mexico and the United States. "Finally, Boss," he concluded, "I believe we are closer to having companion parks [at Big Bend] now than at anytime since the idea was brought to President Roosevelt" in 1935. Nevertheless, the 1980s drew to a close without the consummation of the project. In 1991 a *National Geographic* news story indicated interest in the undertaking was as strong as ever. The editors predicted that the "Border Would Disappear at U.S.-Mexican Park," noting that "the ultimate 'Tex-Mex project'" would be "the biggest international park in the world," with over two million acres.[2] For almost six decades—from the 1930s into the 1990s—the prospect of an international park (or companion parks) on the Rio Grande has kindled the passions (pro and con) of politicians, environmentalists, developers, and numerous others on both sides of the river. It is a still-unfolding story that began during the worst year of the Great Depression.

The establishment in 1932 of the Waterton-Glacier International Peace Park in Montana and the adjacent Canadian province of Alberta was the inspiration for the U.S. National Park Service to propose similar projects with Mexico, including Organ Pipe Cactus Monument in Arizona and Sonora, Coronado Memorial in New Mexico and Chihuahua, and Big Bend in Texas, Chihuahua, and Coahuila.[3] Others outside the agency also had seen the international potential of the Big Bend. Originally commissioned by the Alpine Chamber of Commerce in 1933, Albert W. Dorgan's plan for a "Friendly Nations Park" (discussed in Chapter 5) was merely the first of many proposals to create an international reserve on the Texas-Mexico border. In January 1935 Everett E. Townsend noted the "splendor and grandeur of the scenery" south of the Rio Grande and recommended that the Park Service encourage Mexico likewise to establish a park, which "would create ties of kindly sentiment that would multiply and become stronger between the Mexican and American peoples, now almost unknown to each other." Citizens of both countries would enter a "vast playground," a "zona libre . . . free from all customs and immigration restrictions." At the same time, D. E. Colp, chair of the Texas State Parks Board, unsuccessfully attempted to arrange for the governors of Texas, Chihuahua, and Coahuila to fly over the proposed sites to view firsthand the spectacular scenery in an effort to win their support for the international project.[4]

United States Senator Morris Sheppard of Texas first officially suggested the idea for Big Bend International Park in a letter to Franklin Roosevelt in February 1935. The president, anxious to further his "good neighbor" policy in Latin America, asked Secretary of the Interior Harold Ickes for a report on its feasibility. Ickes obtained an early

Park Service field study, which he forwarded to the White House with a personal recommendation that the "Mexican Government be invited to cooperate with the United States in the establishment of such an international park." In addition, Ickes had the Park Service prepare a press release on the proposed "international peace park," which noted that "the romance of old frontier Mexico is in the atmosphere of the Big Bend region" and that "everything should be done in developing the area to preserve for the tourists seeking rest and recreation the Spanish-Mexican feeling of mañana. As a unit of the national park system the region would be unique in this international flavor." [5]

Another reason Ickes took such an interest in the project was his wish to name the proposed park for Jane Addams, co-founder of Hull House in Chicago's 19th Ward, who had died in 1935. Ickes felt "Jane Addams International Peace Park" would be a fitting memorial to a fellow Chicagoan and the winner of the 1931 Nobel Peace Prize in recognition of her lifelong commitment to international peace and understanding. In particular, she had been the champion of Latinos, who for the last decade of her life constituted the largest ethnic group at Hull House. At Jane Addams's death, Mexican children in the 19th Ward had worn black crepe bows to mourn her passing. Despite having the support of the president, the vice-president, and several members of Congress and other prominent citizens, Ickes's plan had to be abandoned in the face of a determined core of opposition in the Texas delegation. [6]

Nevertheless, Ickes's and Roosevelt's enthusiastic support for the project helped speed the enabling legislation through Congress in sixty-three days. Forty-eight hours after the president signed the Big Bend Act in June 1935, Ickes asked Secretary of State Cordell Hull to contact Mexican officials through the American ambassador to solicit their support for the proposal, which "seems to mean so much in the way of good will and mutual understanding between these two neighboring countries." [7]

The American ambassador in Mexico City was Josephus Daniels, former secretary of the navy in Woodrow Wilson's cabinet under whom young Franklin Roosevelt had served as assistant secretary. Daniels was also a good friend of Arno B. Cammerer, recently appointed director of the National Park Service. The ambassador learned that Mexico had already made plans for a forest reserve and game sanctuary in Chihuahua directly across from the proposed American park. The big game in northwestern Coahuila, "some of the finest in Mexico," including bighorn sheep, deer, antelope, black bear, and cougars, were in danger of extinction from overzealous hunters. Daniels had talked with Miguel A. de Quevedo, Chief of the Mexican Department of Forestry, Fish, and Game, the agency that had jurisdiction over Mexican national parks. He found Quevedo "most enthusiastic" about the idea of a companion national park in Mexico. Two meetings were subsequently scheduled for fall 1935 at El Paso.[8]

The principal negotiators were Quevedo, Daniel Galicia (an engineer in Quevedo's agency), and Herbert Maier and Conrad Wirth of the U.S. National Park Service. It soon became apparent to the Americans that Mexican officials had not yet visited the proposed sites on either side of the Rio Grande and were unfamiliar with U.S. national park policies, especially concerning scenic preservation. Although Mexico had several areas under consideration for national parks, the concept was still so novel that only two had been established, Desert of the Lions near Mexico City and El Chico in the state of Hidalgo. In addition, Maier learned that Quevedo was mainly interested in reforestation programs. Ironically, the Mexican official who had done the most to bring about the conferences, and who was chief of the Mexican agency responsible for his country's national and international parks, was an ardent disciple of Gifford Pinchot, former chief of the U.S. Forest Service, whose conservation policies occasionally clashed with the preservation philosophy of the Park Service.[9]

Quevedo had first met Pinchot when President Theodore Roosevelt invited the Mexican bureaucrat to Washington, D.C. At the time of the El Paso conferences, Quevedo was an honorary member of the Society of American Foresters. His main interest in an international project concerned a massive effort to place tree seedlings, or "forest plantations," in a strip twelve miles wide along the entire length of the border from the Gulf of Mexico to California. Quevedo argued that the greenbelt would add to the health and quality of life in border towns, enhancing recreational and aesthetic values in both countries. Another concern of U.S. Park Service officials was the Mexican government's interest in three power and irrigation dams in Santa Elena, Mariscal, and Boquillas Canyons. Maier cautioned that delicate negotiations were still necessary. "This has taken a little time and has had to be handled carefully, because we do not wish to 'scare' the Mexican officials away from the park idea."[10]

Despite these differences and misunderstandings, conference participants amicably discussed land acquisition, wildlife preservation, tourism, entrance fees, and concession policies, and tentatively agreed to bridge the Rio Grande at the village of Boquillas and to restrict customs and immigration inspections to the entrances of each park to encourage visitors to move freely about the international enclave. And finally, a joint commission was appointed to begin inspections of proposed sites early in 1936. Maier later reported to his superiors that "the attitude of the Mexican representatives at this conference was entirely one of keen enthusiasm. Not the slightest indication of . . . the least selfish motive evidenced itself." Yet he warned that "it is reasonable to assume that the [U.S. NPS], which has instituted the idea of the international park, will lead the way—will have to lead the way"—because of Mexico's inexperience with national parks and preservation policies, a foreshadowing of future conflict.[11]

In February 1936 several of the newly appointed Mexican and American members of the joint international commission met in Alpine, Texas, and then drove to the Chisos Basin at Big Bend. There they left the Civilian Conservation Corps camp in the Basin on horseback and rode to the spectacular South Rim, ascending the "steep trail slowly, stopping frequently to breathe" their mounts while enjoying the "magnificent view" of the Chihuahuan Desert. In the afternoon the party motored from the Basin to the mouth of Santa Elena Canyon, then to the trading post at Castolon for lunch. Later in the afternoon at the landing strip at Elmo Johnson's Ranch, two government biplanes provided commission members aerial views. At a cruising speed of 95 knots (114 miles per hour), each flight covered approximately one hundred miles and lasted an hour as the planes flew down the Rio Grande on the Mexican side, then over Mariscal and Boquillas Canyons, circled over the Chisos Mountains and the Basin CCC camp, winged through the gap in the "Window," and headed back to the landing strip. Although there was a haze over the Chisos Mountains, Roger Toll observed that the "Rio Grande shines in [the] sun like a ribbon of silver." Conrad Wirth was impressed by the bird's-eye view of "mountains and canyons of indescribable beauty." He saw "almost every type of scenery to be found on the North American continent; rushing mountain brooks, thick forests, lovely lakes, rolling plains."

The party next left Johnson's Ranch by government auto and drove to the village of Boquillas on the river near the mouth of the canyon, a distance of just over forty miles. Because of the primitive road, the trip

The village of Boquillas, Mexico. Photo by Jack E. Boucher, National Park Service, Harpers Ferry, West Virginia.

took almost two hours. In Mexico, they drove the length of the Carmel mountain range, likewise forty miles, but this time there were no roads, primitive or otherwise, and the drive took six hours. Crossing the Rio Grande at Boquillas and, later, upstream at Lajitas, nearly every car had to be towed by mules and horses to get to the other side. When water and sand seeped into the crankcases, they had to change the oil. At Boquillas, the river's strong current almost swept away two vehicles.

The hardships and crude conditions remained constant throughout the expedition. At Boquillas they slept on the dirt floor of an adobe house with no window glass and a "rooster in [the] same room." The accommodations at San Carlos, a town with a population of 400, did not have indoor plumbing. As Roger Toll recorded in his trip log: "We slept on [the] dirt floor of [the] house. Washed in street in front

Saddle party at South Rim of the Chisos Mountains. Photo by W. Ray Scott, National Park Concessions, Inc., National Park Service, Harpers Ferry, West Virginia.

Roger Toll, left, and Daniel Galicia stand in front of two U.S. government bi-planes before their flight over the Big Bend Country. Toll died in an automobile accident near Deming, New Mexico, a week later. Photo by George A. Grant, National Park Service, Harpers Ferry, West Virginia.

of 'hotel' with audience of 75 men." All told, the international commission spent three days in Mexico, much of it on horseback. Wirth commented that it was "so primitive" south of the Rio Grande "that Pancho Villa [had] used it as a hideout and remount station," eluding both Mexican and United States troops. On the horseback ride to the summit of Mount Carmel, "deer crossed our path and an occasional bear crashed through the underbrush." In fact, the abundant wildlife, according to Wirth, "seemingly never have seen a human, for they appear unafraid and curious." Unlike the overgrazed American side, there was little evidence of erosion in Mexico, and the mountains were covered with virgin stands of pine trees, some as tall as sixty feet and three feet around at the base. All but Toll agreed that the scenery in Mexico was equal if not superior to that on the American side.[12]

Realization of the goal of an international park seemed to move even closer when Mexico asked Arno B. Cammerer, director of the Park Service, and two other agency men, Roger Toll and George Wright, both members of the international commission, to make a follow-up inspection of the Mexican side. Tragically, the trip never did take place, for Toll and Wright were killed in an automobile accident in New Mexico returning from their initial international inspection. Consequently, the

"The roads in Mexico at present are not the best in the world," wrote photographer George Grant above this photo taken on the Boquillas–San Isidro "highway." Photo by George A. Grant, National Park Service, Harpers Ferry, West Virginia.

Truck and car carrying International Park Commission members stuck in the Rio Grande. Photo by Roger Toll, National Park Service, Harpers Ferry, West Virginia.

official meetings with Mexico did not resume until fall 1936 when Toll's and Wright's positions on the commission were filled.[13]

The new joint commission convened in El Paso on November 8 and 9 of that year. The first night Director Cammerer hosted a dinner in Ciudad Juárez in honor of the Mexican delegation. The next day the commission approved common eastern and western boundary markers for an international park. Discussions continued on the issues of a vehicle bridge, unlimited visitor access to both sides, and the tentative decision of the U.S. Bureau of Reclamation not to construct dams within the park boundaries. It was also decided not to build a road along the Rio Grande since it would hinder the movement of wildlife across the river.[14]

On the surface it appeared that the cooperative effort was succeeding. However, Daniel Galicia candidly told a U.S. Park Service official that the Mexican Forestry Department simply did not have the funds either to acquire the 400,000–500,000 acres for Sierra del Carmen, the Mexican portion of the international park, or to hire and train staff to manage it. Furthermore, the American idea of national parks closed to exploitation had not gained widespread support in a country still developing its frontier resources. To introduce the concept, the U.S. Park Service invited Mexican leaders to tour some of America's more prominent parks at the United States' expense. Concurrently, NPS employees and private citizens traveled to Mexico City, Chihuahua, Saltillo, and elsewhere promoting an international park by distributing brochures explaining United States national park principles, speaking on radio programs, and talking with chamber of commerce directors and members of other civic organizations. Despite these efforts, the decades of the 1930s and 1940s drew to a close and Mexico still had not authorized a companion national park.[15]

A major reason for Mexico's inaction was the state of Texas' nine-year delay in acquiring the Big Bend lands. In October 1935 at the first international meeting in El Paso, and at later conferences, Mexican officials emphasized they would take appropriate steps as soon as Texas deeded the park acres to the federal government, an event that did not occur until June 1944 when the D-Day landings in Europe were taking place during World War II.[16]

Later that summer of 1944, Newton B. Drury, who succeeded Cammerer as director of the Park Service, suggested that Franklin Roosevelt write to Mexican President Miguel Avila Camacho encouraging him to

Members of the International Commission examine grass cover and timber growth on the summit of Picacho de las Vacas in Mexico. Photo by George A. Grant, National Park Service, Harpers Ferry, West Virginia.

establish Sierra del Carmen Park. Roosevelt's letter to Avila Camacho emphasized the former's belief that Big Bend would not be "complete until the entire park area in this region on both sides of the Rio Grande forms one great international park." Moreover, it was Roosevelt's hope that such a park could become a reality "early in the postwar period." Avila Camacho's reply was most encouraging. The Mexican president indicated that he concurred with Roosevelt's wishes and had already asked federal agencies to draw up plans for a companion park across from Big Bend.[17]

Avila Camacho's promise, however, contained little of substance. On a field trip in summer 1945 to Cumbres de Majalca National Park in Chihuahua, Minor R. Tillotson, Southwest regional director, and Ross A. Maxwell, superintendent of Big Bend, learned firsthand that Mexico and its citizens still did not grasp United States national park policies. For example, the cutting of live trees was illegal, but Mexican nationals could gather dead wood. Consequently, enterprising individuals would girdle trees (i.e., cut a ring around the girth and remove the bark, killing the tree) and then harvest them the following season. Later, the Mexican government granted concessions for the outright cutting of timber within its national parks. Furthermore, individuals could buy land inside park boundaries for private homes or businesses. With no building restrictions, run-down shanties stood alongside expensive residences. The two men also found out that an artificial lake was planned to provide recreation for park visitors. Tillotson later told NPS Director Newton Drury that "the possibilities are rather remote" that Mexico would ever have "a sound national park policy." Maxwell agreed and bluntly stated, "From what we saw in Mexico last summer . . . they would encourage all kinds of honky-tonks along our border just in order to get the U.S. tourist dollars."[18]

It appeared that with the exception of a few minor officials, Mexico's national park policies had not evolved since negotiations on the international project began in 1935. Moreover, various secretaries of agriculture, who had jurisdiction over the country's national preserves, expressed little if any interest in Big Bend. The same held true for the governors of Chihuahua and Coahuila.[19] Added to the bureaucratic impasse was one of the main reasons for the stalemate over the international project: Mexico's deep-rooted enmity toward the "Colossus to the North."

In November 1945 William Vogt, chief of the conservation section of the Pan American Union, forwarded to Director Drury and the State Department two controversial documents on the international project prepared by the Mexican Department of Forestry and Hunting. Vogt, who had obtained the confidential reports because of his position with the Pan American Union, commented that the papers exposed "a complete lack of understanding of the Big Bend situation and considerable opposition to going ahead" with the project. One document acknowledged that Big Bend did have unique tourist attractions, but pointed out that its remoteness made it among "the least frequented" of the American national parks and one that was apparently created only because the United States could find no better use for the land. The report also noted that the area in northern Coahuila proposed for a companion park had greater economic potential if used for other purposes. For example, the Sierra del Carmen range had a high density of trees that yielded an excellent timber crop. Not incidentally, an American corporation owned the best wooded section.[20]

International Commission members in Boquillas, Coahuila, Mexico, February 19, 1936. Left to right: R. D. Morgan, superintendent, Chisos Mountains Camp; Dr. W. B. Bell, U.S. Biological Survey; Don Juan Travenia, Mexico Forest Service, Chihuahua City; Roger Toll, superintendent, Yellowstone Park; Daniel Galicia, Mexico Forest Service, Mexico City; Conrad Wirth, assistant director, NPS; Santo Ibarra, Mexico Forest Service; Herbert Maier, NPS, Oklahoma City; and George Wright, chief, Wildlife Division, NPS (Wright died with Toll in the automobile accident near Deming, New Mexico). Photo by George A. Grant, National Park Service, Harpers Ferry, West Virginia.

Another use of the land was for cattle ranching, the focus of the second confidential document. Retired Mexican army General Miguel L. Gonzales owned a successful 300,000-acre cattle ranch in northern Coahuila. Gonzales, a shrewd businessman, practiced conservational ranching methods and did not consider strict preservation of natural resources the best use of his acres. Obviously, if Mexico established a park, he would lose his land. In a memorandum the general warned the director of the Forestry Department of the danger of setting aside a large portion of land for a park, reminding him that the United States had previously violated agreements with Mexico, and that if a large border area were set aside, "the Mexican people will benefit in no way whatsoever."[21]

The first report expanded on the general's conclusions, noting that the tremendous costs of developing and administering an isolated des-

Tiled-roof cottages in the Basin two thousand feet below Casa Grande. Photo by Glenn Burgess, National Park Service, Harpers Ferry, West Virginia.

ert park probably would cause more strife than "good neighborliness" between the two countries. And finally, if the Mexican park were established, exploitation of the forest and cattle resources should continue because "it would not be advisable . . . to segregate something that contributes to the strengthening of the [Mexican] national economy."[22]

An unexpected supporter of the Mexican economic position was Clifford C. Presnall of the U.S. Fish and Wildlife Service. After investigating both sides of the Rio Grande, including the Gonzales ranch, Presnall concluded that Mexican national park policies were a sham and that the best use of the land was conservational cattle ranching as practiced by General Gonzales. Presnall's statement, plus the adverse reports of the Mexican Forestry and Hunting Department and the evidence of abuse of its already existing national parks (now numbering forty-eight), supported the contention that Mexico was primarily responsible for the failure to establish an international park.[23]

The foregoing, of course, was only one side of the story. Strong anti-Mexican sentiments held by many Americans, including public officials, jeopardized the international project. For instance, Park Service reports highlighted the unique Spanish-Mexican atmosphere of the Big Bend area and recommended that the architecture of new park buildings should reflect this heritage. Yet when several influential Texans objected, the agency backed down and eliminated a paragraph on Spanish architectural details from a news release, a foreshadowing of what would follow.[24] Today, a few tile roofs in the Chisos Basin are the only examples of Spanish architectural influence.

A more blatant example of anti-Mexican sentiment occurred in 1947 when United States Senator Tom Connally demanded the construction of a barbed-wire fence along the Rio Grande to keep Mexican livestock and wildlife allegedly infected with hoof-and-mouth disease from entering the park. And earlier, as we have seen, Albert W. Dorgan expressed the ambivalent attitude many Anglo North Americans had for Mexico. If the peaceful objectives of his proposed Pan American Highway failed, the road could always funnel troops and weapons to "subdue Mexico." In subsequent years, conflicts over illegal border crossings, smuggling, drug-related violence, and poaching have reinforced anti-Mexican stereotypes and attitudes, which are hardly conducive to the fulfillment of an international project.[25]

The United States also practiced a double standard when dealing with Mexican lands in which American citizens had an interest. In summer 1947 it appeared that Mexico actually was about to set aside Parque Nacional de la Gran Comba, the new name for its portion of the international project. Although a false alarm, it worried Americans who owned or leased property in Mexico. They were concerned that if the park became a reality, they would not receive fair compensation from the Mexican government. The U.S. State Department consequently instructed consulates in Chihuahua, Coahuila, and Sonora that the United States would have no cause for apprehension provided that Mexican officials would not "interfere with the normal cattle grazing or agricultural pursuits of American citizens owning or controlling lands in the area" of the proposed park. The value of American mining, cattle, and other investments in Sonora, Coahuila, and Chihuahua was estimated at several million dollars. For example, the American Club, a sportsmen's organization headquartered in San Antonio, held 100,000 acres "in probably the most beautiful part of the lovely Carmen Mountains." Dolph and Mason Briscoe of Uvalde, Texas, controlled the Rosita Livestock Company, another American-owned enterprise. As noted above, the area proposed for the Mexican park also contained vast timber resources, some of which were owned by U.S. citizens.[26]

In December 1947, Assistant Park Service Director Hillory Tolson wrote to Carlos Villas Perez, a member of the international commission and the Mexican official most actively working for his country's park. Tolson had an unusual request. He wanted Perez to consider the possibility of authorizing leases for American landowners so that they could "continue to graze cattle or carry on other enterprises," which should not "interfere too greatly with the preservation of the park area." Tolson's letter coincided with his agency's efforts to purchase all the remaining privately owned lands within Big Bend National Park. Apparently, the Park Service could relax its standards when American interests were involved in a foreign country. In any event, Mexico did not respond to the compromise offer.

By December 1948 the State Department had decided to discourage any further action, concluding that American interests would be "adversely affected" by any decrees from Mexico concerning Big Bend and other international projects. The agency agreed with the assessment of its embassy that "the Mexican Government will expropriate whatever . . . properties may fall within the boundaries of the proposed Mexican National Parks . . . whether the interests concerned are owned by American or Mexican citizens." Furthermore, historical precedent taught that "any private interests which may be in conflict with what is considered the National interest will not be held worthy of consideration."[27]

Although the outbreak of the Korean War in 1950 and continuing Cold War tensions further delayed negotiations between the United States and Mexico, efforts continued at the local level on both sides of the border. In 1953, with the backing of the Southwest Regional Office of the Park Service, the Alpine Chamber of Commerce set up an International Affairs Committee whose membership included Mexican and U.S. citizens. In September and October, meetings were held in Saltillo and Chihuahua City, including a session with the governor of Chihuahua. Once again, initial enthusiasm failed to produce concrete results.[28]

At the park dedication in November 1955, Secretary of the Interior Douglas McKay used the occasion to fire a salvo in the Cold War. Observing that the ceremony had been delayed for over ten years because of global conflicts, McKay optimistically speculated that the international park would soon be a reality, "an inspiring example to the troubled peoples behind the iron and bamboo curtains of the way free men and women can live in peace and friendship."[29] Encouraging rhetoric, perhaps, but not enough to bring about the creation of the international reserve.

The idea was revived in the 1960s and 1970s with much fanfare, including visits to Big Bend by federal officials from Mexico and the United States. Not surprisingly, nothing tangible came of the efforts, an all too familiar tale.[30] However, there have been encouraging developments in the 1980s and 1990s.

In February 1988 Eliseo Mendoza Berrueto, governor of Coahuila, visited Big Bend National Park, where he announced a plan to develop tourism at Boquillas del Carmen, a Mexican village on the Rio Grande directly across from the park. Furthermore, Governor Mendoza asked the park staff for suggestions on how to protect the magnificent natural resources of the Sierra del Carmen and Madera del Carmen ranges in his state. He subsequently had meetings with Texas Governor William Clements, U.S. Department of State and Park Service representatives, and officials of SEDUE (Secretaría del Desarrollo Urbano y Ecología [Department of Urban Development and Ecology]), the federal agency in Mexico equivalent to the Department of the Interior.[31] Mendoza's effort was the first time that the governor of a Mexican state had taken the lead in a cooperative proposal involving federal and state agencies in both countries.

Equally significant, on August 5, 1993, at a ceremony in Ciudad Juárez, Mexican President Carlos Salinas de Gortari endorsed setting aside 1.5 million acres for a Mexican Biosphere Reserve in the states of Chihuahua and Coahuila. Protected species would include the mountain lion, Peregrine Falcon, and black bear. The reserve would extend for two hundred miles along the Rio Grande adjacent to Big Bend Ranch State Natural Area, Big Bend National Park, and Black Gap Wildlife Management Area. If the two areas could be combined in a single biosphere, it would embrace over 2.5 million acres, or almost 4,000 square miles.[32]

For the United States, the major development has been an increasing open-mindedness on the part of Park Service personnel toward Mexico's needs and worldview. As we have seen, Park Service officials from the director's office on down historically have tended to regard Mexico's national parks and policies as inferior, an attitude that hindered realization of the goal of companion parks. It also revealed an ignorance on the part of Anglos of the Hispanic (in particular, Mexican) environmental worldview and the cultural and historical forces that shaped it.[33]

Over the last few years there has been growing evidence of a greater cultural awareness and cooperative spirit on behalf of NPS staff at Big Bend. During the 1980s, for instance, the Park Service launched over a half-dozen international programs. Typical are the Goodwill Ambassadors, rangers who are assigned to border villages, which they visit at least once a month "to act as both passers and receivers of information" with local politicians, teachers, and villagers. The rangers also have a

The Sierra del Carmen near Jaleaucillas, Coahuila, Mexico. Photo by George A. Grant, National Park Service, Harpers Ferry, West Virginia.

chance to polish their Spanish while experiencing firsthand the culture of rural Mexico. In a related matter, the NPS has successfully encouraged the hiring of bilingual employees. In the early 1990s there were over three dozen staff members fluent in Spanish and several more with a conversational grasp of the language. Another program provides "hands-on" training for Mexican citizens in resource management techniques such as controlled burning.[34]

Park Service staff are likewise aware of Mexico's concern that its reserve could become a "gringo park," a carbon copy of Big Bend established for the benefit of North Americans, while locking up valuable resources and closing out less affluent Hispanics. Consequently, the NPS no longer looks askance at limited mining, grazing, and timbering in some areas of the proposed biosphere. Leaders on both sides of the border likewise have realized that a companion park, or reserve, in Mexico could help ease several management problems. For instance, increased revenues from tourism and an improved quality of life for Mexico's rural citizens might curb the need to cross illegally into the United States in search of work or to engage in smuggling (e.g., wild animal pelts) or drug trafficking.[35]

Finally, U.S. National Park Service Director of Mexican Affairs Howard Ness offers insight on the significance of political developments in Mexico and the future of the international project. According to Ness, "Environmental issues are near and dear to the heart of President Salinas." The August 5, 1993, ceremony in Ciudad Juárez was more than empty symbolism "because it publicly launched an initiative by a Mexican state, with the blessing of the federal government." Although Salinas constitutionally cannot be re-elected, Ness was confident that the desire to protect environmental resources in Mexico "is real" and "comes from the people," raising the issue above party and candidate. "And make no mistake about it," Ness concluded, "they [Mexican officials and citizens] are doing it for their country, not for anything to do with the U.S." On November 4, 1994, outgoing President Salinas signed decrees setting aside 1.6 million acres for four new wildlife preserves across from Big Bend, thus laying the foundation for cross-border ecosystem management.[36] There's still much to be done, but finally after six long decades the dream of an international reserve on the Rio Grande at Big Bend, "the ultimate 'Tex-Mex project,'" does seem closer to realization than ever before.

 Life and Work in a Desert
Wilderness: Visitor and
Employee Experiences

In a land full of eccentric characters, one of the most colorful in the Big Bend Country was Maggie Smith, an American citizen who had lived in Mexico for a decade and felt more comfortable speaking Spanish than English. Maggie and her husband, Baylor, returned to Texas in 1943 at the invitation of the State Parks Board to operate the hot springs and general store established by J. O. Langford earlier in the century. State officials were concerned that the vacant site would fall prey to vandals during the transition from state to national park. Shortly after the couple's arrival, Baylor Smith died, but Maggie stayed on at Hot Springs until 1952.

Early on, Park Service officials expressed misgivings about Maggie's efficiency as a concessionaire, and asked Superintendent Ross Maxwell to look into the matter. He found that Maggie was indeed a good "horse trader," but knew nothing about bookkeeping. "Mrs. Smith doesn't keep books," Maxwell wrote in his report. "She sends in an order to the wholesaler at Alpine; the mail carrier delivers it to Hot Springs. She pays the bill and if there's any money left, that's profit. A Mexican comes from across the river and trades a goat skin for a sack of flour. The goat skin has a value, but can't be placed as an asset on anybody's books. If [it] is later sold for fifty cents, it goes into the little box and is used to pay for groceries the next week." On Maxwell's recommendation, the Park Service accepted Maggie's unique system until the Hot Springs concession was closed in 1952.

The border frontier could be a dangerous, violent place for man or woman, yet Maggie held her own. She slept with a pistol and a sawed-off shotgun—which she knew how to use—by her side. Once she surprised a man rifling through her cash box. "I put my thirty-eight between his shoulder blades and told him I was going to kill him" if he didn't drop the money and leave quickly. According to Maggie, he ran off faster than any "Olympic varmints could match" as she fired shots at his feet.

Maggie's involvement in wax smuggling also added excitement to her life. The Mexican government held a monopoly on candelilla wax, which forced cash-poor Mexicans to sell the plants they illegally harvested in Mexico to U.S. wax "merchants" such as Maggie Smith, who shipped it to Alpine and Marfa for processing. It was not unusual for six or seven thousand dollars to change hands in one evening. The fact that Maggie Smith was never robbed partly attested to her marksmanship, but probably more so to the love and respect held for her by border residents.

Maggie Smith, called by many the "godmother to the Mexican people," truly was their friend, especially to *los pobres*, the poor ones. Most of her customers were Mexican nationals who traveled great distances to trade and to pick up their mail at Hot Springs, the only store within 175 miles of the border. She paid cash for hogs and chickens, accepted livestock or skins for coffee and flour, and generously granted credit to those who couldn't pay.

She helped in other ways as well. Once a young couple came to Maggie when the woman was already in labor. With Maggie driving them in her pickup, they raced to the doctor in Marathon. When it became obvious that they weren't going to make it in time, Maggie calmly pulled off the road and delivered the baby. The mother and child were fine, but the new father was so overcome by the experience that he was sick during the entire drive back to Hot Springs. Over the years, Maggie estimated that she midwifed so many babies she lost count; she also "stood up" for twenty couples married in front of the store. When she retired, Maggie calculated that her friends still owed her $27,000, yet she did not "regret one minute of it. I said deep down in my heart I feel like . . . I saved many a little child from starving, I saved many a mother from dying, and I've taken [young men] to town all shot to pieces. Some of them died, sure, but some I saved." When called on, she even donated blood. Significantly, when the Park Service closed the Hot Springs concession, fifteen hundred people signed a petition to allow Maggie to stay, but to no avail. She lived out her final years operating stores at San Vicente on the river and Study Butte near the western entrance to the park. Maggie Smith died in 1965.[1]

Another colorful character was Ross A. Maxwell, Big Bend's first superintendent. Appointed in 1943, he would hold the position until 1952, when he joined the faculty at the University of Texas. A tall, ruddy-faced Oklahoma farm boy, Maxwell received his Ph.D. from Northwestern University in 1936. That year the National Park Service employed the young geologist in the Big Bend Country, a landscape whose geology and history he would study for the rest of his life. Stints as regional geologist at Santa Fe (1940) and assistant superintendent, Southwestern National Monuments (1942) preceded his promotion to superintendent at Big Bend. A published scholar and persuasive public speaker, he was especially effective at dealing with local people. A member of the Texas State Parks Board remarked that "Doc . . . is just as plain as an old shoe . . . the salt of the earth," which summed up how many West Texans felt about the superintendent. Maxwell's straightforward, no-nonsense manner and willingness to listen to grievances enabled him to defuse the anger some Texans held toward the federal government and, in particular, the Park Service and its policies (especially with regard to grazing rights and predators). At the same time, he made many friends, even among those who opposed Big Bend. One rancher who steadfastly and loudly protested the presence of the Park Service in Brewster County regularly sent Christmas cards to the Maxwells and entertained them in his home.[2]

These same qualities served Maxwell well in recruiting, training, and retaining competent and loyal employees, a difficult task indeed in the early days at Big Bend. It was one of the most isolated, undeveloped, and least accessible sites in the national park system in the 1940s and early 1950s, and positions often went unfilled for months and were not especially desired by veteran Service employees. Consequently, Maxwell's recruits often were inexperienced and had to learn their jobs in the field. They put in long days with no overtime pay rounding up trespassing stock, fixing broken well pumps, and performing other mundane tasks, which were occasionally punctuated by the excitement of a brush fire or the arrest of a poacher. After ten or more hours on duty, rangers finally returned to their quarters, which consisted of one-room shacks without running water or electricity. Understandably, they sometimes suffered morale problems (dubbed "Big Bend fever" by Maxwell), which the superintendent combated by serving a punch containing a "secret ingredient" that lifted their spirits.[3]

Years later Maxwell reflected on his frontier experiences at Big Bend: "The conditions were not as bad as faced by the people who settled this area from 1840 to 1870. They had oxen and covered wagons—we had cars and trucks." But there weren't many other advantages in the twentieth century.[4]

In the 1940s the nearest physician was over one hundred miles away in Alpine. The need for emergency medical services and facilities for the remote area would remain a major problem for almost forty years. Finally in 1980, John Alexander, a paramedic, established Terlingua Medics to provide emergency medical service to southern Brewster County, Texas, which included the park. In 1982 the park signed an agreement with Alexander that formalized the relationship and pro-

vided $5,000 in financial support. By 1984 the partnership between Terlingua Medics and the Park Service was working so well that Congress appropriated $50,000 to be administered through Big Bend for medical supplies and equipment, training, and vehicle maintenance. One benefit of this arrangement has been cross-training; Terlingua Medics crews, Park Service staff, and others receive instruction in emergency medical procedures and rescue techniques. Consequently, rangers now can be certified as Emer-

Ross A. Maxwell near Boot Spring, Chisos Mountains, January 1940. Big Bend National Park, National Park Service.

Superintendent Maxwell in his office. Archives of the Big Bend, Sul Ross State University, Alpine, Texas.

gency Medical Technicians and Emergency Care Attendants. The effectiveness of the cooperative effort was demonstrated in April 1992 when a school van with fifteen passengers overturned on the road to Chisos Basin, killing one and injuring ten. Emergency units responded from Terlingua Medics, West-Tex Ambulance Service, U.S. Border Patrol, the Park Service, and U.S. Customs Service. The latter provided an aircraft to fly two students to Medical Center Hospital in Odessa, Texas. The other eight were taken to the Big Bend Regional Medical Center in Alpine. All ten of the injured received medical assistance in a timely manner and subsequently recovered. The fatality, a thirteen-year-old boy, died at the accident scene.[5]

Cooperative efforts also have extended south of the border into Mexico. After a couple of medical emergencies in the Mexican towns of Boquillas and Santa Elena in 1990, one of which resulted in the avoidable death of a child, the citizens asked the Park Service for help obtaining general health care instruction. In the fatal incident, a twelve-year-old boy from Boquillas, suffering from flu-like symptoms, was brought by his family to the Rio Grande Village Center for emergency assistance. They were too late, and the child died on New Year's Day, 1991. To avert future tragedies, the Park Service requested assistance from the Texas Department of Health to provide Spanish-speaking instructors to train border residents in general health care.[6]

Big Bend's isolation also made it difficult to educate the children of park and concession personnel. When the park opened in 1944, the closest public school was in Alpine. From 1944 through spring 1947 parents tutored their own children. In fall 1947 the staff reestablished the defunct San Vicente School District, which had closed in the 1930s, and later voted thirteen to eight to raise the tax on each $100 valuation from ten to fifty cents, which qualified the district for state aid. Of the three school trustees appointed by the county judge (who was also the county superintendent), two had Park Service connections: George Sholly, chief park ranger, and Helen Maxwell, the superintendent's wife. The third was William Cooper, Jr., a rancher from nearby Persimmon Gap. The first classroom was half of the old Civilian Conservation Corps mess hall in the Basin. During academic year 1947–1948, there were seven students and one teacher.

In 1952 the school moved into a new building constructed at Panther Junction; two additional structures and a library have been added since then. In the 1960s the school's enrollment reached a high of forty-two students when more employees with school-age children were hired for construction and maintenance projects during Mission 66. The administrative and teaching staff grew proportionately to include three to four teachers, a teachers' aide, a secretary, and a superintendent. In the 1990s, an average of thirty children are enrolled in grades one through eight at Big Bend, but older students attend high school in Alpine, where they either board (returning to the park on weekends) or take the nation's longest daily school bus ride (160 miles round trip, four hours on the road). Because of these hardships, some employees seek transfers to other parks when their children enter high school, just as their predecessors did fifty years earlier.[7]

Employees and spouses over the decades have demonstrated initiative and creativity in overcoming other voids in their lives as well. With no churches in or near the park in the 1940s, various staff members took turns leading nondenominational services, and the women organized Sunday school classes for the children. The first Easter service in 1949 attracted fifty-one people, including most of the local bachelors.

Those who played instruments occasionally got together for informal concerts, and some of the children formed their own band.[8]

Living and working in a desert park without electricity was especially hard on employees and their families in the 1940s and early 1950s. During the hot summer months, for example, it was difficult to obtain fresh meat, milk, and eggs. Although Service regulations forbade it, Maxwell requested permission for his staff to keep chickens and a cow. Unsympathetic Park Service officials suggested that Big Bend's "pioneers" would have to rely on canned goods instead. Once a month Maxwell sent a truck for groceries and supplies to Marathon or Alpine. By 1949 the food bill for the seventeen families and several bachelors was $1,500 to $2,000 monthly, enough to make it profitable for an Alpine grocery to make weekly deliveries.[9]

Finally in 1953 the Rio Grande Electric Cooperative began generating power to most of the park, which considerably helped to bring Big Bend into the twentieth century. To celebrate "when the lights came on," 150 employees, families, and friends gathered for a barbecue in the Basin. The occasion was even more memorable than intended, for dynamite set to go off at the moment the power was turned on (to create a giant firecracker effect) exploded a few seconds early, startling many of the celebrants. Because of the vastness of Big Bend, Rio Grande Village did not get electricity until 1960, and Castolon had to wait until the following year.[10]

Another hardship was the difficulty of communicating with the outside world. For the first six years, mail delivery was once a week. The rural postman put the mail in a box thirteen miles from the Basin and made subsequent stops at Boquillas, San Vicente, and Hot Springs, where Mexican citizens from as far away as one hundred miles south of the border picked up their mail. With the establishment of a fourth-class post office in the Basin in 1950, deliveries increased to twice weekly, if they could get through. During the rainy season from June to September, the unimproved Terlingua–Alpine road could be closed for two weeks at a time. And winter snowfall in the higher elevations infrequently closed the road for as much as ten days. Later, with improved roads and placement of the post office at park headquarters at Panther Junction, mail deliveries were being made daily Monday through Friday.[11]

Throughout much of the 1940s, Big Bend National Park was a hundred miles from the nearest telephone or telegraph station. In 1947, KULF, a commercial radio station in Alpine, volunteered to broadcast emergency radio messages to the park, but the arrangement proved unsatisfactory. The next year the U.S. Border Patrol in Marfa, Texas, began relaying telephone and telegraph messages twice daily over the park's shortwave radio system. In 1949 the Park Service upgraded Big Bend's radio communications so contact could be made during business hours with the regional office in Santa Fe and throughout the park. At last in 1954 telephone lines were installed to Big Bend. In the event of a telephone failure, the Border Patrol radio contact can be used as a backup. Since 1982 all long-distance telephone calls have been transmitted by microwave relays, a noted improvement over the static of previous years, although obsolete switchboard and extension systems continued to cause overloads that tied up the lines.[12]

Because of Big Bend's huge area, it sometimes took longer to extend the amenities of civilization to all corners of the park. An NPS news release in 1985 carried the headline, "Castolon Joins the 20th Century." Located on the road to Santa Elena Canyon in the southwest section of the park, the historic town had received electricity in 1961 (as noted above), but remained "the epitome of isolation," with no mail delivery, newspapers, radio, television, or telephone service. The only communication was via the park radio, which meant "that even 'personal' messages received park-wide attention." At long last Castolonites purchased a satellite dish in summer 1985, which gave them a choice of over one hundred channels. Next, the Big Bend Telephone Company installed phone service by using the existing power lines. For some, the sudden change was too much, and they turned down both conveniences, reasoning that if they "haven't needed it all these years, why start now?"[13]

Further evidence of Big Bend's isolation and frontier character were its place names (or lack thereof), which challenged the creative and research talents of the staff of the United States Board of Geographical Names. Several prominent topographical features had no name, while others had two or three. Names often reflected the Spanish-Mexican heritage of the region, but their anglicized spelling occasionally so distorted the Spanish that the original meaning was lost. For example, the literal translation of Mesa de Anguila is Mesa of the Eels, which hardly suits its arid and lofty location. Overall, the Board made over four dozen decisions for the Big Bend area, some of which upset local resi-

The Chisos Mountains from the southeast with the road between Marathon and Boquillas in the foreground, 1936. Photo by George A. Grant, National Park Service, Harpers Ferry, West Virginia.

dents. Santa Helena, for instance, became Santa Elena, the phonic spelling of the canyon's beautiful Spanish name. Native Big Benders especially objected to decisions that erased local history, such as changing Dead Horse to Boquillas Canyon. Several place names recognized individuals who contributed to the efforts to establish the national park (e.g., Carter and Toll Peaks).[14]

During its first ten years from 1944 to 1954, primitive improvements and facilities gave almost 500,000 visitors to Big Bend a memorable, although not always pleasant, frontier experience. Park concessionaires did stock canned goods and other durable supplies, but not perishable items, which tourists had to purchase outside the park. Toward the end of the 1940s, gasoline was available in Big Bend but at five cents a gallon above Alpine's prices. Motorists unaccustomed to the great distances between service stations were warned by the NPS to "fill your gasoline tanks before leaving" Alpine or Marathon.

Since few of the park's one hundred miles of principal roads had been paved, early visitors had to "eat the dust" of their fellow travelers, except during the rainy season from June through September, when they faced a more dangerous inconvenience: flash floods. Big Bend's brochure advised that "while in the park, you are cautioned regarding washouts and running water during and after a storm." Although the monthly average of precipitation was only about one and one-half inches, it could fall within an hour or two, trapping motorists, or worse, drowning them if caught in one of the fifty or so arroyos that criss-crossed the main roads. Measuring sticks indicated when waters had subsided enough for fording, which, unfortunately, did not help hapless drivers surprised at the bottom of a creek. The entire road system contained only three culverts.[15]

In 1956 the NPS launched Mission 66, a ten-year master plan to upgrade the national park system scheduled for completion in 1966, the fiftieth anniversary of the agency. Congress appropriated over one billion dollars for physical improvements, protection, conservation, and interpretation of natural, historical, and cultural resources, and for the hiring and training of personnel to carry out these programs. The $14 million received by Big Bend helped pave one hundred miles of roads, constructed bridges over the more difficult arroyos, and dynamited a tunnel through a ridge, which eliminated Dead Man Curve in Ernst Gap. Other projects included the building of hiking trails, an orientation and administration center at Panther Junction, and air-conditioned cabins with private bathrooms and a lodge in the Basin. In the lodge's restaurant was a huge window that provided diners views of the Basin's spectacular sunsets.[16]

Over subsequent decades additional improvements have been made. In 1979 the Park Service removed the frame "Dallas Huts" with their common showers and bathrooms, and finally replaced them ten years later with new motel facilities with private bathrooms. For campers and recreational vehicle users, new overnight facilities were opened in the Basin, Rio Grande Village, and Castolon. Present overnight facilities at the park include a 58-room motel complex, eight lodge units, four cottages, a group campground, and a 62-site Class A campground in the Basin and a total of 332 Class A and B campsites at Rio Grande Village and Castolon (in addition, the former has a 25-site concession-operated recreational vehicle campground). The popularity of the lodging facilities (especially during spring break, Thanksgiving, and Christmas) has exceeded their capacity, with the consequence that reservations sometimes must be made three years in advance to ensure a room during peak holiday periods. By the 1990s, the park contained over 400 miles of roads (161.81 paved, 256.86 unpaved), quite an improvement since the "dust-eating" days of the 1950s.[17]

An arroyo near Boquillas, Mexico. Photo by George A. Grant, National Park Service, Harpers Ferry, West Virginia.

The amenities of civilization—paved roads, indoor plumbing, and air-conditioned cabins—might temporarily conceal the region's true character, but its rugged frontier qualities and occasionally violent heritage lie just below the surface. In 1899 Robert T. Hill called the area "the Bloody Bend," and with good reason. On his expedition that year through the canyons of the Rio Grande, the explorers stopped at a small store at Polvo a few miles below Presidio. There the shopkeeper showed Hill "splotches of blood upon the floor and wall behind the counter, where his predecessor had been robbed and murdered" by an outlaw. Before 1899 was over, the shopkeeper would suffer a similar fate. Not surprisingly, Hill and his companions kept their weapons by their sides for the rest of the trip.[18]

The image and the reality of the "Bloody Bend" have continued well into the twentieth century. One of the most infamous local incidents occurred in May 1916 when Mexican bandits during the Revolution raided Glenn Springs, killing three soldiers of the Fourteenth Infantry, United States Army and several civilians. Fifty years later in 1966

The Tornillo Creek Bridge, a Mission 66 project, spans a dry stream for most of the year, but sudden rains can turn the dry bed into a raging torrent. An ocotillo plant is in the foreground. Photo by Jack E. Boucher, National Park Service, Harpers Ferry, West Virginia.

Another Mission 66 project was Park Headquarters at Panther Junction. The Chisos Mountains are in the background. Photo by M. Woodbridge Williams, National Park Service, Harpers Ferry, West Virginia.

when Lady Bird Johnson took a float trip through Mariscal Canyon, Secret Service agents were concerned about how easy it would be for a sniper to fire from the cliffs, a fear realized in 1988 when gunmen killed a man on a raft trip west of the park.[19] Although two Mexican nationals were arrested, convicted, and imprisoned in Mexico for the shooting, this case was an exception. More often, suspects disappear into the mountains and canyons, and many crimes remain unsolved.

"I don't think this is an unduly unsafe park," said Jim Northrup, the chief ranger in charge of law enforcement at Big Bend in 1994. "But people should remember that this is a remote wilderness area along an uncontrolled international border."[20]

More and more frequently, park rangers have had to curtail other duties to concentrate on law enforcement, including protecting campsites and automobiles from looters, patrolling the river for "wetbacks," and trying to stem the increasing flow of marijuana, heroin, cocaine, and other drugs from Mexico. In 1972 Ranger George Howarth surprised "Bronco," a well-known drug smuggler, crossing the Rio Grande. The two men drew their weapons and locked eyes as Bronco slowly retraced his steps across the shallow river. "It's probably a good thing George didn't try to stop him," Superintendent Joe Carithers said

"Dallas Huts" in the Basin. Photo by George A. Grant, National Park Service, Harpers Ferry, West Virginia.

The view from Rio Grande Village: Sierra del Carmen range and pond.
Photo by Roland H. Wauer, National Park Service, Harpers Ferry, West
Virginia.

Camping in the Basin before improvements: A family with trailer at the foot of Casa Grande, 1945. Photo by Matt Dodge and Isabelle Story, National Park Service, Harpers Ferry, West Virginia.

Mission 66 provided the Chisos Basin campground ramadas with tables and charcoal broilers, restrooms, and campsites for tents and trailers. Photo by Jack E. Boucher, National Park Service, Harpers Ferry, West Virginia.

with characteristic Western understatement. "Someone would've gotten hurt."[21]

Occasionally, individuals have been apprehended. In the 1980s, for example, U.S. Border Patrol agents stopped a couple towing a forty-foot-long mobile home on the highway to Fort Stockton, and seized over 660 pounds of cocaine with an estimated street value of $148 million. The pair had picked up the valuable cargo in the park, which Drug Enforcement Administration officials suspected had been flown from Colombia to one of many small airfields on ranches in Mexico adjacent to Big Bend. The arrest and seizure were the result of a cooperative investigation between the Border Patrol and the National Park Service.[22]

Also assisting with law enforcement has been "Judge Roy Bean," a canine trained to sniff out narcotics, who deserved his namesake's reputation as the "law west of the Pecos." In 1989 "Roy" was brought to Castolon to check out a suspicious vehicle. His keen nose discovered 337 pounds of marijuana concealed in a compartment under the bed of a pickup truck. The Park Service later equipped the confiscated vehicle with an air compressor and power tools for cutting through metal. When "Roy" or other dogs in the K-9 drug corps pick up the scent of narcotics, rangers can then cut open suspected vehicles on the site.[23]

Park Service, Border Patrol, and other law enforcement officials of-

The Glenn Springs Store, site of border violence in 1916. Big Bend National Park, National Park Service.

ten refer to the Boquillas and San Vicente "connections" for drugs and stolen goods, and "wetbacks" frequently cross the Rio Grande at the two Mexican villages adjacent to the park. Once a stolen tractor-trailer rig transporting stereo components into Mexico bogged down in the river and had to be abandoned by its illicit entrepreneurs. Although most illegal aliens have been from Mexico and other Latin American countries, there have been surprises. From 1984 to 1985, for instance, there were several cases involving Polish "wetbacks." It seems that naturalized Poles living in New Jersey recruited Polish citizens in Europe. They each paid $800–$900 to their Polish-American padrones, obtained travel visas, and flew to Mexico City, where their New Jersey contacts met them and assisted with the trip northward to the border. At Boquillas, the Poles were smuggled across the river and through the park on their way to destinations in the United States. Unfortunately for them, they only got as far as Alpine before they were arrested.[24]

As the park staff gears up for the rest of the 1990s and plans for the twenty-first century, some of the same problems persist that challenged Ross Maxwell fifty years before. The authors of the latest *Statement for Management* (1992) note that "Big Bend is a remote duty location, which presents challenges to residents in need of market, medical, educational, and recreational facilities." The management plan continues, "With great travel distances to towns and cities [and] little employment opportunity for spouses with dual careers . . . it is difficult to maintain employee and family morale." In an extreme case, one individual suffered severe bouts of depression because his spouse had taken the couple's two children and relocated to a city in another southwestern state. She had moved to afford her children better schooling and to further her own career. The nearest Texas city to Big Bend that could provide the therapy that her husband needed for his depression was Midland, Texas, five hundred miles round-trip from the park. He consequently requested a transfer from Big Bend to be near his family, where he could also receive treatment for his condition. More common are the overheard conversations of some Park Service staff counting the days left in their "sentences" before they can transfer to a less isolated assignment. One frequent complaint is the lack of leisure facilities. An NPS employees recreation building, complete with a gymnasium and an outdoor 35' × 60' swimming pool and 12' × 35' wading pool, was proposed in 1981, but fell victim to budget "belt tightening." And finally, traditionally low pay rates in the Park Service, especially for rangers, makes recruitment and retention particularly difficult. The "Employee Roster" for June 1, 1991, for instance, listed 128 full- and part-time positions, 39 of which were vacant, or just over 30 percent. Of the unfilled positions, 17 were for rangers.[25]

Adding to morale problems are inadequate housing and office spaces. At the park headquarters at Panther Junction many employees and their families reside in a "trailer ghetto," poorly insulated mobile homes unattractively grouped together without landscaping, storage, or garages, where utility lines crisscross the desert sky overhead. For the time being, older trailers are gradually being replaced by modular landscaped housing.[26]

At work, employees share office space with the staff of the Big Bend Natural History Association (BBNHA), squeezing between filing and storage cabinets and doubling up on desks. The only facility for group work projects, team, and staff meetings is the headquarters auditorium, which is also used for visitor and interpretive programs. Although as early as 1981 the *General Management Plan* called for a new visitor center and office space of 3,100 square feet, budget cutbacks have pushed the project back to 1999 or later. As an interim measure, the BBNHA, a nonprofit organization, is proceeding with plans to construct a 2,000-square-foot office at Panther Junction, which will free 720 square feet in the headquarters office to be used by NPS interpretation and visitor services staff.[27]

Upstream view of the Rio Grande from Boquillas, Mexico. National Park Service, Harpers Ferry, West Virginia.

EPILOGUE

Big Bend at Fifty: Into the Twenty-first Century

In May 1994, a month before the celebration of the fiftieth anniversary of Big Bend's establishment, a newspaper reporter interviewed Superintendent Rob Arnberger about some of the problems facing the park as it approached the twenty-first century. The superintendent's list included the familiar and the not so ordinary, ranging from drug smugglers to car thieves, from air pollution to trespassing livestock, from marauding black bears to four-wheel-drive vehicles scarring the fragile desert surface. Arnberger warned, "It's becoming more clear with every day that goes by that this wild national park" in the Chihuahuan Desert "is being impacted by things that are far beyond our control, some of them hundreds of miles away."

Arnberger identified the most urgent crisis as air pollution. In the state of Coahuila, Mexico, 125 miles to the southeast, Carbón II, a coal-burning power facility, was under construction. Scheduled for completion in 1995, it will join the nearby Carbón I plant, and together they will annually emit an estimated 230,000–300,000 tons of sulfur dioxide, a clear gas that causes haze and acid rain. If the plants were in the United States, they would be the largest source of the toxic gas in the country. That huge volume, coupled with pollutants already in the atmosphere, could cut visibility in the park and its environs from one hundred to forty miles, or a reduction of 60 percent. According to John

Forsythe, a technician who monitors the park's air quality, "There are days when you can't see the outline of mountains 20 miles away." Although the emissions meet Mexico's standards, they far exceed those of the U.S. Environmental Protection Agency. "It's going to be a hazy day forever," Arnberger lamented.[1]

The North American Free Trade Agreement (NAFTA), signed on January 1, 1994, further complicated matters. Intended primarily to boost economic development, its effect on fragile resources could be devastating. Realizing this, NAFTA officials included a provision to establish a Commission for Environmental Cooperation with members from Canada, Mexico, and the United States. A joint advisory committee will have the authority to resolve environmental controversies. The commission and Mexico's establishment in November 1994 of four new wildlife preserves comprising 1.6 million acres across from Big Bend bode well for the future. In the meantime, Carbón I in Mexico continues to pump tons of sulfur dioxide into the atmosphere.[2]

Big Bend is not the only Park Service site suffering from air pollution. The views at Great Smoky Mountains, the most visited national park (over nine million people in 1993) are hazed over 90 percent of the time by a combination of sulfate particles (similar to those emitted by the Carbón I plant) and ground-level ozone (air pollution caused by automobiles and power plants emitting nitrogen oxide and hydrocarbons). The natural haze (the Cherokees called it the "Place of Blue Smoke") has been replaced by "Smog Alley." Views are not the only casualties of the chemical pollutants. At the higher elevations of the southern Appalachians, acid rain from almost two dozen fossil fuel plants in the Tennessee and Ohio valleys has decimated red spruce tree populations. Elsewhere in the park, ozone has damaged the leaves or stunted the growth of over one hundred species of plants and trees. Tragically, the problem of "dirty air" affects almost all national park sites from Maine to California.[3]

Another major systemwide problem identified by Secretary of the Interior Bruce Babbitt is an "alarming lack of financial support" for the national parks. The National Park Service's physical plant is valued in excess of $40 billion, yet the agency's annual operating budget is only $1 billion, 40 percent of which goes for "Band-Aid" maintenance ("paint, nails, and lawnmowers"); the funds simply are not there for basic repairs and improvements. "Maintenance continually deferred has created a construction and repair time bomb," warned Babbitt. In

1994 there was a $5 billion backlog of repairs and improvements. The construction budget of $200 million in 1994 was for 80 separate projects; another 220 awaited funding at a projected cost of $3 billion, which will double to $6 billion by 1996. Grand Canyon National Park, a priority site visited by almost five million people in 1993, requested $19 million to resurface roads and $24 million to construct employee housing. Congress appropriated almost $6 million for employee housing; no funds were provided for roads.[4]

Big Bend does not have the visitation of Grand Canyon or Great Smoky Mountains. As one of the remotest and least frequented of the parks, it sometimes seems to the staff that they are "more and more isolated from any external help." The annual operating budget for 1994 was $3.6 million, an amount that has remained stable but inadequate for several years. Many of the facilities date from the 1950s and 1960s and suffer from the "deferred maintenance" malady affecting the rest of the system. In 1993, 41 percent of maintenance projects at Big Bend were postponed, and half or more were delayed in 1994.[5]

The record for cultural resources was much worse. With no permanent funds available for preservation maintenance, the staff had to rely on grants. Of fifty-four historic structures eligible from 1987 to 1992, only one received funding. The remaining fifty-three, including nine National Register properties, continued to deteriorate. Only a fraction of Big Bend's archaeological resources (estimated at over ten thousand sites) has been inventoried and documented. Lacking funds and staff (one archaeologist doubles as the park historian), long-term monitoring procedures—essential for the preservation of irreplaceable artifacts and sites—have not yet been put in place for historic or archaeological resources. Because of insufficient staff, budget constraints, and inadequate storage facilities for historic and natural resource collections, approximately 24,000 artifacts were stored outside of the park and have not been catalogued.[6]

The rangers' responsibilities and workload have grown heavier in other areas as well. In 1988 there were 26 bear sightings in Big Bend. Five years later there were 502 sightings, and bear contacts with vehicles, tents, and people have risen accordingly. In 1993 forty bear incidents were reported, half of which occurred in December. Criminal activity on the border also has escalated. In 1993 forty burglaries or larcenies were reported, many involving unattended vehicles. Smuggling of goods, livestock, and people across the river and occasional

A family visits a "hermit's hut" in June 1959. Photo by Jack E. Boucher, National Park Service, Harpers Ferry, West Virginia.

violent crimes continue to take a disproportionate share of NPS employees' time. As a result of downsizing and the site's limited appeal to career employees, there are not enough law enforcement personnel. In 1985 twenty rangers patrolled the park's 1,252 square miles; the number had shrunk to ten by 1994.[7]

As noted above, the difficulty of recruiting and retaining qualified employees at the remote desert park further adds to Big Bend's problems. In 1994 there were ninety-three full-time positions, yet Superintendent Arnberger estimated he would require twenty more positions just to deal with minimum needs. As Dennis Vasquez, the park's chief naturalist, observed, "It takes a special kind of person to work here. Not everyone can do it." And they are getting more and more difficult to find as advertised positions at Big Bend, particularly for rangers, go unfilled.[8]

One of the most successful programs at Big Bend designed to supplement declining numbers of full-time staff has been the Volunteers-in-Parks (VIPs). In 1990, 203 volunteers donated 20,752 hours, the equivalent of ten employee years of work. The Park Service provided VIPs housing, uniforms, and limited expenses up to $10 per day. The volunteers in turn ran the Persimmon Gap Visitor Center, helped at the Panther Junction headquarters, conducted interpretive programs, and assisted with resource and maintenance activities, among other duties. One of the more unusual projects had an international flavor when four adobe masons from Mexico, all volunteers, restored the Alvino House, the oldest adobe structure in the park. At the same time, another team of VIPs interpreted to visitors the restoration work underway and the significance of the house as representative of border life in the early twentieth century. Yet even such an efficient and economical program as VIPs felt the budget-cutters' ax in 1992 when it lopped off the $12,500 allotted for VIPs expenses.[9]

The problems facing Big Bend and the entire national park system on the eve of the twenty-first century are the greatest challenges yet faced by America's democratic experiment to preserve wild areas for enjoyment by present and future generations. In the 1950s, 50 million visitors poured into parks equipped for half that number, jeopardizing natural and cultural resources as Americans almost "loved to death" their national parks. For about a billion dollars spread over ten years, Mission 66 temporarily shored up the system. In 1993 the annual operating budget for all the parks was one billion dollars, and it's not even enough to do the job. That same year, 270 million people visited the national parks, with 340 million and 500 million visitors projected for the years 2000 and 2010 respectively. Consequently, the Park Service is considering new controls to limit the numbers, including higher user fees and visitation caps, neither of which is especially popular with the public or Congress. As noted, construction expenses alone for the system are estimated at $6 billion in 1996. And the cost of providing protection against environmental threats to the parks defy rational budget projections.[10]

Historian Roderick Nash considers national parks an "American invention," an idea that we successfully "have exported . . . around the world." The problems are indeed global, affecting other nations' parks from Japan to Africa, from Canada to Mexico. The solutions will require international cooperation and understanding, as the Big Bend case study demonstrates. Other nations continue to look to the United

States for leadership in the stewardship of the national park ideal, just as foreign visitors regularly flock to America's national parks for recreation and inspiration.[11]

Numerous scientists, poets, and philosophers have offered logical and eloquent reasons for preserving wild areas. The most compelling arguments come from those who have personally experienced nature. Henry David Thoreau's voluntary exile to Walden Pond in 1845 led him to observe that "in Wildness is the preservation of the World." A century and a half later in spring 1994, Andy Arkell, a London tourist, was midway through a six-month motorcycle trek to America's national parks. Traveling alone, he camped in Big Bend's back country for three days. His only companion was a rattlesnake, which emerged daily from its den to sun itself. As he left, Arkell told a ranger that the wild and rugged park in the Chihuahuan Desert was his favorite so far. "This whole part of the country is the most magical that I've seen," a sentiment shared by the Chisos Indians, the old forgotten cowboy, Lady Bird Johnson, and thousands of others over the years who have made the effort to visit the Big Bend Country on the Rio Grande. Whether or not the magic in that "fabulous corner of the world" endures into the twenty-first century depends on a lot of factors. Whatever the outcome, it will reveal much about the human species' values, quality of life, and ability to adapt and survive in a global community.[12]

NOTES

Abbreviations

ACM   Amon Carter Museum, Fort Worth, Texas

BBNHA   Big Bend Natural History Association

BBNP   Big Bend National Park

BBNP-NA   Records of Big Bend National Park, Record Group 79, National Archives, College Park, Maryland

BBSPP   Big Bend State Park Papers, Texas Parks and Wildlife Department, Austin, Texas

Drury File, BBNP-NA   Records of Newton B. Drury, Director's Personal File, Big Bend National Park, 1940 to March, 1951, Record Group 79, National Archives, College Park, Maryland

LBJ Library   Lyndon Baines Johnson Library, Austin, Texas

NPS   National Park Service

NPS Files, BBPIP-NA   Records of the National Park Service, Central Classified Files, 1907–1949, File 0-32, Big Bend Proposed International Park, Part I, Record Group 79, National Archives, College Park, Maryland

PR-BBNP   Park Records at Big Bend National Park, Texas

Secretary of the Interior, Central Classified Files, Big Bend, RG 48, NA   Records of the Office of the Secretary of the Interior, Central Classified Files, 12-29, National Parks, Big Bend, Texas, General, Parts I and II, Record Group 48, National Archives, College Park, Maryland

TPWD   Texas Parks and Wildlife Department, Austin, Texas

Webb Papers, American History Collection Walter Prescott Webb Papers, The
Center for American History, University of Texas, Austin
Webb Papers, TSA   Walter Prescott Webb Papers, Texas State Archives,
Austin

Prologue

1. Nathaniel T. Kenney, "Big Bend: Jewel in the Texas Desert," *National Geographic* 133 (January 1968): 133; from Stewart L. Udall's introduction in Virginia Madison, *The Big Bend Country of Texas,* p. vii.

2. "Trails through Texas" Trip Itinerary, April 2, 1966, White House Social Files, Box 21, Liz Carpenter Subject File, Lyndon Baines Johnson Library, Austin, Texas (hereafter cited as LBJ Library). Once journalists arrived at the park, they had access to telephone lines and Western Union.
Shana Alexander, "Lady Bird's Boat Ride," *Life* 60 (April 15, 1966): 34; "The First Lady: Home on the Range," *Time* 87 (April 8, 1966): 26–27; Frances Coltun, "Let's Travel: With Mrs. LBJ to Big Bend," *Mademoiselle* 63 (July 1966): 26, 28, 30.

3. "First Lady Begins Trip into the Big Bend Country," *New York Times,* April 3, 1966.

4. William M. Blair, "First Lady Rafted Down Rio Grande in Tour of Canyon," *New York Times,* April 4, 1966; Blair, "Plant Smugglers Plunder U.S. Park," *New York Times,* April 10, 1966; Alexander, "Lady Bird's Boat Ride," *Life*: 34.

5. LBJ Library: Press Release, March 12, 1966, White House Social Files, Box 21, Liz Carpenter Subject File; Mrs. Johnson to Conrad Wirth, April 25, 1966, White House Social Files, Box 201, Beautification-Wirth.

6. Frank Collinson, *Life in the Saddle,* pp. 209, 212, 214.

7. From Everett Townsend to "Max," September 1, 1943, quoted in Madison, *Big Bend Country,* p. 230; C. B. Casey to the author, February 21, 1973.

8. Robert T. Hill, "Running the Cañons of the Rio Grande: A Chapter of Recent Exploration," *Century Magazine* 61 (January 1901): 372, 377, 380–381.

9. The length of the boundary on the Rio Grande fluctuates as the river changes its course.

10. Roland H. Wauer, *Naturalist's Big Bend;* David J. Schmidly, *The Mammals of Trans-Pecos Texas; Big Bend National Park: Statement for Management,* 1992, pp. 1–2, 11, 14.

11. Wauer, *Naturalist's Big Bend,* p. 61. The most recent insect addition was a species of beetle, *Leptopinara fleminga,* named for Carl M. Fleming, a National Park Service (NPS) resource management specialist. See "News Release," October 27, 1993, File K3415, Park Records at BBNP (hereafter cited as PR-BBNP). The National Park Service and the Big Bend Natural History Association (BBNHA) provide brochures and other publications on the park's history, geology, flora, fauna, and general information, including checklists (*Bird Checklist,* revised 1988; *Mammal Checklist,* 1989; *Amphibians and Reptiles Checklist,* 1989).

12. *BBNP: Statement for Management*, 1992, pp. 1, 15; *Archaeology Brochure*.

13. *Geology Brochure;* Ross A. Maxwell, *The Big Bend of the Rio Grande: A Guide to the Rocks, Geologic History, and Settlers of the Area of Big Bend National Park;* "Home on the Range," *Time: 27.*

14. *Geology Brochure;* Maxwell, *Big Bend of the Rio Grande.*

15. Rosemary Williams, "Tops in Texas," *Texas Highways* 39 (July 1992): 12–17. The 230,000 annual average of visitors is based on visitation records from 1981 to 1990 kept by the superintendent's office, BBNP. In 1993 visitation was 330,000, considerably above the average, and the numbers are rising.

1. The Campaign for Texas' First National Park

1. *Fort Worth Star-Telegram,* October 10, 1937; April 6, 1958; Jodie P. Harris, "Protecting the Big Bend—A Guardsman's View," *Southwestern Historical Quarterly* 78 (January 1975): 292.

2. *El Paso Daily Times,* June 10, 1883; June 12, 1883; Ronnie C. Tyler, "Robert T. Hill and the Big Bend: An 1899 Expedition That Helped Establish a Great National Park," *American West* 10 (September 1973): 36.

3. U.S. Congress, House, H.R. 11749, 60th Cong., 1st sess., 1908, p. 480; U.S. Congress, House, H.R. 13651, 60th Cong., 2d sess., 1908, p. 706; U.S. Congress, House, H.R. 4734, 62d Cong., 1st sess., 1911, p. 245; U.S. Congress, House, H.R. 330, 64th Cong., 1st sess., 1915, p. 21; U.S. Congress, House, 64th Cong., 2d sess., 1917, Appendix and Index, p. 305; Dan Flores, "The Grand Canyon of Texas: How Palo Duro Just Missed Becoming Texas's Third Great National Park," *Texas Parks and Wildlife* (September 1993): 4–15; Roderick Nash, *Wilderness and the American Mind,* Chapter 10.

4. Victor H. Schoffelmayer, "The Big Bend Area of Texas," *Texas Geographic* 1 (May 1937): 5; William J. Lawson and Will Mann Richardson, "The Texas State Park System: A History, Study of Development and Plans for the Future of the Texas State Parks," *Texas Geographic* 2 (December 1938): 1–12; *Journal of the Senate of Texas,* S.C.R. 9, 42d Legislature, reg. sess., pp. 97–98.

5. John A. Salmond, *The Civilian Conservation Corps, 1933–1942: A New Deal Case Study,* p. 26; James Steely and Joseph Monticone, *The Civilian Conservation Corps in Texas State Parks.*

6. *Journal of the Senate of Texas,* S.C.R. 9, 42d Legislature, reg. sess., pp. 97–98; *Journal of the Senate of Texas,* S.C.R. 73, 43d Legislature, reg. sess., p. 1935; U.S. Congress, Senate, 71st Cong., 3d sess., 1931, p. 4001; U.S. Congress, House, 71st Cong., 3d sess., 1931, p. 6213; Sheppard to Wilbur, February 24, 1931, File 0-32, Part I, Records of Big Bend National Park, Record Group 79, National Archives, College Park, Maryland (hereafter cited as BBNP-NA).

7. BBNP-NA (File 0-32, Part I): Albright to Vance Prather, February 3, 1931.

8. Ibid.; C. B. Casey and Lewis H. Saxton, "The Life of Everett Ewing Townsend," *West Texas Historical and Scientific Society Publication* No. 17 (1958):

54. For the origins of Albright's aestheticism, see Donald Swain, *Wilderness Defender: Horace M. Albright and Conservation*, p. 89.

9. Department of the Interior, *Annual Report of the Secretary of the Interior, Fiscal Year 1933*, p. 65; *Annual Report of the Secretary of the Interior, Fiscal Year 1934*, p. 176; Judith K. Fabry, *Guadalupe Mountains National Park: An Administrative History*, pp. 22–23.

10. BBNP-NA: "Review of Proposed Big Bend National Park," May 1, 1934, File 0-32, Part I; "Status Report on Texas National Park," (no date), File 0-32, Part VIII. U.S. Congress, House, H.R. 9193, 68th Cong., 1st sess., 1924, p. 8497; U.S. Congress, House, H.R. 3590, 71st Cong., 1st sess., 1929, p. 2303.

11. *Abilene Reporter-News*, June 11, 1944; R. M. Wagstaff, "Beginnings of the Big Bend Park," *West Texas Historical Association Year Book* 44 (October 1968): 3–14.

12. Casey and Saxton, "Life of Townsend," p. 52; Madison, *Big Bend Country*, p. 230. BBNP-NA (File 207): Townsend to Col. Robert H. Lewis, November 25, 1933.

13. Wagstaff, "Beginnings," pp. 7–12; Casey and Saxton, "Life of Townsend," p. 54; Casey, "The Big Bend National Park," *West Texas Historical and Scientific Society Publication* No. 13 (1948): 30; *Vernon's Texas Statutes*, 1948, Art. 6077b; Ronnie C. Tyler, *The Big Bend: A History of the Last Texas Frontier*, pp. 192–193.

14. Casey, "Big Bend National Park," p. 31; Wagstaff, "Beginnings," pp. 12–14; *Vernon's Texas Statutes*, 1948, Art. 6077c.

15. For examples of Smithers's photographs, see W. D. Smithers, *Chronicles of the Big Bend*.

16. *Alpine Avalanche*, September 3, 1948. BBNP-NA: "Report on the Proposed Big Bend National Park," March 3, 1934, File 207; Toll to Herbert Maier, February 19, 1934, File 0-32, Part I.

17. Robert Shankland, *Steve Mather of the National Parks*, pp. 247–248; A. N. Marquis, ed., *Who's Who in America, 1936–1937*, p. 2430; Obituary in *Trail and Timberline* 209 (March–April 1936): 27–28.

18. Department of the Interior, *Annual Report of the Secretary of the Interior, Fiscal Year 1933*, p. 153. BBNP-NA (File 0-32, Part I): Cammerer memorandum to Arthur E. Demaray, Conrad Wirth, and Harold C. Bryant, April 2, 1934.

19. Casey, "Big Bend National Park," pp. 32–35. BBNP-NA: Ben H. Thompson to Director, NPS, April 18, 1934; "Report on the Proposed Big Bend National Park," March 3, 1934, File 207; "Review of Proposed Big Bend National Park," May 1, 1934, File 0-32, Part I.

20. BBNP-NA (File 0-32, Part I): W. G. Carnes to L. I. Hewes, May 4, 1934; Maier to Wirth, December 22, 1934.

21. BBNP-NA (File 207): "Report of the Big Bend Area, Texas," January 1935.

22. Ibid.

23. Ibid.; "An Act to Establish a National Park Service" (39 Stat. 535); *Vernon's Texas Statutes*, 1948, Art. 6077c.

24. Madison, *Big Bend Country*, p. 232; Casey, "Big Bend National Park," p. 37; Thomason to Townsend, January 28, 1935, Box A-1, Big Bend State Park

Papers, Texas Parks and Wildlife Department, Austin, Texas (hereafter cited as BBSPP). BBNP-NA (File 0-32, Part I): G. A. Moskey memorandum to Wirth, Hillory Tolson, and Arthur Demaray, February 8, 1935.

25. BBNP-NA (File 0-32, Part I): Sheppard to President Roosevelt, February 16, 1935; Roosevelt memorandum to the Secretary of the Interior and the Secretary of State, February 19, 1935; Ickes to the Secretary of State, March 8, 1935; Ickes to President Roosevelt, February 27, 1935.

26. U.S. Congress, House, H.R. 6373, 74th Cong., 1st sess., 1935, p. 2916; U.S. Congress, Senate, S.B. 2131, 74th Cong., 1st sess., 1935, p. 2822. BBNP-NA (File 0-32, Part I): D. E. Colp to Wirth, March 11, 1935; Grady Chandler and William McGraw to Colp, March 6, 1935. The estimated acreage for Big Bend was revised down from 1.5 million to 1 million acres.

27. PR-BBNP: Ross A. Maxwell, "History of Big Bend National Park" (ms.), 1952. BBNP-NA (File 0-32, Part I): Demaray to Robert P. Allen, May 17, 1935. U.S. Congress, Senate, 74th Cong., 1st sess., 1935, pp. 9620, 9818; *United States Statutes at Large*, Vol. 49, Part I, pp. 393–394.

2. Texas Politics and the Park Movement, 1935–1944

1. BBNP-NA: Conrad Wirth telegram to Roger Toll, June 29, 1935; Wirth telegram to Herbert Evison, June 26, 1935, File 0-32, Part I; "Report on Field Investigation Together with Recommendations for the Establishment of a Boundary Line for the Big Bend National Park Project," September 9, 1935; Charles West to Allred, October 14, 1935, File 0-32, Part II.

2. BBNP-NA: Townsend to Herbert Maier, November 29, 1935, File 0-32, Part II; Alexander Brooks memorandum to G. A. Moskey, March 11, 1936; Wirth to Gerald Mann, February 11, 1936, File 0-32, Part III. James G. Anderson, "Land Acquisition in the Big Bend National Park of Texas," M.A. thesis, p. 41.

3. BBNP-NA: Maier to Wirth, September 13, 1935; Maier to Townsend, September 11, 1935, File 0-32, Part II; Regional Director, Region III, to Arno B. Cammerer, November 16, 1936; Ben F. Tisinger telegram to Senator Morris Sheppard, February 14, 1936; Tisinger to Sheppard, February 15, 1936; J. O. Guleke and Members of the Texas Board of Education to Sheppard, February 21, 1936, File 0-32, Part III.

4. BBNP-NA: L. T. Burrow to Carroll H. Wegemann, September 19, 1935; Wegemann to Earl Trager, September 25, 1935, File 0-32, Part II; Maier to Cammerer, January 4, 1937, File 0-32, Part IV. *Alpine Avalanche*, October 2, 1936.

5. BBNP-NA: Maier to Director, NPS, November 13, 1936; Cammerer telegram to Maier, November 19, 1936, File 0-32, Part III; Arthur Demaray telegram to Maier, January 6, 1937, File 0-32, Part IV.

6. BBNP-NA (File 0-32, Part IV): Maier to Director, NPS, January 27, 1937; January 28, 1937.

7. BBNP-NA (File 0-32, Part IV): Maier to Director, NPS, attention of Moskey, February 18, 1937. *Fort Worth Star-Telegram*, March 3, 1937.

8. BBNP-NA (File 0-32, Part IV): Stevenson's Press Release, February 21, 1937. *Fort Worth Star-Telegram*, February 20, 1937.

9. BBNP-NA (File 0-32, Part IV): Maier to Director, NPS, attention of Wirth, March 27, 1937.

10. *Austin Dispatch*, May 17, 1937. BBNP-NA (File 0-32, Part IV): Maier to Director, NPS, attention of Wirth, May 1, 1937; April 16, 1937.

11. BBNP-NA (File 0-32, Part IV): Maier to Director, NPS, attention of Wirth, May 31, 1937; Maier to Departamento Forestal, Caza y Pesca, attention of Daniel F. Galicia or Juan Zinser, May 26, 1937; M. A. de Quevedo to Pierre del Boal, June 4, 1937; Boal telegram to Daniels, June 5, 1937; Cammerer telegram to Allred, June 5, 1937.

12. PR-BBNP: "Legislative Messages of Governor James V. Allred," 1935–1939. BBNP-NA (File 0-32, Part IV): Allred to Daniels, June 15, 1937; Leo McClatchy, "Big Bend Campaign," (ms.), August 18, 1937.

13. *Fort Worth Star-Telegram*, June 11, 1937; Maier to Record, July 13, 1937, Amon Carter Museum (hereafter cited as ACM). BBNP-NA (File 0-32, Part IV): Morelock to *Fort Worth Star-Telegram*, June 12, 1937; J. M. North to Morelock, June 21, 1937; Maier to Director, NPS, attention of Wirth, July 13, 1937.

14. *Fort Worth Star-Telegram*, July 25, 1937; September 8, 1937; September 16, 1937; October 3, 1937; October 9, 1937.

15. BBNP-NA (File 0-32, Part V): *Dallas Morning News*, July 25, 1937; *El Paso Times* (date obscured); Morelock to Harold Ickes, October 25, 1937; Maier telegram to Director, NPS, attention of Fred T. Johnston, November 20, 1937.

16. *Houston Chronicle*, July 25, 1937; *Fort Worth Star-Telegram*, September 1, 1937; November 20, 1937; November 25, 1937. BBNP-NA (File 0-32, Part V): NPS Press Release, December 11, 1937; Wirth to Thomason, November 10, 1937.

17. BBNP-NA (File 0-32, Part IV): Adams to Cammerer, June 18, 1937; Johnston to Regional Director, Region III, June 25, 1937; Demaray to Daniels, July 2, 1937; Cammerer memorandum to Ickes, August 8, 1937. *Fort Worth Star-Telegram*, September 4, 1937; *Alpine Avalanche*, November 5, 1937; *Vernon's Texas Statutes*, 1948, Art. 6077c.

18. BBNP-NA (File 0-32, Part V): Morelock to Carter, March 10, 1938.

19. *Fort Worth Star-Telegram*, May 24, 1938. BBNP-NA (File 0-32, Part VII): Maier to Director, NPS, May 28, 1938. The Permanent Executive Committee eventually grew to a membership of fifty directors by 1941.

20. ACM: Minutes of the Executive Board, Texas Big Bend Park Association, May 23, 1938. BBSPP (Box A-7): Wychgel to Allred, May 28, 1938.

21. BBNP-NA (File 0-32, Part VI): Maier memorandum to Director, NPS, November 22, 1938.

22. BBNP-NA (File 0-32, Part VII): Thomason to Morelock, July 1, 1938; Cammerer memorandum to Maier and the Files, July 11, 1938.

23. *Galveston News*, August 8, 1938; *Dallas Morning News*, September 9, 1938; *San Antonio Light*, August 15, 1938; *Goose Creek Sun*, October 19, 1938. BBNP-

NA (File 0–32, Part VI): Maier memorandum to Director, NPS, November 22, 1938; O'Daniel to Demaray, December 20, 1938. O'Daniel received 573,166 votes out of 1,114,885 cast; see *Texas Almanac, 1956–1957*, p. 73.

24. BBNP-NA (File 0–32, Part VI): Maier memorandum to Director, NPS, January 24, 1939; Maier to Winfield, January 24, 1939. *Fort Worth Star-Telegram*, April 5, 1939.

25. BBNP-NA (File 0 32, Part VI): Draft of S.B. 123. *San Antonio Express*, March 4, 1939.

26. *Austin Times*, March 7, 1939; *Journal of the Senate of Texas*, 46th Legislature, reg. sess., March 1, 1939, pp. 476–478; Edgar B. Nixon (ed.), *Franklin D. Roosevelt and Conservation, 1911–1945*, vol. 2, pp. 298–299.

27. *Alpine Avalanche*, May 2, 1939; *Temple Telegraph*, May 2, 1939; *Fort Worth Star-Telegram*, May 2, 1939; *Del Rio Herald*, April 7, 1939; *Texarkana News*, June 22, 1939. BBNP-NA: Wirth telegram to Regional Director, Region III, May 19, 1939, File 0–32, Part VI; NPS Press Release, June 30, 1939, File 501-03, Part II.

28. BBNP-NA: Maier memorandum to Director, NPS, November 22, 1938; May 13, 1939, File 0–32, Part VI; Tolson memorandum to Johnston, November 10, 1939, File 0–32, Part VII; Milton McColm memorandum to Director, NPS, August 13, 1940; Carter to Members of Executive Committee, BBPA, October 22, 1940; McColm telegram to Director, NPS, April 10, 1940, File 0–32, Part VIII; Maxwell memorandum to Director, NPS, July 26, 1948, File 601; M. R. Tillotson memorandum to Director, NPS, February 27, 1943, File 601, Part I. *Fort Worth Star Telegram*, August 25, 1940; May 16, 1941. Carter said the land purchase program would begin as soon as the BBPA raised $100,000 through popular subscription (exclusive of the working fund). Since it never began, the figure of $100,000 would be the maximum estimation.

29. BBNP-NA (File 0–32, Part VIII): A. J. Wirtz to Morelock, August 20, 1940; Townsend to Tillotson, January 17, 1941; L. C. Fuller memorandum to Tillotson, January 20, 1941; Tillotson memorandum to Director, NPS, March 6, 1941; Tillotson, "The Big Bend National Park as an Asset to the State of Texas" (ms.), March 27, 1941; Tillotson telegram to Director, NPS, March 20, 1941.

30. BBNP-NA (File 0–32, Part IX): John C. Diggs memorandum to Regional Director, Region III, June 9, 1941; Frank Quinn to Tillotson, December 18, 1941. PR-BBNP: Ross Maxwell, "History of Big Bend National Park" (ms.). *Fort Worth Star-Telegram*, August 8, 1941.

31. BBNP-NA: Tillotson memorandum to Director, NPS, November 10, 1942; Carter to Newton B. Drury, April 15, 1943; Moskey memorandum to Wirth, May 1, 1943, File 601, Part I; Drury memorandum to Secretary of the Interior, June 7, 1943, File 601, Part II.

32. BBNP-NA: Tolson memorandum to Solicitor General, August 31, 1944, File 601, Part II; Harry Connelly to Drury, June 11, 1942, File 0–32, Part IX. *Washington Star*, June 7, 1944.

3. A Park for the People from the People

1. BBNP-NA (File 610): Norah Walker to President of the United States of America, February 7, 1942.

2. BBNP-NA (File 610, Part III): Mrs. W. T. Burnham to Roosevelt, March 5, 1945. The Burnham family left the Big Bend area in 1945.

3. BBNP-NA (File 610): Lilla C. Singleton to Department of the Interior, March 5, 1943. Madison, *Big Bend Country*, p. 238.

4. BBNP-NA: Maier to Wirth, December 22, 1934, File 0-32, Part I; "Report on the Proposed Big Bend National Park," March 3, 1934; "Report on the Big Bend Area, Texas," January, 1935, File 207.

5. John Ise, *Our National Park Policy: A Critical History*, pp. 376, 380.

6. BBNP-NA: "Report on Field Investigation Together with Recommendations for the Establishment of a Boundary Line for the Big Bend National Park Project," September 9, 1935, File 0-32, Part II; Acting Director, NPS, to Director, Geological Survey, March 11, 1936, File 0-32, Part III; "Status of Approved Land Acquisition Programs," February 8, 1943; Newton B. Drury memorandum to Secretary of the Interior, December 22, 1942; Eugene Thompson to M. R. Tillotson, August 23, 1943, File 601, Part II.

7. BBNP-NA: Maier to Wirth, October 30, 1936; Hillory Tolson memorandum to Director, NPS, February 1, 1939, File 0-32, Part III; Thompson memorandum to Wirth, May 10, 1941; NPS Press Release, July 18, 1941; Frank Quinn to Tillotson, December 18, 1941, File 0-32, Part IX. "Final Report of Big Bend Land Department," April 1, 1949, from files of the Texas Parks and Wildlife Department, Austin, Texas (hereafter TPWD); *Fort Worth Star-Telegram*, August 24, 1941. Frank Quinn was originally appointed to head the Big Bend Land Department, but he resigned after a few weeks and instead coordinated the Texas State Parks Board land acquisition activities from Austin.

8. *Fort Worth Star-Telegram*, December 9, 1941; Anderson, "Land Acquisition," pp. 94–95; *Dallas Morning News*, February 17, 1942.

9. BBNP-NA (File 601, Part I): Decision Number 9260, A. H. King, Appellant, versus George H. Sheppard, Appellee, from District Court of Travis County, Texas, filed December 3, 1941 (transcript of decision in File 601, Part I); Carter to Drury, February 23, 1942; Frederick B. Isely to Donald E. Lee, March 9, 1942; Lee to Isely, March 24, 1942; Theodore Spector memorandum to Director, NPS, May 23, 1942.

10. BBNP-NA: Quinn to Tillotson, December 18, 1941; Quinn and Thompson to All Members of the Texas State Parks Board, December 15, 1941, File 0-32, Part IX; Carter to Drury, February 23, 1942, File 601, Part I. Anderson, "Land Acquisition," p. 95.

11. BBNP-NA: Thompson to D. M. Bennett, September 8, 1942; Milton McColm memorandum to Director, NPS, September 2, 1941; Drury memorandum to Secretary of the Interior, December 22, 1942; Tillotson memoranda to Director, NPS, August 31, 1942, and November 10, 1942, File 601, Part I;

Thompson to Tillotson, August 23, 1943, File 601, Part II; Quinn to Tillotson, August 18, 1941; December 18, 1941, File 0-32, Part IX. "Final Report of Big Bend Land Department," April 1, 1949, TPWD.

12. BBNP-NA (File 601, Part I): Tillotson to Thompson, September 23, 1942; Drury memorandum to Regional Director, Region III, January 20, 1943; Drury to Quinn, March 11, 1943.

13. BBNP-NA (File 601, Part I): Tillotson memorandum to Director, NPS, February 6, 1943; Drury memorandum to Regional Director, Region III, February 25, 1943; Quinn to Drury, March 25, 1943; Tillotson memorandum to Director, NPS, March 26, 1943; Drury to Carter, March 20, 1943; Carter to Drury, April 15, 1943.

14. BBNP-NA: Lindsay C. Warren to Thomason, April 22, 1943; Thompson, "Probable Funds to Complete Program," August 1, 1942; "Excerpts from Minutes of the Meeting of the Texas State Parks Board, August 14, 1942, Austin, Texas"; Quinn to Drury, March 25, 1943; Quinn to Drury, April 1, 1943; Drury memorandum to Regional Director, Region III, January 20, 1943, File 601, Part I; Drury memorandum to Secretary of the Interior, June 7, 1943, File 601, Part II; Drury to Wirth, October 14, 1943; Tolson Departmental Memorandum, October 21, 1943, File 610.

15. BBNP-NA (File 601): Arthur Demaray to Thompson, July 7, 1943.

16. BBNP-NA: H. L. Winfield to Quinn, April 2, 1945, File 601, Part III; Ross Maxwell memorandum to Regional Director, Region III, March 31, 1947; April 22, 1947; Tillotson memorandum to Director, NPS, March 27, 1946; Tillotson to James Record, June 11, 1947; Thompson to Maxwell, January 13, 1949, File 610; "Annual Report for Big Bend National Park, 1947," July 7, 1947, File 207. "Final Report of Big Bend Land Department," April 1, 1949, TPWD.

17. PR-BBNP: Maxwell, "Remarks to be Given before the Appropriations Committee, State Legislature—in Support of a Bill to Appropriate $100,000 with which to Purchase the Remaining Private Lands in Big Bend National Park," April 13, 1949.

18. United States Statutes at Large, Vol. 63, pp. 679–680. PR-BBNP: Lemuel Garrison memorandum to Regional Director, Region III, January 29, 1954.

19. PR-BBNP: Garrison memorandum to Regional Director, Region III, January 29, 1954. TPWD: "Final Report of Big Bend Land Department," April 1, 1949.

20. United States Statutes at Large, Vol. 67, p. 497; Joe Brown, NPS, to the author, December 13, 1973; January 10, 1974; J. F. Carithers, NPS, to the author, December 6, 1973.

21. BBNP: Statement for Management, 1992, pp. 6–7, 17–18.

4. Promoting a Park to "Excel Yellowstone"

1. Maier to Webb, April 26, 1937, Box 2M260, General Correspondence, Walter Prescott Webb Papers, The Center for American History, University of Texas, Austin (hereafter cited as Webb Papers, American History Collection).

2. Ibid.; Leo McClatchy to Webb, (no date), File 4, Walter Prescott Webb Papers, Texas State Archives, Austin (hereafter cited as Webb Papers, TSA). BBNP-NA (File 501): Webb, "The Big Bend of Texas," NPS Press Release, April 18, 1937. Webb originally had written one article, but its length necessitated dividing it into two parts.

3. BBNP-NA (File 501): Webb, "The Big Bend of Texas," NPS Press Release, April 25, 1937. Webb Papers, TSA (File 2): Thomas Skaggs to E. E. Townsend, March 30, 1937. The quote is from Larry McMurtry, *In a Narrow Grave: Essays on Texas*, p. 43.

4. In addition to Townsend, Webb asked others for reports on canyon passages (cited below). Webb Papers, TSA: Townsend, "Data on Passages Made Through the Canyons of the Rio Grande," August 1936; H. W. Johnson and Henry M. Zellar memorandum to Commanding Officer, Fort D. A. Russell, Texas, April 28, 1930, on the subject "Reconnaissance of Grand Canyon of Santa Helena"; and Nick D. Collaer to District Director, U.S. Immigration Service, El Paso, July 30, 1930, File 2.

5. BBNP-NA (File 0-32, Part IV): Maier to Director, NPS, April 24, 1937; Wirth to Regional Director, Region III, April 27, 1937; NPS Press Release, May 7, 1937.

6. Webb Papers, TSA: Skaggs to Webb, April 11, 1937, File 1; May 11, 1937, File 2. The capped words are in the original.

7. Webb Papers, TSA: Webb, "Materials Prepared as a Basis for a Guide to Points of Interest in the Proposed BBNP," File 2; Skaggs to Webb, April 3, 1937, File 1; May 9, 1937, File 1; May 11, 1937, File 2.

8. BBNP-NA (File 0-32, Part IV): NPS Press Release, May 7, 1937. *Austin Dispatch*, May 16, 1937; Skaggs to Webb, April 29, 1937, File 1, Webb Papers, TSA.

9. Skaggs to Webb, May 2, 1937, File 1, Webb Papers, TSA.

10. *Fort Worth Star-Telegram*, May 18, 1937; *Oklahoma City Times*, May 18, 1937; *El Paso Times*, May 17, 1937; *Oklahoma City Oklahoman*, May 19, 1937; *Austin Statesman*, May 17, 1937; Webb, "Materials Prepared as a Basis for a Guide to Points of Interest in the Proposed BBNP," File 2, Webb Papers, TSA.

11. *Fort Worth Star-Telegram*, July 28, 1937; September 10, 1937; September 19, 1937; *Palestine Herald Press*, April 17, 1938; *Austin American*, April 14, 1936; *San Antonio News*, November 3, 1937; *San Angelo Standard-Times*, March 3, 1939; *Colorado City Record*, April 28, 1939; *Amarillo News*, April 15, 1939; *Corpus Christi Caller-Times*, April 15, 1939; *Shamrock Texan*, July 28, 1937; *Alpine Avalanche*, March 5, 1937; *Woodville Booster*, June 1, 1939. Morelock gave credit for the statement to Herbert Maier of the Park Service; see BBNP-NA (File 0-32, Part V): "Big Bend National Park Bulletin of Information," September 10, 1937. Santa Elena is often referred to as the "Grand Canyon of the Rio Grande."

12. BBNP-NA: Leo A. McClatchy, "Interesting Things About the Big Bend" (ms.), File 501-04; Erle Kauffman, "The Big Bend of the Rio," *American Forests* (advance proof), File 0-32, Part I; NPS Press Release, April 26, 1936, File 0-32,

Part III. *Fort Worth Star-Telegram*, April 26, 1936; September 29, 1940; *Dallas Morning News*, April 26, 1936; *Alpine Avalanche*, May 8, 1942.

13. Madison, *Big Bend Country*, p. 240. BBNP-NA (File 501-02): Maxwell memorandum to Regional Director, Region III, October 5, 1944. Jack Hope, "Big Bend: A Nice Place to Visit," *Audubon* 75 (July 1973): 38–39; J. O. Langford, *Big Bend: A Homesteader's Story*, p. 20; Arthur R. Gomez, *A Most Singular Country: A History of Occupation in the Big Bend*, p. 125.

14. *Austin American*, May 1, 1936; *Alpine Avalanche*, May 14, 1936; *Fort Worth Star-Telegram*, February 28, 1937; December 6, 1937; December 2, 1938; *Dallas Morning News*, February 28, 1937; October 31, 1937; *Galveston Tribune*, September 11, 1937; *Denver Post*, March 7, 1937; *San Antonio Express*, February 28, 1937; March 7, 1937; *New York Times*, November 24, 1935; *Butte* (Montana) *Daily Post*, March 14, 1936; *Miami* (Florida) *News*, September 27, 1942; *Christian Science Monitor*, July 21, 1944; *San Francisco Call Bulletin*, June 20, 1944. BBNP-NA: Leo McClatchy, "Interesting Things About Big Bend" (ms.), June 5, 1936, File 501-04; NPS Press Release, April 26, 1936, File 0-32, Part III.

15. BBNP-NA: NPS Press Release, September 2, 1937; Hillory Tolson to Maier, November 12, 1937, File 0-32, Part V; W. B. McDougall memorandum to Victor Cahalane, January 9, 1940, File 0-32, Part VIII.

16. *Dallas Morning News*, January 17, 1945. BBNP-NA: Maier to E. E. Townsend, April 20, 1936, File 0-32, Part III; Tillotson memorandum to Director, NPS, January 22, 1945, File 501-03.

17. BBNP-NA (File 0-32, Part V): Sheppard to Arno B. Cammerer, December 17, 1937; Arthur Demaray to Sheppard, December 31, 1937. *Houston Press*, August 13, 1938; *El Paso Herald-Post*, August 18, 1938; *Fort Worth Star-Telegram*, August 21, 1938.

18. *Dallas Morning News*, October 26, 1942. BBNP-NA (File 501): Eugene Thompson to J. V. Ash, November 1, 1942.

19. Shankland, *Steve Mather of the National Parks*, p. 246. BBNP-NA: Story to Carl P. Russell, March 7, 1938, File 0-32, Part V; Wirth to Regional Director, Region III, August 7, 1937, File 0-32, Part IV. The following represent only a sample of the non-Texas newspaper coverage on Big Bend: *New York Times*, November 24, 1935; *Christian Science Monitor*, January 30, 1936; July 21, 1944; *Butte* (Montana) *Daily Post*, March 14, 1936; *Denver Post*, January 31, 1936; March 7, 1937; September 27, 1942; *Philadelphia Evening Public Ledger*, January 10, 1938; *Miami News*, September 27, 1941; *Oakland* (California) *Tribune*, July 28, 1944; *New York Herald Tribune*, September 12, 1944; *Detroit News*, January 21, 1945; *Cumberland* (Maryland) *Times*, November 13, 1944; *Charleston* (West Virginia) *Gazette*, November 12, 1944; *Mankato* (Minnesota) *Free Press*, November 11, 1944; *Alexandria* (Louisiana) *Town Talk*, November 9, 1944; *Portsmouth* (Virginia) *Star*, November 11, 1944.

20. BBNP-NA: Cammerer memorandum to E. K. Burlew, November 12, 1935, File 0-32, Part II; Earl Trager memorandum to Russell, May 9, 1936, File 0-32, Part III; H. L. Winfield to W. F. Ayres, March 13, 1939; Tom L. Beauchamp to

Ayres, March 14, 1939, File 0-32, Part VI. *San Angelo Standard-Times*, April 12, 1938; *Alpine Avalanche*, April 15, 1938; March 2, 1939; *Fort Worth Star-Telegram*, June 4, 1938; March 30, 1939; *Fort Stockton Pioneer*, April 7, 1939; *Eden Echo*, May 25, 1939; *Wichita Falls Times*, June 4, 1939.

21. *Balmorhea Texan*, February 24, 1939. BBNP-NA: Maxwell to Director, NPS, attention of Trager, March 7, 1938, File 0-32, Part V; Trager memorandum to Regional Director, Region III, January 16, 1939, File 0-32, Part VI; Tillotson to Bolton, June 6, 1944; Herbert Kahler to Drury, June 23, 1944; Kahler to Bolton, June 23, 1944, File 204.

22. *Austin State Observer*, June 12, 1939; *Harlingen Valley Morning Star*, May 13, 1939; *Galveston News*, May 13, 1939; *Fort Worth Star-Telegram*, May 14, 1939. BBNP-NA (File 0-32, Part VIII): O'Daniel to Roosevelt, October 17, 1940.

23. *Dallas Morning News*, October 31, 1937; April 24, 1938; September 25, 1938; October 30, 1938; October 1, 1940; July 6, 1944; July 7, 1944; July 9, 1944; July 10, 1944; *Austin Statesman*, April 7, 1939; *Houston Press*, April 17, 1939; *Wichita Falls Record News*, May 22, 1939; *Amarillo Daily News*, November 25, 1938; *El Paso Times*, October 17, 1937; August 21, 1939; *Houston Chronicle*, November 28, 1937; *Galveston Tribune*, September 11, 1937; *Austin American*, May 1, 1936; *Alpine Avalanche*, May 14, 1936; January 1, 1937; *Yoakum Herald*, November 10, 1938; *Marshall News-Messenger*, March 14, 1939; *San Angelo Standard-Times*, March 6, 1939; *Journal of the Senate of Texas*, 46th Legislature, reg. sess., March 1, 1939, p. 478; *Fort Worth Star-Telegram*, June 11, 1942; Nixon, ed., *Franklin D. Roosevelt and Conservation*, vol. 2, pp. 298–299, 367, 471.

24. Speech delivered by Secretary of the Interior Ickes at the dedication of the Buchanan and Inks Dams, October 16, 1937, Records of the Office of the Secretary of the Interior, Central Classified Files, 12-29, National Parks, Big Bend, Texas, General, Part II, RG 48, National Archives, College Park, Maryland (hereafter cited as Secretary of the Interior, Central Classified Files, Big Bend, RG 48, NA).

25. *El Paso Herald-Post*, November 10, 1936. BBNP-NA (File 0-32, Part VIII): Tillotson, "The Big Bend National Park as an Asset to the State of Texas" (ms.), March 27, 1941.

26. The following is a representative sample of the Texas newspapers that emphasized economic arguments for a national park at Big Bend: *El Paso Herald-Post*, November 10, 1936; *Galveston Tribune*, December 12, 1936; *Houston Post*, May 28, 1937; *Houston Press*, October 21, 1937; *San Angelo Times*, February 23, 1938; *San Antonio Evening News*, November 16, 1938; *Del Rio Evening News*, December 12, 1938; *Abilene Reporter-News*, December 1, 1938; *Dallas Times-Herald*, December 1, 1938; *San Antonio Express*, September 12, 1938; *Dallas Morning News*, March 3, 1939; *Colorado City Record*, April 28, 1939; *Dallas Dispatch-Journal*, May 18, 1939; *Graham Reporter*, June 24, 1939; *Fort Worth Star-Telegram*, January 26, 1937; July 31, 1938; *San Antonio Express*, March 24, 1937; February 25, 1939.

27. *Fort Worth Star-Telegram*, February 20, 1937; August 24, 1937; *San Antonio Express*, February 23, 1937; April 12, 1937; June 6, 1937; June 10, 1937; *Houston*

Post, February 22, 1937; April 12, 1937; May 28, 1937; *Tyler Morning Telegraph,* April 13, 1937; *Alpine Avalanche,* May 14, 1936; December 4, 1936; January 1, 1937; *El Paso Herald-Post,* May 28, 1937; *Dallas Times-Herald,* June 9, 1937; *Brownwood Bulletin,* June 11, 1937; *El Paso Times,* June 9, 1937; October 17, 1937; *Dallas Morning News,* October 31, 1937; April 24, 1938; September 25, 1938; October 30, 1938; October 1, 1940; July 6, 1944; July 7, 1944; July 9, 1944; July 10, 1944; *Austin Statesman,* April 7, 1939; *Houston Press,* April 17, 1939; *Wichita Falls Record News,* May 22, 1939; *Amarillo Daily News,* November 25, 1938; *Houston Chronicle,* November 28, 1937; *Galveston Tribune,* September 11, 1937; *Austin American,* May 1, 1936; *Yoakum Herald,* November 10, 1938; *Marshall News-Messenger,* March 14, 1939.

28. *Fort Worth Star-Telegram,* October 24, 1937; *Tyler Morning Telegraph,* May 29, 1939; *Albuquerque Journal,* May 29, 1939; *Corpus Christi Caller-Times,* May 28, 1939; *Dallas Times-Herald,* May 30, 1939; *Amarillo Daily News,* April 15, 1939; *Corpus Christi Caller-Times,* April 15, 1939; *Shamrock Texan,* April 15, 1939; *San Angelo Standard-Times,* April 7, 1939. BBNP-NA (File 501-03, Part II): NPS Press Release, August 13, 1939.

29. BBNP-NA (File 0-32, Part VIII): Clark to Tillotson, September 29, 1940.

30. Pete Williams, "The Big Bend," *Sparks* (January 1944): 5.

31. "Park for 'Texico': Big Bend International Reservation for Texas and Mexico," *Literary Digest* (March 26, 1936): 3; *Fort Worth Star-Telegram,* February 27, 1938; Frederick Simpich, "Down the Rio Grande: Taming This Strange, Turbulent Stream on Its Long Course from Colorado to the Gulf of Mexico," *National Geographic* 76 (October 1939): 430, 439.

32. "Big Bend, A Texas Wonderland Is the Country's Newest National Park," *Life* (September 3, 1945): 68–73; John Kord Lagemann, "Beauty on a Bend," *Collier's* (January 31, 1938): 13–15, 67–68; "Big Bend Is a National Park," *Parade* (March 28, 1948): 19–21; Kenneth Foree, Jr., "Our New National Park on the Rio Grande," *Saturday Evening Post* (December 2, 1944): 26–27, 106; Dee Woods, "The Dusty River Region," *South* (December 1946): 11, 23, 26; Minor R. Tillotson, "Newest National Park—Big Bend," *National Motorist* (June 1945): 10, 17–18; *Alpine Avalanche,* September 7, 1945. BBNP-NA: Walter P. Taylor, "The Big Bend" (reprinted from *American Forests* [July 1946]), File 501-04; Drury to P. P. Patraw, Tolson, and Herbert Evison, September 8, 1945, File 501-02.

33. BBNP-NA (File 501-02): Foree to Maxwell, September 30, 1944; Maxwell to Foree, October 5, 1944; Story handwritten note, October 13, 1944.

34. *Pecos Enterprise,* April 8, 1938; *Marlin Democrat,* May 23, 1939; *Fort Worth Star-Telegram,* March 7, 1939; May 21, 1939. BBNP-NA (File 0-32, Part IX): Morelock to Drury, January 6, 1942.

35. Official Annual Visitation Figures, 1944–1993, can be obtained from the Superintendent, Big Bend National Park.

36. PR-BBNP (File K3415): News Releases, August 15, 1990; April 1, 1991; October 5, 1992; October 21, 1992; January 11, 1993; January 25, 1993; March 30, 1987; April 13, 1987.

37. PR-BBNP (File K3415): News Release, April 13, 1987.

38. PR-BBNP (File K3415): News Release, August 4, 1992.

39. Arnberger's original estimate of Big Bend's economic benefits to local communities had been $25 million (PR-BBNP [File K3415]: News Releases, April 2, 1992; January 25, 1993; July 11, 1994). Ironically, at the same time Arnberger announced cutbacks in visitor services because of the harsh economic climate of the 1990s (PR-BBNP [File K3415]: News Release, May 10, 1993).

5. From Dude Ranches to Haciendas

1. BBNP-NA (File 0–32, Part I): Dorgan to Ickes, October 8, 1934; Dorgan to Senators Morris Sheppard and Tom Connally, August 28, 1935. Dorgan further elaborated on his plans for Big Bend in the second letter to the senators, which was sent after Congress passed the enabling legislation for the park.

2. BBNP-NA (File 600–01): Minor Tillotson memorandum to Director, NPS, September 28, 1944. The Lone Star State had retained ownership of its public domain when it entered the Union in 1845. A delaying factor affecting land purchase was the outbreak of World War II.

3. BBNP-NA (File 0–32, Part I): Herbert Maier to Conrad Wirth, May 31, 1935. Two recent books that describe the "trial and error" planning at their respective parks are Duane Smith, *Mesa Verde National Park: Shadows of the Centuries,* and Alfred Runte, *Yosemite: The Embattled Wilderness.*

4. Robert Shankland notes that master plans for each park are "now the main instrument for reconciling preservation with use"; see his *Steve Mather of the National Parks,* p. 256. Another planning tool, discussed later, is the *Big Bend National Park: Statement for Management,* revised every few years, which applies management objectives to the problems of the park within the framework of NPS goals and policies. For further reading on the importance of planning to sound resource management in the parks, see Eugenia Horstman Connally, ed., *National Parks in Crisis;* The Conservation Foundation, *National Parks for a New Generation: Visions, Realities, Prospects;* Ronald A. Foresta, *America's National Parks and Their Keepers;* Gary E. Machlis and David L. Tichnell, *The State of the World's Parks: An International Assessment for Resource Management, Policy, and Research;* National Parks and Conservation Association, *National Parks: From Vignettes to a Global View.* For a summary of NPCA's study, see the "Perspective" column in the *Public History News* 9 (Summer 1989): 2, 9. Two well-done overviews of the National Park Service (the agency and the system) are William C. Everhart, *The National Park Service,* and Alfred Runte, *National Parks: The American Experience* (rev. ed., 1987).

5. For a thorough analysis of one era, see Donald C. Swain, "The National Park Service and the New Deal, 1933–1940," *Pacific Historical Review* 41 (August 1972): 312–332. Swain contends that before 1933, NPS directors had political motives when they encouraged Americans to visit national parks "to demonstrate to Congress that the voters were using and enjoying the parks and that the Park

Service should receive larger appropriations for park protection and development." After 1933, the objective shifted to an economic one. Increased visitation to parks would stimulate local communities stricken by the depression and would indirectly contribute to national recovery (p. 317).

6. BBNP-NA (File 0-32, Part V): NPS Press Release, December 11, 1937. *San Antonio Express,* September 12, 1938. BBNP-NA (File 857): Ward P. Webber memorandum to Thomas Vint, May 2, 1947. PR-BBNP: Dedication Speech for Big Bend National Park by Douglas McKay, November 21, 1955. See "Official Annual Visitation Figures for Big Bend National Park," which can be obtained from the superintendent.

7. Max Bentley, "Big Bend Park: Regional Executive Gets His First Look, Views It as 'Utterly Different' Among National Parks," *West Texas Today* (October 1940): 7.

8. BBNP-NA (File 620): Tillotson to W. W. Thompson, December 22, 1942. E. R. Beck of Fort Worth first suggested the "Jersey Lilly" idea.

9. BBNP-NA: J. D. Coffman, "Report on the Forest and Vegetative Aspect," August 9, 1935, File 0-32, Part I; Maier to State Park ECW, attention of Wirth, October 30, 1935; Wirth to Will C. Burnes, September 21, 1935; Wright memorandum to Arthur Demaray, October 17, 1935, File 0-32, Part II; W. B. McDougall, "Preliminary Report on a Plant Ecological Survey of the Big Bend Area, November 30, 1935, File 207. Walter Prescott Webb to W. R. Hogan, September 5, 1937, Webb Papers, American History Collection.

10. BBNP-NA: "Report on the Field Investigation Together with Recommendations for the Establishment of a Boundary Line for the Big Bend National Park Project," September 9, 1935, File 0-32, Part II; Maxwell and Borell, "Special Report: Longhorn Cattle Range Studies, Big Bend Area, Texas," June 10, 1937, File 0-32, Part IV; "The Big Bend National Park Project, Texas," 1939, File 501. *Fort Worth Star-Telegram,* August 8, 1938.

11. BBNP-NA (File 601, Part II): Pat McCarran to Harold Ickes, April 25, 1944. McCarran was United States Senator from Nevada and a member of the Committee on Public Lands and Surveys.

12. BBNP-NA: W. B. McDougall, "Texas Longhorn Cattle: A Brief Report from the Point of View of Animal Husbandry," May 8, 1936, File 207; Wirth to R. E. Thomason, March 10, 1944, File 900-01; Walter P. Taylor, McDougall, and William B. Davis, "Preliminary Report of an Ecological Survey of Big Bend National Park, March–June, 1944," File 204. Big Bend remained overgrazed throughout the time the longhorn proposal was discussed. A Park Service study found that fifty to one hundred acres would be required to sustain each longhorn and this was only after substantial recovery of the depleted range.

13. BBNP-NA: Drury memorandum to Regional Director, Region III, June 8, 1942; Hillory Tolson memorandum to Regional Director, Region III, May 30, 1944, File 600-01; Taylor, McDougall, and Davis, "Preliminary Report of an Ecological Survey of Big Bend National Park, March–June, 1944," File 204. J. Frank Dobie, *The Longhorns.* Historian Robert Utley, however, argues convincingly that

longhorns did indeed once roam Brewster County; see his "The Range Cattle Industry in the Big Bend of Texas," *Southwestern Historical Quarterly* 49 (April 1966): 419–441.

14. BBNP-NA (File 601-01): Tillotson memorandum to Director, NPS, September 28, 1944.

15. BBNP-NA: "Report of the Big Bend Area, Texas," January, 1935, File 207; Manbey, "Proposed Big Bend National Park Report on Suggested Park Boundary, Engineering Requirements and General Notes," August 19, 1935, File 0-32, Part IX; "The Big Bend National Park Project, Texas," 1939, File 501; Tolson memorandum to Regional Director, Region III, May 30, 1944, File 601-01; Tillotson, "Suggested Outline of Concessionaire Operations in Big Bend National Park," March 29, 1944, File 900-03.

16. *BBNP: Statement for Management*, 1992, p. 11. PR-BBNP: James W. Carrico to Lawrence Villalva, July 27, 1990, File P4417; W. Philip Koepp to United States Immigration and Naturalization Service at Presidio, Texas, May 24, 1990, File P94; Carrico memorandum to Assistant Regional Director, Planning, Southwest Regional Office, Santa Fe, February 5, 1990, File A3817. BBNP-NA (File 0-32, Part III): J. T. Roberts, "Special investigation of Proposed Mexican Big Bend National Park," September 1936.

17. BBNP-NA: Oliver G. Taylor, "Comment on Big Bend National Park Master Plan," August 26, 1944, File 600-01; W. W. Thompson to Director, NPS, June 27, 1944; Ross A. Maxwell memorandum to Regional Director, Region III, January 12, 1948, File 900-05.

18. See sources cited in note 15.

19. BBNP-NA: "Big Bend National Park: Its Future," September 20, 1948, File 501-04; NPS Press Release, December 11, 1937, File 0-32, Part V; Wirth memorandum to Regional Director, Region III, February 23, 1940, File 0-32, Part VIII. Maxwell memorandum to Regional Director, Region III, June 20, 1949, Records of Newton B. Drury, Director's Personal File, Big Bend National Park, 1940 to March, 1951, RG 79, National Archives (hereafter cited as Drury File, BBNP-NA); various clippings from the *Fort Worth Star-Telegram*, July 25, 1937; December 12, 1937.

20. BBNP-NA: Tillotson memorandum to Director, NPS, July 11, 1945, File 900-05; Wirth memorandum to Director, NPS, May 22, 1945; Maxwell memorandum to Regional Director, Region III, May 7, 1945, File 600-03, Part I; Tillotson memorandum to Director, NPS, November 11, 1944, File 718.

21. BBNP-NA: Manley W. Allen to C. L. Andrews, April 26, 1948; Tolson memorandum to Regional Director, Region III, June 9, 1944, File 900-02; Demaray to Thomason, January 30, 1946, File 900-05; Chris E. Taylor memorandum to Director, NPS, May 12, 1949, File 900-06. Drury File, BBNP-NA: Demaray memorandum to Regional Director, Region III, September 12, 1949; Maxwell memorandum to Regional Director, Region III, June 20, 1949; Tillotson memorandum to Director, NPS, July 11, 1949; Demaray to H. S. Sanborn,

August 4, 1949; Demaray memorandum to Regional Director, Region III, August 4, 1949; Sanborn to Demaray, September 5, 1949. Maxwell, *Big Bend Country*.

22. BBNP-NA: Tillotson memorandum to Director, NPS, April 28, 1942, File 600-03, Part I; Maxwell memorandum to Regional Director, Region III, November 6, 1947, File 900-05; "Superintendent's Monthly Narrative Report, May 1947," June 6, 1947, File 207-02.3; Maxwell memorandum to Director, NPS, May 28, 1947, File 204. Maxwell, "History of Big Bend National Park" (ms.), 1952, PR-BBNP.

23. PR-BBNP: Official Annual Visitation Figures, 1944–1993.

24. Concerning range recovery, see BBNP-NA: File 718; Maxwell memorandum to Director, NPS, October 5, 1945, File 720-04. An examination of the "Annual Animal Census Reports," "Biennial Annual Census Reports," and "Wildlife Inventories" in the PR-BBNP also reveals a relative stability of wildlife populations.

25. Conrad Wirth, "The Mission Called 66," *National Geographic* 130 (July 1966): 11, 15–16.

26. Presley Bryant, state editor for the *Fort Worth Star-Telegram*, quoted in Virginia Madison, *The Big Bend Country of Texas*, p. 249.

27. Wilderness Study: Big Bend National Park, p. 20. Big Bend National Park: Final Environmental Statement; Proposed Wilderness Classification, p. 1. The following definition of wilderness is from the 1964 congressional act creating a national wilderness preservation system: "an area where the earth and its community of life are untrammeled by man, where man himself is a visitor who does not remain . . . an area of undeveloped Federal land retaining its primeval character and influence, without permanent improvements or human habitation, which is protected and managed so as to preserve its natural conditions" (*United States Statutes at Large*, Vol. 78, p. 891). Background on the Wilderness Act can be found in Michael McCloskey, "The Wilderness Act of 1964: Its Background and Meaning," *Oregon Law Review* 45 (1966): 288–321.

28. *Big Bend National Park Master Plan: Preliminary Draft*.

29. *Big Bend National Park: Final Environmental Statement*, pp. 131–132, 153–170; *Odessa American*, January 16, 1972; Newell to the author, May 29, 1974. Later, other state agencies—some of which had not been contacted in 1972—voiced support for the wilderness proposal. These included the Historical Commission, Department of Agriculture, Industrial Commission, Water Quality Board, Air Control Board, Water Rights Commission, and the Highway Department's engineering division. The Texas Tourist Development Agency continued to oppose the proposal.

The Big Bend National Parks Development Committee, with headquarters in Alpine, Texas, states its purpose as "the growth and progress" of Big Bend National Park, Fort Davis Historic Site, Amistad Recreation Area, and Guadalupe Mountains National Park.

30. *Odessa American*, January 16, 1972; *Wilderness Study: BBNP*, p. 18; *Wilder-*

ness Recommendation: Big Bend National Park, Texas, Appendix, Hearing Officer's Report.

31. *Odessa American,* January 16, 1972.

32. *Big Bend National Park Master Plan,* pp. 20–21; *BBNP Master Plan: Preliminary Draft,* pp. 21–23. On August 15, 1994, the horse concession expired after over forty years of operation and was not renewed. The Park Service "will conduct an assessment to determine the future of commercial horseback ride services" in the park (PR-BBNP [File K3415]: News Release, August 22, 1994).

33. *Odessa American,* January 16, 1972; *Wilderness Recommendation: BBNP,* Appendix, Hearing Officer's Report; Dorothy L. McBride, Mayor of Alpine, to Bill Rabenstein, Chief Park Naturalist, BBNP, March 4, 1974; and Newell to Robinstein (*sic*), March 1, 1974, in *BBNP: Final Environmental Statement,* pp. 172–177.

34. See *BBNP: Statement for Management,* 1992, pp. 26–28 for descriptions and a map of each of these zones.

35. Stephen Harrigan, "Wild Forever: A Sneak Preview of Big Bend Ranch, Texas' Rugged New Parkland," *Texas Monthly* (December 1989): 100, 152; Texas Parks and Wildlife Department, Public Lands Division, *Big Bend Ranch State Natural Area: Planning Document.*

6. The "Predator Incubator" and Other Controversies

1. BBNP-NA (File 900-01): G. A. Morriss to Ross Maxwell, August 18, 1946. Other parks likewise had "predator sanctuary" controversies; for example, see Duane Smith, *Mesa Verde National Park,* p. 152.

2. William O. Douglas, *Farewell to Texas: A Vanishing Wilderness,* pp. 52–53. BBNP-NA: George F. Baggley memorandum to Wirth, March 9, 1936, File 0-32, Part III; NPS Press Release, January 15, 1937, File 0-32, Part IV; Maier memorandum to Director, NPS, November 12, 1937, File 0-32, Part IX.

3. PR-BBNP: Ross A. Maxwell, "History of Big Bend National Park" (ms.), 1952. BBNP-NA (File 0-32, Part IV): Conrad Wirth to Regional Director, Region III, June 2, 1937. Maxwell, *Big Bend Country,* p. 87.

4. "The Big Bend Park Incubator," *Sheep and Goat Raisers Magazine,* February 1948 (typed copy of editorial in BBNP-NA [File 719]); Simpich, "Down the Rio Grande," p. 430; *San Angelo Standard-Times,* December 14, 1947; January 28, 1948.

5. *San Angelo Standard-Times,* January 28, 1948. BBNP-NA (File 0-32, Part IV): NPS Press Release, May 8, 1937; BHT [Ben H. Thompson] to Connie [Conrad Wirth], (no date).

6. BBNP-NA (File 719): Maxwell memorandum to Regional Director, Region III, April 16, 1948.

7. Ibid.; Langford, *Big Bend,* p. 153.

8. Madison, *Big Bend Country,* p. 151.

9. PR-BBNP: "Annual Animal Census Report for Big Bend National Park, 1950." *El Paso Herald-Post,* December 3, 1947; *San Angelo Standard-Times,* De-

cember 7, 1947; December 14, 1947. BBNP-NA (File 719): E. E. Townsend to Maxwell, December 17, 1947.

10. *San Angelo Standard-Times*, December 14, 1947; January 28, 1948.

11. BBNP-NA (File 719): Maxwell memorandum to Regional Director, Region III, February 1, 1948.

12. BBNP-NA: Vestal Askew to Director, NPS, December 22, 1947, File 719; "Superintendent's Monthly Narrative Report, December 1947," January 8, 1948, File 207-02.3.

13. BBNP-NA (File 719): Demaray to Askew, January 19, 1948.

14. BBNP-NA (File 719): P. P. Patraw to Superintendent, BBNP, January 23, 1948.

15. *El Paso Daily Times*, February 17, 1948. BBNP-NA (File 719): "Big Bend Incubator," *Sheep and Goat Raisers Magazine*, February 1948 (typed copy of editorial in File 719); Newton B. Drury memorandum to Regional Director, Region III, March 15, 1948; Patraw memorandum to Director, NPS, April 30, 1948.

16. BBNP-NA: "Superintendent's Monthly Narrative Report, November 1947," December 5, 1947; "Superintendent's Monthly Narrative Report, January 1948," February 4, 1948, File 207-02.3; Maxwell memorandum to Regional Director, Region III, December 23, 1947; January 23, 1948, File 719.

17. BBNP-NA (File 719): Maxwell memorandum to Regional Director, Region III, January 23, 1948.

18. BBNP-NA (File 719): Maxwell memorandum to Regional Director, Region III, April 16, 1948.

19. BBNP-NA (File 719): Maxwell to the author, August 6, 1973; Ernest Williams to Demaray, June 28, 1948.

20. BBNP-NA (File 719): Tolson to Williams, July 15, 1948.

21. BBNP-NA (File 719): Director, NPS, memorandum to Director, Fish and Wildlife Service, January 25, 1949.

22. BBNP-NA: Maxwell memorandum to Regional Director, Region III, February 10, 1949, File 204; Director, Fish and Wildlife, to Director, NPS, March 16, 1949, File 719; "Superintendent's Monthly Narrative Report, March 1949," April 6, 1949, File 207-02.3. *San Angelo Standard-Times*, March 13, 1949. PR-BBNP: Maxwell, "History of Big Bend National Park" (ms.), 1952.

23. PR-BBNP: "Annual Animal Census Report for Big Bend National Park, 1951"; "Biennial Animal Census Reports for Big Bend National Park, 1952–1953; 1954–1955"; O. C. Wallmo, "Work Study Report on Mountain Lions in Big Bend National Park, December 1952 to January 1959."

24. PR-BBNP: News Release, March 20, 1990, File K3415; Chief Ranger memorandum to All Chisos Area Employees, May 7, 1990, File N1615; Chief Ranger memorandum to All Employees, January 18, 1991; Raymond Skiles to Jack Cook, August 3, 1990, File N1427.

25. Drury File, BBNP-NA: Ernest Williams to Tom Connally, October 17, 1950. PR-BBNP: "Annual Animal Census Report for Big Bend National Park, 1951."

26. *Dallas Times-Herald,* June 24, 1990. PR-BBNP: "Superintendent's Annual Report, 1990," February 19, 1991, File A2621; Resource Management Trainee memorandum to Chief Ranger, December 17, 1990, File N1427. Scientists consider a sow with cubs evidence of a resident rather than a transitory population, since females seldom roam far from their mothers' territories. Males, on the other hand, range over a territory encompassing forty to fifty square miles.

27. PR-BBNP (File N1427): Resource Management Trainee memorandum to Chief Ranger, December 17, 1990; Robert Rothe to William T. Smaltz, November 28, 1990.

28. PR-BBNP (File A2621): "Superintendent's Annual Report, 1979." For information on the proposals for the Bolson tortoise and bighorn sheep, see PR-BBNP: File N2219 (tortoise) and Files N1422 and N1615 (sheep).

29. *Dallas Times-Herald,* September 2, 1990. PR-BBNP: Robert L. Arnberger to Steve Schaps, September 10, 1991, File N1621; Roy Given memorandum to Jeff Selleck, May 1, 1991, no file; Arnberger to Rick LoBello, June 7, 1991, File A3821; Arnberger memorandum to Regional Director, SWRO, June 7, 1991, File A42; Arnberger to Elizabeth Sizemore, September 12, 1991, File N1415; News Release, January 11, 1993, File K3415.

30. PR-BBNP (no file): Joe Carrico to Sue Tenthorey, October 29, 1990.

31. PR-BBNP (File N1621): Carrico memorandum to Regional Director, SWRO, October 28, 1990.

32. PR-BBNP: News Releases, January 31, 1990; January 25, 1993, File K3415; Arnberger to Larry McKinney, October 21, 1991; David H. Dreier to J. W. Clifford, February 2, 1990, File N1621; J. R. Skiles, "Status of Peregrine Falcons in Big Bend National Park and Along the Rio Grande Wild and Scenic River from 1973 to 1992," File A3615.

33. BBNP-NA (File 715-04): Matt N. Dodge memorandum to Superintendent, BBNP, July 21, 1945; F. M. Shigley, "Report on White-tail Deer Deaths," September 4, 1948; Sholly memorandum to Superintendent, BBNP, September 8, 1948; W. T. Hardy to E. G. Marsh, Jr., September 8, 1948; Maxwell memorandum to Regional Director, Region III, October 14, 1948; Victor H. Cahalane memorandum to Chief, Division of Wildlife Research, Fish and Wildlife Service, October 26, 1948.

34. BBNP-NA (File 715): Harold Ratcliff memorandum to Regional Forester, Region III, November 24, 1948; Maxwell memorandum to Regional Director, Region III, December 27, 1948; Director, NPS, memorandum to Regional Director, Region III, January 27, 1949.

35. BBNP-NA: Drury to Ken Regan, May 11, 1949, File 204; "Superintendent's Monthly Narrative Report, May 1947," June 6, 1947; "Superintendent's Monthly Narrative Report, November 1947," December 5, 1947, File 207-02.3; Maxwell's Advance Report, May 21, 1948, File 207; Maxwell memorandum to Regional Director, Region III, October 29, 1947; John M. Davis to John A. Grambling, February 25, 1949, File 208-48.

36. BBNP-NA: H. W. Patterson to Regan, April 18, 1949, File 208-48; Max-

well's Advance Report, May 21, 1948; "1945 Annual Report, BBNP," July 6, 1945, File 207. Nevertheless, trespass stock remained an expensive problem. In 1948, when illegal grazing was the lowest it had been since the park opened in 1944, 423 head of trespassing stock were removed at a cost of $4,500.

37. BBNP-NA: "Superintendent's Monthly Narrative Report, February 1948," March 8, 1948; "Superintendent's Monthly Narrative Report, April 1947," May 9, 1947, File 207-02.3; Maxwell memoranda to Regional Director, Region III, February 28, 1947; August 3, 1948, File 208-48.

38. BBNP-NA: José Pontones to Superintendent, BBNP, April 21, 1949; Maxwell to Pontones, April 27, 1949, File 208-06; "Superintendent's Monthly Narrative Report, February 1949," March 9, 1949, File 207-02.3.

39. "Blue Creek Fire" Brochure, BBNHA, 1989.

40. BBNP-NA (File 883-05, Part I): "Statement of Elmer Davenport, Project Superintendent, Museum Fire of December 26, 1941," December 29, 1941. Underlining in "Preliminary Report of an Ecological Survey of Big Bend National Park" (1945), quoted in *Environmental Assessment: Fire Management Program Big Bend National Park*, August 2, 1993, pp. 5–6.

41. For a photographic and narrative overview, see Alan and Sandy Carey, *Yellowstone's Red Summer; Environmental Assessment: Fire Management Program Big Bend National Park*, pp. 11–12; and PR-BBNP (File K3415): News Release, July 11, 1994.

7. "The Ultimate 'Tex-Mex Project'"

1. PR-BBNP (File L62): Frome to Walker, December 20, 1973.

2. *National Geographic* 179 (February 1991): 140. PR-BBNP (File A4037): Cook memorandum to Director, NPS, June 24, 1988.

3. BBNP-NA (File 504): Hillory Tolson to Richard Kendrick, January 13, 1945. Rotarians first suggested the concept of an international park on the Canadian–United States border. Both Waterton and Glacier had "existed previously and each continued under its own national administration."

4. BBNP-NA (File 207): "Report of the Big Bend Area, Texas," January 1935. BBSPP (Box A-1): Colp to Sam Rayburn, January 17, 1935; Josephus Daniels to Rayburn, January 31, 1935.

5. BBNP-NA (File 0-32, Part I): Sheppard to Roosevelt, February 16, 1935; Ickes to Roosevelt, February 27, 1935; Department of the Interior Memorandum for the Press, March 3, 1935.

6. J. W. Linn, "Biography of Jane Addams," (typescript), July 12, 1935, Secretary of the Interior, Central Classified Files, Big Bend, RG 48, NA.

7. BBNP-NA (File 0-32, Part I): Ickes to Secretary of State, June 22, 1935.

8. BBNP-NA (File 0-32, Part I): Daniels to Cordell Hull, Secretary of State, July 27, 1935; August 16, 1935.

9. Quevedo's Department of Forestry, Fish, and Game was an agency in the Mexican Department of Agriculture.

10. BBNP-NA (File 0-32, Part II): Maier to Wirth, October 21, 1935.

11. PR-BBNP: "Report on Conference with Mexican Representatives in Connection with Proposed Big Bend National Park," October 5, 1935. BBNP-NA (File 0-32, Part II): "Report on Conference with Mexican Representatives Relative to the Proposed Big Bend International Park and Other Border Areas," November 24, 1935.

12. BBNP-NA: Roger Toll Travel Itinerary Notes, February 13–25, 1936; Department of Interior Press Release, February 16, 1936, File 0-32, Part III; Carroll Wegemann, "Diary of a Trip from Alpine to Big Bend and Old Mexico with the International Park Commission," February 17, 1936, File 207. Wirth quoted from *Philadelphia Evening Public Ledger*, August 29, 1936, in *Alpine Avalanche*, September 18, 1936.

13. *Alpine Avalanche*, September 3, 1948. BBNP-NA (File 0-32, Part III): Director, NPS, memorandum to Ickes, February 29, 1936; Wirth to Regional Director, Region III, June 29, 1936.

14. BBNP-NA (File 0-32, Part III): Maier to Director, NPS, November 13, 1936.

15. BBNP-NA: Maier to Wirth, July 3, 1936, File 0-32, Part IV; "Partial Text of Radio Speech Broadcast over Mexican Station XEFI, Chihuahua City, Chihuahua, 6:00 P.M.," June 18, 1945; Tillotson memorandum to Director, NPS, June 30, 1945, File 207. Tillotson memorandum to Director, NPS, December 14, 1935, Records of the National Park Service, Central Classified Files, 1907–1949, File 0-32, Big Bend Proposed International Park, Part I, Record Group 79, National Archives, College Park, Maryland (hereafter cited as NPS Files, BBPIP-NA). PR-BBNP: L. A. Garrison, "A History of the Proposed Big Bend International Park," July 6, 1953 (revised April 1, 1954).

16. PR-BBNP: "Report on Conference with Mexican Representatives in Connection with Proposed Big Bend National Park," October 5, 1935. BBNP-NA: Newton B. Drury telegram to Associate Director, NPS, September 7, 1943, File 601, Part II; Department of the Interior Press Release, July 21, 1941, File 501.

17. Drury File, BBNP-NA: Camacho to Roosevelt, November 30, 1944.

18. NPS Files, BBPIP-NA: Tillotson memorandum, June 30, 1945; Tillotson memorandum to Director, NPS, December 14, 1945; William Vogt to Victor Cahalane, March 25, 1945. PR-BBNP (File L62): Maxwell memorandum to Tillotson, December 17, 1945.

19. BBNP-NA: Maurice Minchen to Mae M. Ament, March 18, 1945, File 501; Wirth to Glenn Burgess, October 5, 1944, File 601, Part II; Tillotson memorandum to Director, NPS, September 25, 1944, File 718.

20. Drury File, BBNP-NA: Vogt to Drury, November 6, 1945; "Report of the Study Made in La Sierra del Carmen, Coahuila, for the Creation of an International Park between the United States and Mexico," n.d.

21. Drury File, BBNP-NA: Memorandum to Director General, Directorate General of Forestry and Hunting, June 12, 1945.

22. Drury File, BBNP-NA: "Report of the Study Made in La Sierra del Car-

men, Coahuila, for the Creation of an International Park between the United States and Mexico," n.d.

23. NPS Files, BBPIP-NA: Presnall to Devereaux Butcher, November 26, 1945.

24. BBNP-NA: "Report of the Big Bend Area, Texas," January, 1935, File 207; J. D. Coffman, "Report on the Forest and Vegetation Aspect," August 9, 1935; Maier to State Park ECW, June 8, 1935; NPS Press Release, March 3, 1935, File 0-32, Part I; Bernard F. Manbey, "Proposed Big Bend National Park Report on Suggested Park Boundary, Engineering Requirements and General Notes," August 19, 1935, File 0-32, Part IX; Isabelle F. Story memorandum to William E. Warne, June 26, 1943, File 501.

25. *Chicago Daily News*, January 29, 1947. BBNP-NA (File 0-32, Part I): Dorgan to Ickes, October 8, 1934. The files at the park contain ample documentation of these activities. In particular, see PR-BBNP (File K3415): News Media, Press Releases, General Correspondence.

26. NPS Files, BBPIP-NA: M. L. Stafford to Stephen E. Aguirre, American Consul, Ciudad Juárez, September 5, 1947; American Embassy in Mexico's Despatch Number 4790, "Development of International Parks in Big Bend and Coronado International Memorial Areas," October 6, 1947. BBNP-NA (File 702-04): Ernest Marsh, Jr., "A Preliminary Report on a Biological Survey of the Santa Rosa and Del Carmen Mountains of Northern Coahuila, Mexico," October 11, 1936.

27. NPS Files, BBPIP-NA: Tolson to Carlos Villas Perez, December 18, 1947; Assistant Secretary of State to Secretary of the Interior, November 26, 1947; Assistant Secretary of State to J. A. Krug, December 3, 1948.

28. PR-BBNP: Garrison, "A History of the Proposed Big Bend International Park," July 6, 1953 (revised April 1, 1954).

29. PR-BBNP: Dedication Speech for Big Bend National Park by Douglas McKay, November 21, 1955.

30. W. J. Newell to the author, April 26, 1973; Stanley W. Hulett, Associate Director, NPS, to the author, April 4, 1973. Hulett wrote that "Mexico has taken no further action" on the park proposal, indicative that the Park Service blamed Mexico for the delay.

31. PR-BBNP (File A4037): "Briefing Statement Regarding Proposed Sierra del Carmen Protected Area in State of Coahuila, Mexico," July 1988.

32. Author's interview with Ramón Olivas, June 5, 1991; Laurence Parent, "Mountains Across the River," *Texas Parks and Wildlife* (April 1990): 6–8; Jean Hardy, "Two Nations, One Land," *Texas Parks and Wildlife* (April 1994): 29.

33. The classic (and prophetic) *Road to Survival* (1948) by William Vogt contains a perceptive discussion of the cultural and historical roots of the Latin American environmental worldview. In particular, see Chapter 7, "The Land on Edge."

34. PR-BBNP (File L66): "National Park Service U.S.-Mexico Border Activities," January 26, 1984. Other activities have included: International Good Neighbor Day Festival involving schoolchildren from the U.S. and Mexico; El Dia de los Reyes (Epiphany or Twelfth Night Party), at which used toys and clothes are

given to the children of the three Mexican villages adjacent to the park; and the Regional Marketing Plan for Southwest Texas and Adjacent Mexican Border, which focused on tourism for the area.

35. Author's interview with Ramón Olivas, June 5, 1991; Parent, "Mountains Across the River," pp. 6–8.

36. Hardy, "Two Nations," pp. 32–33; "News Update," *National Parks* (January/February 1995): 13.

8. Life and Work in a Desert Wilderness

1. NPS interview of Maggie Smith, no date, BBNP Library; Maxwell, *Big Bend Country*, pp. 25, 32; Douglas, *Farewell to Texas*, pp. 94–95, 97–98; Virginia Madison and Hallie Stillwell, *How Come It's Called That? Place Names in the Big Bend Country*, pp. 49–50. BBNP-NA (File 900): Maxwell memorandum to Regional Director, Region III, December 11, 1946.

2. BBNP-NA: Isabelle F. Story memorandum to Horton, October 19, 1943, File 201-06; Maxwell memorandum to Regional Director, Region III, January 23, 1948, File 719; *Dallas Morning News* (clipping with no date), File 201-06; Frank Quinn to M. M. Harris, September 23, 1943, File 201-06; M. R. Tillotson memorandum to Director, NPS, September 23, 1943, File 201-06. For a selected list of Maxwell's Big Bend publications, see Bibliography.

3. BBNP-NA: Maxwell to Bernard DeVoto, November 22, 1948, File 504; Maxwell memorandum to Director, NPS, May 28, 1947, File 204; Maxwell's Advance Report, May 21, 1948, File 207. Author's interview with Robert Wear, September 21, 1972.

4. Maxwell to the author, August 6, 1973.

5. PR-BBNP (File H3415): News releases, January 19, 1984; April 13, 1992.

6. PR-BBNP: Fernando G. Sanchez, Jr., memorandum to Acting Chief, Interpretation and Visitor Services, January 3, 1991, File A3821; Dennis Vasquez to Ray Charro, Office of Texas-Mexico Health and Environmental Issues, Texas Department of Health, May 26, 1992, File A3817.

7. Author's interview with Robert Wear, September 21, 1972. BBNP-NA: Maxwell memorandum to Regional Director, Region III, June 17, 1946, File 843-03; "Superintendent's Monthly Narrative Report, August 1947," September 4, 1947, File 207-02.3; "Superintendent's Monthly Narrative Report, September 1947," October 1, 1947, File 207-02.3; "Superintendent's Monthly Narrative Report, April 1948," May 6, 1948, File 207-02.3. Everhart, *The National Park Service*, p. 159; Maxwell, *Big Bend Country*, pp. 72, 76; *Dallas Morning News*, February 19, 1995.

8. BBNP-NA (File 843-03): Maxwell memorandum to Regional Director, Region III, April 19, 1949. Author's interview with Robert Wear, September 21, 1972; Robert Wear, "Where the Pavement Ends," *Texas Star* (May 21, 1972): 9.

9. BBNP-NA: Maxwell memorandum to Regional Director, Region III, September 27, 1944; Tolson memorandum to Regional Director, Region III, File 201-

10; Maxwell memorandum to Regional Director, Region III, February 11, 1949; Tillotson memorandum to Superintendent, BBNP, February 15, 1949, File 900-05. Maxwell to the author, August 6, 1973.

10. Maxwell, *Big Bend Country*, pp. 71–72.

11. BBNP-NA: Tolson to First Assistant Postmaster General, November 27, 1946; Maxwell to H. K. Coale, June 27, 1947, File 204; "Superintendent's Monthly Narrative Report, August 1947," September 4, 1947, File 207-02.3. Maxwell, *Big Bend Country*, p. 72.

12. BBNP-NA (File 660-04.3): Maxwell memorandum to Director, NPS, July 21, 1944; Tillotson to Glenn Burgess, March 13, 1947; Maxwell memorandum to Regional Director, Region III, March 6, 1948. Maxwell, *Big Bend Country*, p. 72; *BBNP: Statement for Management*, 1992, p. 40. The park also has telegraph service.

13. PR-BBNP (File K3415): News Release, June 19, 1985.

14. BBNP-NA (File 731-01): Maxwell memorandum to Edmund Rogers, Superintendent, Yellowstone NP, May 20, 1946. Maxwell, *Big Bend of the Rio Grande*, pp. 3–4; *Decisions of the United States Board of Geographical Names: Decisions Rendered Between July 1, 1938 and June 30, 1939.* Other possible translations for Mesa de Anguila were Mesa of the Angels or Eagles since *anguila* could be the English corruption of the Spanish for angel (*ángel*) or eagle (*águila*).

Amon Carter was publisher of the *Fort Worth Star-Telegram* and led the Big Bend National Park Association; Roger Toll, Yellowstone's superintendent, was chief investigator of proposed sites for the NPS.

15. BBNP-NA: Maxwell to DeVoto, November 22, 1948, File 504; Tolson memorandum to Director, NPS, and Regional Offices, July 15, 1944, File 601, Part II. Big Bend National Park brochure, revised 1956, File K3819, Records of Big Bend National Park, Record Group 79, Federal Records Center, Fort Worth, Texas; Maxwell, *Big Bend Country*, pp. 66–67.

16. Everhart, *The National Park Service*, pp. 34–37; Madison, *Big Bend Country*, p. 250; Maxwell, *Big Bend Country*, pp. 74–75.

17. *BBNP: Statement for Management*, 1986, p. 21; *BBNP: Statement for Management*, 1992, pp. 20–21, 25.

18. Hill, "Running the Cañons of the Rio Grande," pp. 371, 376. For additional details on Hill's expedition, see Nancy Alexander, *Father of Texas Geology: Robert T. Hill*, Chapter 11, especially pp. 125–126.

19. O. L. Shipman, *Taming of the Big Bend*, p. 148; Madison and Stillwell, *How Come It's Called That?*, p. 42; Kenney, "Big Bend: Jewel in the Texas Desert," pp. 112, 119; *Dallas Morning News*, May 15, 1994.

20. *Dallas Morning News*, May 15, 1994.

21. Hope, "Big Bend: A Nice Place to Visit," p. 46.

22. PR-BBNP (File K3415): News Release (undated in 1983 folder).

23. PR-BBNP: Robert Arnberger memorandum to Drug/ARPA Program Manager, WASO, December 30, 1991, File W34; James Carrico to Larry Smith, President, AARP, Alpine Chapter, April 30, 1990, File A3823.

24. *Dallas Morning News,* May 15, 1994. PR-BBNP (File K3415): photocopied documents of clippings (undated in 1983 folder).

25. *BBNP: Statement for Management,* 1992, p. 39; *BBNP: Statement for Management,* 1981, p. 27. PR-BBNP: Donna K. Lowin, Acting Superintendent, BBNP memorandum to Regional Director, SWRO, December 26, 1989, File P4015; "Employee Roster," June 1, 1991.

26. *BBNP: Statement for Management,* 1992, p. 41. PR-BBNP (File S7421): Carrico memorandum to Regional Director, SWRO, May 10, 1990.

27. *Environmental Assessment for Construction of a New Office Building and Parking Area to House Big Bend Natural History Association Operations in the Panther Junction Developed Area of BBNP,* p. 1.

Epilogue

1. Randy Lee Loftis, "A Fierce, Fragile Beauty: Big Bend National Park Struggles to Survive Amid Thieves, Pollution and Bureaucracy," *Dallas Morning News,* May 15, 1994.

2. Ron Steffens, "Bridging the Border," *National Parks* 68 (July/August 1994): 37–38; "News Update," p. 13; Hardy, "Two Nations," pp. 26–33.

3. "National Parks and Conservation Association News: Views Threatened at Two National Parks," *National Parks* 70 (November/December 1994): 11; National Parks and Conservation Association, *Parks in Peril: The Race Against Time Continues;* John G. Mitchell, "Our National Parks: Legacy at Risk," *National Geographic* 186 (October 1994): 29, 35.

4. Mitchell, "Our National Parks," pp. 12, 30, 45.

5. Loftis, "A Fierce, Fragile Beauty"; *BBNP: Statement for Management,* 1992, p. 39.

6. *BBNP: Statement for Management,* 1992, pp. 17, 35–36, 40.

7. Loftis, "A Fierce, Fragile Beauty"; Eduardo Montes, "Big Bend's Birthday," *Dallas Morning News,* June 11, 1994. Incidents enforcing the stereotype of the "Bloody Bend" continue to surface. In November 1994 a forty-three-year-old man was murdered in the park. The NPS offered a $5,000 reward for information or evidence leading to a conviction for the crime (PR-BBNP [File K3415]: News Release, January 31, 1995).

8. PR-BBNP: Loftis, "A Fierce, Fragile Beauty"; "Employee Roster," June 1, 1991.

9. PR-BBNP: "Superintendent's Annual Report for 1990," February 19, 1991, File A2621; Roy Given, VIP coordinator, memorandum to Division Chiefs, BBNP, November 15, 1991, File P94.

10. Mitchell, "Our National Parks," pp. 30, 32, 40, 45. To appreciate the massive scale of the problems faced by national parks in the 1990s, compare Mitchell's article with Conrad Wirth, "The Mission Called 66," *National Geographic* 130 (July 1966): 6–47.

11. Roderick Nash, "The American Invention of National Parks," *American*

Quarterly 22 (Fall 1970): 726–727. Of the Grand Canyon's five million visitors in 1993, for example, 30 percent (or 1.5 million) were citizens from foreign countries (Mitchell, "Our National Parks," 45).

12. Loftis, "A Fierce, Fragile Beauty." Thoreau's quotation is from his essay "Walking," as excerpted in Eliot Porter, *"In Wildness Is the Preservation of the World,"* p. 1.

BIBLIOGRAPHY

Primary Materials

SPECIAL COLLECTIONS

Big Bend National Park File, Amon Carter Museum, Fort Worth, Texas.

Big Bend National Park Land Acquisition File, Texas Parks and Wildlife Department, Austin, Texas.

Big Bend State Park Papers, Texas Parks and Wildlife Department, Austin, Texas.

Park Records at Big Bend National Park, Texas.

Records of Big Bend National Park, Record Group 79, National Archives, College Park, Maryland.

Records of Big Bend National Park, Record Group 79, Federal Records Center, Fort Worth, Texas.

Records of Newton B. Drury, Director's Personal File, Big Bend National Park, 1940 to March, 1951, Record Group 79, National Archives, College Park, Maryland.

Records of the National Park Service, Central Classified Files, 1907–1949, File 0-32, Big Bend Proposed International Park, Part I, Record Group 79, National Archives, College Park, Maryland.

Records of the Office of the Secretary of the Interior, Central Classified Files,

12-29, National Parks, Big Bend, Texas, General, Parts I and II, Record Group 48, National Archives, College Park, Maryland.

Walter Prescott Webb Papers, General Correspondence, 1937, The Center for American History, University of Texas, Austin, Texas.

Walter Prescott Webb Papers, Texas State Archives, Austin, Texas.

White House Social Files, Lyndon Baines Johnson Library, Austin, Texas.

CORRESPONDENCE

Brown, Joe, Assistant Director, National Park Service. Letters to author: November 23, 1973; December 13, 1973; January 10, 1974.

Carithers, J. F., Superintendent, Big Bend National Park. Letters to author: December 6, 1973; August 14, 1975.

Casey, Clifford B., Alpine, Texas. Letter to author, February 21, 1973.

Collins, Bill M., Head, Concession Management and Contracts Section, Texas Parks and Wildlife Department. Letters to author: May 23, 1973; August 16, 1973; November 6, 1973.

Hulett, Stanley W., Associate Director, National Park Service. Letters to author: April 4, 1973; May 4, 1973.

Maxwell, Ross A., Austin, Texas. Letters to author: October 2, 1972; May 17, 1973; August 6, 1973.

Morris, Robert C., Acting Superintendent, Big Bend National Park. Letter to author, April 4, 1973.

Newell, W. J., Alpine, Texas. Letters to author: April 26, 1973; May 29, 1974; December 5, 1974.

Sutton, Myron D., Acting Chief, Division of International Park Affairs, National Park Service. Letter to author, May 24, 1974.

Torrey, Charles P., Director, Office of Mexican Affairs, Department of State. Letter to author, May 15, 1974.

Wear, Robert, Arlington, Texas. Letters to author: July 8, 1972; July 27, 1972.

Wilson, Caroline C., Park Technician, Big Bend National Park. Letters to author: August 19, 1973; September 14, 1973.

INTERVIEWS AND ORAL HISTORIES

Maxwell, Ross A. Interview with author. Austin, Texas, December 21, 1972.

Olivas, Ramón. Interview with author. Big Bend National Park, Texas, June 5, 1991.

Smith, Maggie. National Park Service Oral History Interview, Big Bend National Park, Texas, no date.

Tyler, Ronnie C., Curator of History, Amon Carter Museum. Interview with
    author. Fort Worth, Texas, October 10, 1973.
Wear, Robert. Interview with author. Arlington, Texas, September 21, 1972.

DOCUMENTS

Congressional Record. Vols. 42, 47, 52, 55, 65, 67, 71, 74, 79. Washington, D.C.
Journal of the Senate of Texas, 1931; 1933; 1939.
United States Statutes at Large. Vols. 49, 63, 67, 77, 78. Washington, D.C.
Vernon's Texas Statutes, 1948.

Secondary Materials

ARTICLES, CHAPTERS IN BOOKS, AND OTHER SOURCES

Alexander, Shana. "Lady Bird's Boat Ride." *Life* 60 (April 15, 1966): 34.
*An Alternative to the Master Plan and Wilderness Proposal for Big Bend National
    Park.* Temple, Tex.: Americans Backing Better Park Development, 1972.
Anderson, James G. "Land Acquisition in the Big Bend National Park of
    Texas." M.A. thesis, Sul Ross State University, 1967.
Bentley, Max. "Big Bend Park: Regional Executive Gets His First Look,
    Views It as 'Utterly Different' Among National Parks." *West Texas Today*
    (October 1940): 6–7.
"Big Bend, A Texas Wonderland Is the Country's Newest National Park." *Life*
    39 (September 3, 1945): 68–73.
"Big Bend Is a National Park." *Parade* (March 28, 1948): 19–21.
Big Bend Natural History Association. *Amphibians and Reptiles Checklist.* Big
    Bend National Park, Texas, 1989.
———. *Archaeology Brochure.* Big Bend National Park, Texas, 1990.
———. *Bird Checklist.* Big Bend National Park, Texas, revised 1988.
———. *Blue Creek Fire.* Big Bend National Park, Texas, 1989.
———. *Geology Brochure.* Big Bend National Park, Texas, 1989.
———. *Guide to the Backcountry Roads and the River: Big Bend National Park.*
    Big Bend National Park, Texas, 1970.
———. *Hiker's Guide to the Developed Trails and Primitive Routes: Big Bend
    National Park.* Big Bend National Park, Texas, 1971.
———. *Mammal Checklist.* Big Bend National Park, Texas, 1989.
———. *Road Guide to the Paved and Improved Dirt Roads: Big Bend National
    Park.* Big Bend National Park, Texas, 1969.

"Border Would Disappear at U.S.-Mexican Park." *National Geographic* 179 (February 1991): 140.

Brown, William E., and Roland Wauer, with the assistance of Roy E. Appleman and Benjamin Levy. *Historic Resources Management Plan: Big Bend National Park*. Washington, D.C.: Department of the Interior/National Park Service, 1968.

Burgess, Glenn. "The Big Bend Deed is Passed." *West Texas Today* (September 1943): 6, 20.

Casey, Clifford B., "The Big Bend National Park." *West Texas Historical and Scientific Society Publication* No. 13 (1948).

―――. *Soldiers, Ranchers and Miners in the Big Bend*. Washington, D.C.: Department of the Interior/National Park Service, 1969.

―――, and Lewis H. Saxton. "The Life of Everett Ewing Townsend." *West Texas Historical and Scientific Society Publication* No. 17 (1958).

Cole, John N. "The Return of the Coyote." *Harper's Magazine* (May 1973): 48–51.

Coltun, Frances. "Let's Travel: With Mrs. LBJ to Big Bend." *Mademoiselle* 63 (July 1966): 26, 28, 30.

Connelly, Harry. "Big Bend National Park Project Reality at Last." *West Texas Today* (September 1941).

Decisions of the United States Board of Geographical Names: Decisions Rendered Between July 1, 1938 and June 30, 1939. Washington, D.C.: Government Printing Office, 1939.

Department of the Interior. *Annual Reports of the Secretary of the Interior, for the Fiscal Years Ended June 30, 1933, 1934, 1935*. Washington, D.C.: Government Printing Office, 1933, 1934, 1935.

Department of the Interior/National Park Service. *Big Bend National Park: Final Environmental Statement; Proposed Wilderness Classification*. Washington, D.C.: Department of the Interior/National Park Service, 1975.

―――. *Big Bend National Park: Statement for Management*. Washington, D.C.: Department of the Interior/National Park Service, 1981; 1986; 1992.

―――. *Big Bend National Park Master Plan*. Washington, D.C.: Department of the Interior/National Park Service, 1975.

―――. *Big Bend National Park Master Plan: Preliminary Draft*. Washington, D.C.: Department of the Interior/National Park Service, 1971.

―――. *Part One of the National Park System Plan: History*. Washington, D.C.: Department of the Interior/National Park Service, 1972.

―――. *Part Two of the National Park System Plan: Natural History*. Washington, D.C.: Department of the Interior/National Park Service, 1972.

————. *Wilderness Recommendation: Big Bend National Park, Texas*. Washington, D.C.: Department of the Interior/National Park Service, 1973.

————. *Wilderness Study: Big Bend National Park*. Washington, D.C.: Department of the Interior/National Park Service, 1971.

Dobie, J. Frank. "A Texan Part of Texas." *Nature* (December 1930): 343–346.

Edwards, Cas. "Needed: A Good Dam." *Texas Game and Fish* (May 1945): 4–5.

Environmental Assessment: Fire Management Program Big Bend National Park. BBNP: Division of Science and Resource Management, 1993.

Fabry, Judith K. *Guadalupe Mountains National Park: An Administrative History*. Santa Fe: Department of the Interior/National Park Service, 1990.

"The First Lady: Home on the Range." *Time* (April 8, 1966): 26–27.

Fleming, Carl M., W. Philip Koepp, and David W. Corrick, preparers. *Environmental Assessment for Construction of a New Office Building and Parking Area to House Big Bend Natural History Association Operations in the Panther Junction Developed Area of Big Bend National Park*. BBNP: Division of Science and Resource Management, 1994.

Flores, Dan. "The Grand Canyon of Texas: How Palo Duro Just Missed Becoming Texas's Third Great National Park." *Texas Parks and Wildlife* (September 1993): 4–15.

Foree, Kenneth, Jr. "Our New National Park on the Rio Grande." *Saturday Evening Post* (December 2, 1944): 26–27, 106.

Gard, Wayne. "Where the Mountains Meet: The Big Bend Today." *Southwest Review* 26 (Winter 1941): 203–210.

George, Jean. "What's Ahead for Our National Parks?" *National Wildlife* 10 (February–March 1972): 36–41.

Hardy, Jean. "Two Nations, One Land." *Texas Parks and Wildlife* (April 1994): 26–33.

Harrigan, Stephen. "Wild Forever: A Sneak Preview of Big Bend Ranch, Texas' Rugged New Parkland." *Texas Monthly* (December 1989): 98–109, 152, 154.

Harris, Jodie P. "Protecting the Big Bend—A Guardsman's View." *Southwestern Historical Quarterly* 78 (January 1975): 292–302.

Hearings before a Subcommittee of the Committee on Appropriations, House of Representatives, 93d Cong., 1st sess., Part II; Department of the Interior and Related Agencies Appropriations for 1974. Washington, D.C.: Government Printing Office, 1973.

Hill, Robert T. "Dabs of Related Geology, Geography and History along the Southwestern Border Region of the United States and Adjacent Mexico." *Texas Geographic* 1 (May 1937): 26–34.

————. "Running the Cañons of the Rio Grande: A Chapter of Recent Exploration." *Century Magazine* 61 (January 1901): 371–387.

Hope, Jack. "Big Bend: A Nice Place to Visit." *Audubon* 75 (July 1973): 36–49.

Ironside, R. G. "Private Development in National Parks: Residential and Commercial Facilities in the National Parks of North America." *Town Planning Review* 16 (October 1970): 305–316.

Jameson, John. "From Dude Ranches to Haciendas: Master Planning at Big Bend National Park, Texas." *Forest and Conservation History* 38 (July 1994): 108–117.

————. "An International Peace Park on the Rio Grande: A Study of Cultural Differences." In *The American West: Essays in Honor of W. Eugene Hollon,* edited by Ronald Lora. Toledo, Ohio: University of Toledo Press, 1980.

————. "The National Park System in the United States: An Overview with a Survey of Selected Government Documents and Archival Materials." *Government Publications Review* 7A (1980): 145–158.

————. "The Quest for a National Park in Texas." *West Texas Historical Association Year Book* 50 (1974): 47–60.

————. "Walter Prescott Webb, Public Historian." *Public Historian* 7 (Spring 1985): 47–60.

Kenney, Nathaniel T. "Big Bend: Jewel in the Texas Desert." *National Geographic* 133 (January 1968): 104–133.

————. "Our Wild and Scenic Rivers: The Rio Grande." *National Geographic* 152 (July 1977): 46–51.

Lagemann, John Kord. "Beauty on a Bend." *Collier's* 121 (January 31, 1948): 13–15, 67–68.

Lawson, William J., and Will Mann Richardson. "The Texas State Park System: A History, Study of Development and Plans for the Future of the Texas State Parks." *Texas Geographic* 2 (December 1938): 1–12.

Long, George W. "Many Splendored Glacierland." *National Geographic* 119 (May 1956): 589–636.

Martinson, Arthur D. "Mountain in the Sky: A History of Mount Rainier National Park." Ph.D. diss., Washington State University, 1966.

McCloskey, Michael. "The Wilderness Act of 1964: Its Background and Meaning." *Oregon Law Review* 45 (1966): 288–321.

Mitchell, John G. "Our National Parks: Legacy at Risk." *National Geographic* 186 (October 1994): 2–55.

Nash, Roderick. "The American Invention of National Parks." *American Quarterly* 22 (Fall 1970): 726–735.

"National Parks and Conservation Association News: Views Threatened at Two National Parks." *National Parks* (November/December 1994): 10–11.

"News Update." *National Parks* (January/February 1995): 13.

Paige, John C. *The Civilian Conservation Corps and the National Park Service, 1933–1942: An Administrative History*. Washington, D.C.: Department of the Interior/National Park Service, 1985.

Parent, Laurence. "Mountains Across the River." *Texas Parks and Wildlife* (April 1990): 4–11.

"Roger Toll Obituary." *Trail and Timberline* 209 (March–April 1936): 27–28.

Roth, Daniel L. "Mexican and American Policy Alternatives in the Big Bend Region: An Updated Study of the Proposed Mexican National Park in the Sierra del Carmen." Professional Report, Master of Public Affairs, University of Texas at Austin, 1992.

Schoffelmayer, Victor H. "The Big Bend Area of Texas." *Texas Geographic* 1 (May 1937): 1–25.

Simpich, Frederick. "Down the Rio Grande: Taming This Strange, Turbulent Stream on Its Long Course from Colorado to the Gulf of Mexico." *National Geographic* 76 (October 1939): 415–454.

Steffens, Ron. "Bridging the Border." *National Parks* 68 (July/August 1994): 36–41.

Strong, Douglas Hillman. "A History of Sequoia National Park." Ph.D. diss., Syracuse University, 1964.

Swain, Donald C. "The National Park Service and the New Deal, 1933–1940." *Pacific Historical Review* 41 (August 1972): 312–332.

Texas Parks and Wildlife Department, Public Lands Division. *Big Bend Ranch State Natural Area: Planning Document Draft*. Austin: Texas Parks and Wildlife Department, 1992.

Thompson, Roger C. "The Doctrine of Wilderness: A Study of the Policy and Politics of the Adirondack Preserve Park." Ph.D. diss., Syracuse University, 1961.

Tillotson, Minor R. "Newest National Park—Big Bend." *National Motorist* (June 1945): 10, 17–18.

Tyler, Ronnie C. "Robert T. Hill and the Big Bend: An 1899 Expedition That Helped Establish a Great National Park." *American West* 10 (September 1973): 36–43.

———, ed. "Exploring the Rio Grande: Lt. Duff C. Green's Report of 1852." *Arizona and the West* 10 (Spring 1968): 43–60.

Utley, Robert. "The Range Cattle Industry in the Big Bend of Texas." *Southwestern Historical Quarterly* 49 (April 1966): 419–441.

Wagstaff, R. M. "Beginnings of the Big Bend Park." *West Texas Historical Association Year Book* 44 (October 1968): 3–14.

Wear, Robert. "Where the Pavement Ends." *Texas Star* (May 21, 1972): 8–9.

Williams, Pete. "The Big Bend." *Sparks* (January 1944): 5.

Williams, Rosemary. "Tops in Texas." *Texas Highways* 39 (July 1992): 12–17.

Wirth, Conrad. "The Mission Called 66." *National Geographic* 130 (July 1966): 6–47.

Woods, Dee. "The Dusty River Region." *South* (December 1946): 11, 23, 26.

BOOKS

Alexander, Nancy. *Father of Texas Geology: Robert T. Hill.* Dallas: Southern Methodist University Press, 1976.

Bartlett, Richard A. *Yellowstone: A Wilderness Besieged.* Tucson: University of Arizona Press, 1985.

Bernstein, Marvin D. *The Mexican Mining Industry, 1890–1950.* Albany: State University of New York, 1964.

Campbell, Carlos C. *Birth of a National Park in the Great Smoky Mountains.* Knoxville: University of Tennessee Press, 1960.

Carey, Alan and Sandy. *Yellowstone's Red Summer.* Flagstaff, Ariz.: Northland Publishing, 1989.

Casey, Robert J. *The Texas Border and Some Borderliners: A Chronicle and a Guide.* Indianapolis: The Bobbs-Merrill Company, Inc., 1950.

Chase, Alton. *Playing God in Yellowstone: The Destruction of America's First National Park.* New York: Harcourt, Brace Jovanovich, 1986.

Collinson, Frank. *Life in the Saddle.* Edited and arranged by Mary Whatley Clarke. Norman: University of Oklahoma Press, 1963.

Connally, Eugenia Horstman, ed. *National Parks in Crisis.* Washington, D.C.: National Parks and Conservation Association, 1982.

The Conservation Foundation. *National Parks for a New Generation: Visions, Realities, Prospects.* Washington, D.C.: The Conservation Foundation, 1985.

———. *National Parks for the Future.* Washington, D.C.: The Conservation Foundation, 1972.

Darling, F. Fraser, and Noel D. Eishhorn. *Man and Nature in the National Parks.* 2d ed. Washington, D.C.: The Conservation Foundation, 1969.

Dilsaver, Lary M., and William C. Tweed. *Challenge of the Big Trees: A Resource History of Sequoia and Kings Canyon National Parks.* Three Rivers, Calif.: Sequoia Natural History Association, Inc., 1990.

Dobie, J. Frank. *The Longhorns.* New York: Bramhall House, 1941.

Doughty, Robin W. *Wildlife and Man in Texas: Environmental Change and Conservation*. College Station: Texas A&M University Press, 1983.

Douglas, William O. *Farewell to Texas: A Vanishing Wilderness*. New York: McGraw-Hill Book Company, 1967.

Dugger, Ronnie, ed. *Three Men in Texas: Bedichek, Webb, and Dobie. Essays by Their Friends in the Texas Observer*. Austin: University of Texas Press, 1967.

Everhart, William C. *The National Park Service*. Rev. ed. New York: Praeger Publishers, 1983.

Foresta, Ronald A. *America's National Parks and Their Keepers*. Washington, D.C.: Resources for the Future, 1984.

Gomez, Arthur R. *A Most Singular Country: A History of Occupation in the Big Bend*. Provo: Brigham Young University Press, 1990.

Hampton, H. Duane. *How the U.S. Cavalry Saved Our National Parks*. Bloomington: Indiana University Press, 1971.

Hartzog, George B., Jr. *Battling for the National Parks*. Mt. Kisco, N.Y.: Moyer Bell Limited, 1988.

Horgan, Paul. *Great River: The Rio Grande in North American History*. New York: Rinehart and Company, Inc., 1954.

Ise, John. *Our National Park Policy: A Critical History*. Baltimore: Johns Hopkins Press, 1961.

Jameson, John R. *Big Bend National Park: The Formative Years*. El Paso: Texas Western Press, 1980.

Langford, J. O. *Big Bend: A Homesteader's Story*. Austin: University of Texas Press, 1955.

Machado, Manuel A., Jr. *The North Mexican Cattle Industry, 1910–1975: Ideology, Conflict, and Change*. College Station: Texas A&M University Press, 1981.

Machlis, Gary E., and David L. Tichnell. *The State of the World's Parks: An International Assessment for Resource Management, Policy, and Research*. Boulder, Col.: Westview Press, 1985.

Madison, Virginia. *The Big Bend Country of Texas*. 2d ed. New York: October House, Inc., 1968.

———, and Hallie Stillwell. *How Come It's Called That? Place Names in the Big Bend Country*. Rev. ed. New York: October House, Inc., 1968.

Marquis, A. N., ed. *Who's Who in America, 1936–1937*. Chicago: A. N. Marquis, Inc., 1936.

Maxwell, Ross A. *Big Bend Country: A History of Big Bend National Park*. Big Bend National Park: Big Bend Natural History Association, 1985.

———. *The Big Bend of the Rio Grande: A Guide to the Rocks, Geologic His-*

tory, and Settlers of the Area of Big Bend National Park. Austin: University of Texas, Guidebook 7, Bureau of Economic Geology, 1968.

————, John T. Lonsdale, Roy T. Hazzard, and John A. Wilson. *Geology of Big Bend National Park, Brewster County, Texas*. Austin: University of Texas, Publication No. 6711, Bureau of Economic Geology, 1967.

McCloskey, Maxine E., ed. *Wilderness the Edge of Knowledge*. New York: Sierra Club, 1970.

————, and James P. Gilligan, eds. *Wilderness and the Quality of Life*. New York: Sierra Club, 1969.

McMurtry, Larry. *In a Narrow Grave: Essays on Texas*. New York: Simon and Schuster, 1968.

Nash, Roderick. *The American Environment: Readings in the History of Conservation*. Reading, Mass.: Addison-Wesley Publishing Company, 1968.

————. *Wilderness and the American Mind*. Rev. ed. New Haven: Yale University Press, 1982.

National Parks and Conservation Association. *National Parks: From Vignettes to a Global View*. Washington, D.C.: National Parks and Conservation Association, 1989.

————. *Parks in Peril: The Race Against Time Continues*. Washington, D.C.: National Parks and Conservation Association, 1992.

Nixon, Edgar B., ed. *Franklin D. Roosevelt and Conservation, 1911–1945*. 2 vols. Washington, D.C.: Government Printing Office, 1957.

Porter, Eliot. *"In Wildness Is the Preservation of the World."* New York: Ballantine Books, 1967.

Pyne, Stephen J. *Fire in America*. Princeton: Princeton University Press, 1982.

Ragsdale, Kenneth Baxter. *Wings Over the Mexican Border: Pioneer Military Aviation in the Big Bend*. Austin: University of Texas Press, 1984.

Raht, Carlysle Graham. *The Romance of the Davis Mountains and Big Bend Country: A History*. El Paso: The Rahtbook Company, 1919.

Righter, Robert W. *Crucible for Conservation: The Creation of Grand Teton National Park*. Denver: Colorado Associated University Press, 1982.

Rothman, Hal. *Preserving Different Pasts: The American National Monuments*. Urbana: University of Illinois Press, 1989.

Runte, Alfred. *National Parks: The American Experience*. Rev. ed. Lincoln: University of Nebraska Press, 1987.

————. *Yosemite: The Embattled Wilderness*. Lincoln: University of Nebraska Press, 1990.

Salmond, John. *The Civilian Conservation Corps, 1933–1942: A New Deal Case Study*. Durham: Duke University Press, 1967.

Schmidly, David J. *The Mammals of Trans-Pecos Texas*. College Station: Texas A&M University Press, 1977.

Shankland, Robert. *Steve Mather of the National Parks*. 3d ed. New York: Alfred A. Knopf, 1970.

Shipman, O. L. *Taming of the Big Bend*. Marfa, Tex.: (privately published), 1926.

Smith, Duane A. *Mesa Verde National Park: Shadows of the Centuries*. Lawrence: University Press of Kansas, 1988.

Smithers, W. D. *Chronicles of the Big Bend: A Photographic Memoir of Life on the Border*. Austin: Madrona Press, Inc., 1976.

Steely, James, and Joseph Monticone. *The Civilian Conservation Corps in Texas State Parks*. Austin: Texas Parks and Wildlife Department, 1986.

Swain, Donald. *Wilderness Defender: Horace M. Albright and Conservation*. Chicago: University of Chicago Press, 1970.

Tebeau, Charlton W. *Man in the Everglades: 2000 Years of Human History in the Everglades National Park*. Coral Gables, Fla.: University of Miami Press, 1968.

Tyler, Ronnie C. *The Big Bend: A History of the Last Texas Frontier*. Washington, D.C.: Department of the Interior/National Park Service, 1975.

Vogt, William. *Road to Survival*. New York: William Sloane Associates, Inc., 1948.

Warnock, Barton H. *Wildflowers of the Big Bend Country, Texas*. Alpine, Tex.: Sul Ross State University, 1970.

Wauer, Roland H. *Naturalist's Big Bend*. College Station: Texas A&M University Press, 1973.

Webb, Walter Prescott. *The Great Plains*. Boston: Ginn and Company, 1931.

———. *An Honest Preface and Other Essays*. Boston: Houghton Mifflin, 1959.

———. *The Texas Rangers: A Century of Frontier Defense*. 2d ed. Austin: University of Texas Press, 1980.

Weintraub, Sidney. *A Marriage of Convenience: Relations Between Mexico and the United States*. New York: Oxford University Press, 1990.

Wirth, Conrad L. *Parks, Politics, and the People*. Norman: University of Oklahoma Press, 1980.

Work Projects Administration. *Texas: A Guide to the Lone Star State* (Work Projects Administration Writers' Program). New York: Hastings House, 1940.

INDEX

(Illustrations are in *italics*)

Abilene, Texas, 23
Adams, Dom, 36
Addams, Jane, 104
Africa, 145
agave (Century Plant), *9*
Agriculture, U.S. Department of, 18, 100
Alaska, 58, 71
Alberta, province of (Canada), 103
Albright, Horace M.: opposed to establishment of inferior parks, 19–20; origins of his aestheticism, 150n.54
Alexander, John, 124
Allred, James V., 31–32, 33, 34, 35, 36, 38, 39, 64
Alpine, Texas, 24, 25, 30, 31, 38, 47, 57, 81, 96, 106, 121, 122, 124, 125, 126, 127, 128, 129, 137, 163n.29
Alpine Avalanche, 66, 95
Alpine Chamber of Commerce, 36–37, 103, 118

Alps, 57
Alto Frio Canyon National Park (proposed), 19
Alvino House, 145
Amarillo, Texas, 18
American Airlines Electra, 5
American Club, 117
Amistad National Recreation Area, 163n.29
Apache Indians, 11, 54; creation legend, 12; firefighters, 99
Appalachian Mountains, 142
Argentina, 71
Arizona, 26, 57, 95, 103
Arizona cypress, 10
Arkell, Andy, 146
Arnberger, Robert, 69, 95, 141–142, 144
arroyo, *131*
Asia, 57
Atomic Energy Commission, 77
Austin, Texas, 22, 48
Avila Camacho, Miguel, 111–112

Babbitt, Bruce, 142
badgers, 10
Banta Shut-In, 73
Bassett, C. H., 38
Bean, Judge Roy, 72
Beaumont, Texas, 38
beavers, 10
Bell, W. B., *114*
Big Bend (boat), 55, *56*
Big Bend Country, xiii, 3, 7, 8–9, 22;
    first humans in, 11; first mammals
    in, 14
Big Bend gambusia (fish), 11, 95
Big Bend International Park (proposed),
    47; Dorgan's "Friendly Nations
    Park," 70–71; first proposed by E. E.
    Townsend, 27; historical develop-
    ments, 102–120; negative impact of
    appropriation veto on, 35; President
    Roosevelt's support, 62; visit of Inter-
    national Commission, 106–107, 109,
    110, 111, 114
Big Bend Land Department, 47
Big Bend Museum building, *98, 99*
Big Bend National Park, xiii, xiv, xv; air
    pollution at, 141–142; appropriation
    for, 32–33, 34, 35–36, 40–43; astro-
    nauts' visit, 14; the "Bloody Bend"
    (violence at), 131, 133, 172n.7; cam-
    paign for Texas' first national park,
    17–30; canine corps at, 136; care of
    cultural resources at, 143; CCC camp,
    27, *28*, 37–38; climate, 10; concession
    franchise at, 77–78; court injunction
    against, 47–48; difficulty filling jobs
    at, 123–124; dinosaurs, 12; Dorgan's
    "Friendly Nations Park, "70–71;
    economic arguments for, 32, 33–34,
    62–63, 69, 78–79, 82, 160n.39; elec-
    tricity, 127; employee morale at, 123–
    124, 137– 138; erosion, 15; fire dan-
    gers and policies, 99–101; flash floods
    at, 129–130; fluctuating visitation,
    77–78, 149n.15; frontier conditions
    at, 126–127; geological overview, 11–
    12; greatest challenges yet at, 145–

146; horse concession at, 82, 164n.32;
    illegal immigration at, 136–137; in-
    adequate budget at, 143; increasing
    ranger work loads, 143–144; Lady
    Bird Johnson's visit, 3–7, 131, 133;
    land acquisition, 27–29, 43, 45–52;
    law enforcement at, 133, 136–137;
    legislation, 9; longhorn cattle and
    dude ranch, 72–74, 161n.12, 161–
    162n.13; Maier report, 27–28; man-
    aging natural resources, 85–101;
    medical services and facilities at,
    124–126; mineral rights controversy,
    28, 32, 33, 34, 40; Mission 66 (master
    plan), 79, 130; natural, historic, and
    cultural resources stable, 79; place
    names at, 128–129; planning, 27, 70–
    84; planning for international park,
    74–75; politics and park move-
    ment, 31–44; postal service at, 127;
    protection of endangered species, 95–
    96; publicity, 53–69; radio, tele-
    phone, and telegraph, 127–128; repa-
    triation of species, 94–95; Roosevelt's
    support, 41, 62; schools at, 126; tec-
    tonic forces, 12, 14; Toll report, 26,
    27; transfer of title, 43–44; trespass-
    ing livestock, 96–99; vandalism at,
    40–41, *41;* varieties of species, 10–
    11; visitor activities, 15; volcanoes,
    14–15; Volunteers-in-Parks program
    at, 144–145; wilderness classification,
    79, 81–82; wildlife survey, 27
Big Bend National Parks Development
    Committee, 81, 82, 163n.29
Big Bend Natural History Association
    (BBNHA), 95, 138
Big Bend Ranch State Natural Area,
    83–84, 119
Big Bend Regional Medical Center (Al-
    pine), 125
Big Bend State Park: campaign for, 22–
    25; CCC camp in, 25; called Texas
    Canyons State Park, 23; managing
    natural resources, 85–86; water dis-
    covered in Basin, 27

Big Bend Telephone Company, 128
bighorn sheep, 85, 94, 104–105
Biological Survey, U.S., *114*
black bears, 58, 87, 93, 94, 95, 105, 118
Black-capped Vireo, 11, 95
Black Gap Wildlife Management Area, 119
Blair, William, 6–7
bluebonnets, 10
blue catfish, 10
Blue Creek, 99
bobcats, 10, 87
Bolson tortoise, 94
Bolton, Herbert, 61–62
Bonham, Texas, 38
Boot Spring, *124*
Boquillas Canyon, 20, *22*, 46, 50, 105, 106, 129
Boquillas, Mexico, 75, 100, 102, 106, 107, *107, 114*, 118, 125, 127, *129, 131*, 136–137, *140*
Boquillas-San Isidro "highway," *110*
Border Patrol, U.S., 54, 125, 128, 136
Boston, Massachusetts, 89
Brazos River, 62
Brewster County, Texas, 9–10, 20, 60, 67, 86, 90, 123, 124
Brewster County Chamber of Commerce, 25, 36–37
Briscoe, Dolph, 117
Briscoe, Mason, 117
Brown, Rollo Walter, 64
Brownsville, Texas, 54
Brownwood, Texas, 38
Buchanan Dam, 62
buffalo, 73
Bureau of Animal Industry, U.S., 98
Bureau of Reclamation, U.S., 111
burros, feral, 7, 96

cacti, 10–11, 95–96
California, 61, 62, 105, 142
Cammerer, Arno B., 26–27, 32–33, 35, 63, 104, 109, 111
Canada, 142, 145
candelilla plants, 51, 60

candelilla wax, 7, 122
Canyon Wrens, 7
Carbon I plant, 141, 142
Carbon II plant, 141
Carithers, Joe, 102, 133, 136
Carlsbad Caverns National Park, 34
Carmel Mountains, 107
Carpenter, John W., 38
Carpenter, Liz, 3–4, 7
Carrico, Joe, 68–69, 84
Carter, Amon, 38–39, 40, 42, 44, 47, 48, 171n.14
Carter Peak, 129, 171n.14
Casa Grande, *77, 80, 115, 135*
Casner, James E., 31, 36
Castolon, 49, 50–51, 70, 81, 106, 127, 128, 130, 136
Castolon Historic District, 11
Castolon store, *10*
Cauthorn, Albert R., 42
Ceniza Flat, 82
Century Magazine, 9, 23
chamosaurus, 12
Channel Islands, 72
Cheri, Kevin, 100
Cherokee Indians, 142
Chicago, Illinois, 104
Chihuahua, Mexico, 111, *114*, 118
Chihuahua, state of (Mexico), 103, 104, 112, 113, 116–117, 118
Chihuahuan Desert, 10, 11, 60, 106, 141, 146
Chihuahuan Desert Research Institute, 96
Chillicothe, Texas, 47
Chisos Basin, *xii*, 6, *28*, 75, 76, *77, 80*, 81, 82, 83, 93, 94, 106, *115*, 126, 127, 130, 133, *135*
Chisos Basin Loop Trail, 93
Chisos Basin "Window," *xii*, xiv, 72, 106
Chisos Indians, 11, 146
Chisos Mountains, *xii*, xiv, *2, 7–8, 9*, 14, 20, *21*, 46, 57, 58, *59*, 60, 64, 73, 75, 81, 86, 94, 99, 101, 106, *108, 124, 129, 132*

Cinco de Mayo (boat), 55, *56*
Civilian Conservation Corps (CCC), 19,
    25, *28*, 37–38, 76, 106, 126
Civil War, U.S., 54, 87
claret cup cactus, 10
Clark, Nolan, 65–66
Clements, William, 118
Cliff Swallows, 10
Coahuila, state of (Mexico), 7, 75, 103,
    104, 112, 114, *114*, 116–117, 118,
    119, 141
Coast Guard, U.S., 55, 56
Cold War, 117–118
Colima Warbler, 10, 58, 85
Collier's, 66
Collinson, Frank, 7
Colombia, 136
Colorado, 34, 62
Colp, D. E., 21, 103
Comanche Indians, 11
Commission for Environmental Coop-
    eration, 142
Connally, Tom, 116; sponsored Big
    Bend legislation in U.S. Senate, 29
Cook, John E., 95, 102
Cooper, William, Jr., 126
Cooperative Club, 68
copperheads, 10
Coronado, 62
Coronado Memorial, 103
cottontail rabbits, 10
coyotes, 10, 87, 91, 92, 93
creosote bushes, *59*
Cumbres de Majalca National Park
    (Mexico), 112
Customs Service, U.S., 125

Dagger Flats, *67*
Dallas, Texas, xiii, 5, 34, 38, 61, *77*
"Dallas Huts," *77*, *133*
Daniels, Josephus, 35, 104
Daniels and Graham Ranch, 75, 76
Daughters of the American Revolution,
    68
Davis Mountains National Park (pro-
    posed), 19

D-Day landings, 111
Dead Horse Canyon, 129
Dead Horse Mountains, xiv, 46
Dead Man Curve, 130
deer, 10, 96, *97*
Del Rio, Texas, 81
Demaray, Arthur, 40, 89–90
Deming, New Mexico, *109, 114*
Denton, Texas, 38
Denver Service Center (NPS), 75, 79, 81
Desert of the Lions National Park
    (Mexico), 105
Dia de los Reyes (Epiphany or Twelfth
    Night Party), 169–170n.34
dinosaurs, 12
Disney, Walt, 71
Dobie, J. Frank, 22, 23–24, *24*, 61, 74,
    88–89
Doran, Hilary, Jr., 81
Dorgan, Albert W., xiv–xv, 70–71, 72,
    84, 103, 116
Douglas fir, 10
drooping juniper, 10, 58
Drug Enforcement Agency, U.S., 136
Drury, Newton B., 43, 48–49, 66, 74,
    75, 76, 92, 111–112, 113

Eisenhower, Dwight D., 44, 79
El Chico National Park (Mexico), 105
El Paso, Texas, xiv, 9, 17, 20, 25, 29, 38,
    54, 63, 105, 111
El Paso Daily Times, 17, 64
endangered species, 11
Environmental Protection Agency,
    U.S., 142
Epcot Center, 71
Ernst Gap, 130
Estufa Fire, 100
Europe, 57
Everglades National Park, 20, 46

Ferguson, Miriam, 24
Field and Stream, 102
Fish and Wildlife Service, U.S., 92,
    95, 115
fishing, *14*

Florida, 20, 61
Foree, Kenneth, 66–67
Forest Service, U.S., 105
Forsythe, John, 141–142
Fort Davis, Texas, 3
Fort Davis National Historic Site,
   163n.29
Fort Stockton, Texas, 25, 30, 136
Fort Worth, Texas, 34, 38, 63
Fort Worth Star-Telegram, 34, 36, 38, 63
foxes (gray and kit), 10
France, 44
Frome, Michael, 102

Galicia, Daniel, 105, *109*, 111, *114*
Galveston, Texas, 38
General Management Plan, 138
Geological Survey, U.S., 61
Giant Dagger, *67*
Glenn Springs, 131, *136*
goats, feral, 96
Golden Eagles, 10, 87, 88
Gonzales, Miguel L., *114*, 116
Goodwill Ambassadors, 119
Grand Canyon, 26, 57
Grand Canyon National Park, xiv, 18,
   143, 173n.11
Grand Teton National Park, 63
Great Smoky Mountains National Park,
   62, 142–143
Green Gulch, 5–6
Greenville, Texas, 43, 47
Green-winged Teals, 10
Guadalupe Mountains National Park,
   19, 20, 27, 163n.29
guayule plants, 50
Gulf of Mexico, 105

Hagan, William R., 55
Haley, J. Evetts, 25, *26*
Harris, Jodie P., 17
Harte Ranch, 50
Hawaii, 25
Hetch Hetchy controversy, 18
Hidalgo, state of (Mexico), 105
Hill, Reverend and Mrs. Milton, 64

Hill, Robert T., xv, 23, 54, 61; the
   Bloody Bend," 131; Rio Grande ex-
   pedition, 8–9, 18
hoof-and-mouth disease, 98, 116
Hot Springs, xiv, 121–123, 127
Hot Springs Historic District, 11
Houston, Texas, 38, 63
Howarth, George, 133, 136
Hudspeth, C. B., 20
Hull, Cordell, 104
Hull House, 104
Humble Oil and Refining Company, 32
Hunter, W. B., 48

Ibarra, Santo, *114*
Ickes, Harold, 27, 29, 31, 43, 44, 62–63,
   70, 103–104
Inks Dam, 62
Interior, U.S. Department of, 3, 18,
   32, 100
International Good Neighbor Day Fes-
   tival, 169n.34
International Parks Highway Associa-
   tion, 68
Interstate Highway System, 71
Isle Royale National Park, 46

jackrabbits, 10
Jaleaucillas, Mexico, *119*
Japan, 145
javelinas, 10
Jersey Lilly saloon, 72, *73*
Johnson, Lady Bird, xv, *2*, 61, 146; con-
   cern about snipers on float trip, 131,
   133; trip to park, 3–7
Johnson Ranch, Elmo, 106
Jones, Jesse H., 38
Jornado Mogollon Indians, 11
Josey, J. E., 38
Juárez, Ciudad, 111, 118, 120
"Judge Roy Bean" (dog), 136
Jumano Indians, 11
Juniper Canyon, 5

kangaroo rats, 10
Kentucky, 39

Kimsey, J. Edgar, 64
King, J. H., 47–48
King, John E., 38
Kings Canyon National Park, 30
Kiwanis, 68
Korean War, 117
KULF Radio Station, 128

Lajitas, Texas, 107
Lane, Joe, 54–55
Langford, J. O., 121
Langtry, Lily, 72
"Las Vegas Kim." *See* Kimsey, J. Edgar
lechuguilla plants, 10
leopard frogs, 10
Leptopinara fleminga, 148n.11
Life, 60, 66
Lions Club, 68
Literary Digest, 66
LoBello, Rick, 95
Local Park Committees, 36
long-nosed gars, 10
Lost Mine Trail, 5
Louisiana, 18
Love Field, 5
Lufkin Daily News, 64
Luna's Jacal, 11

Madera del Carmen Mountains, 118
Maier, Herbert, 32, 33, 35, 36, 105, 106,
    114; head of NPS study team for pro-
    posed Big Bend park, 27–29
Maine, 142
Mammoth Cave National Park, 39
Marathon, Texas, 122, 127, 129
Marfa, Texas, 25, 30, 36, 64, 122, 128
Mariscal anticline, 12
Mariscal Canyon, *4,* 6–7, *16,* 20, 46, 64,
    72, 105, 106, 131
Mariscal Mining District, 11
Mather, Stephen, 25, 61
Maxwell, Helen, 126
Maxwell, Ross, xv, 50, 57–58, 67, 76–
    77, 78, 85, 90–91, 92, 97, 112–113,
    121, 122, 123–124, *124, 125,* 127, 137

Mayes, Wendell, 38
McCamey, Texas, 54
McKay, Douglas, 72, 118
McKittrick Canyon National Park (pro-
    posed), 19
Medical Center Hospital (Odessa,
    Texas), 125
Mendoza Berrueto, Eliseo, 118
Mesa de Anguila, 14, 128
Metcalf, James A., 55
Mexican Biosphere Reserve, 118
Mexican Department of Agriculture,
    167n.9
Mexican Department of Forestry, Fish,
    and Game, 105, 111, 113, *114,* 116,
    167n.9
Mexican long-nose bat, 11, 95
Mexican nationals, 7, 122, 133
Mexican Revolution, 17, 131
Mexican Wolf Coalition of Texas, 94
Mexico City, 105, 111, *114,* 137
Midland, Texas, 81, 137
Mineral Wells, Texas, 17
Mission 66 (master plan), 79, 126, 130,
    132, 135, 145
Moffett, George, 47
Montana, 63, 103
Montezuma quail, 94
Moody, W. L., III, 38
Morelock, Horace, 36–37, *37,* 38, 47, 57
Morgan, R. D., 114
Mormons, 63
Morris, G. C., 43, 47
Moskey, George, 32–33
mountain lions, 10, 66, 86, 87, 90, 91,
    92–93, 105, 118
Mount Carmel, 109
Mount Rainier, 26
Mount Rainier National Park, 25
Mule Ear Peaks, *12,* 15

Nail, Sam, 86
Nash, Roderick, xiii–xiv, 145
National Audubon Society, 94
National Geographic, 61, 66, 86, 103

National Park Concessions, Inc., 77–78
National Park Service (NPS), xiv, 3,
    21–22, 25, 27, 31, 32, 37, 39, 42–43,
    46, 50–51, 61, 63, 71–72, 75, 82–83,
    86, 87, 91–92, 100, 103, 105, 111,
    118, 119–120, 121–122, 125, 127,
    130, 136; air pollution, 142; effect of
    North American Free Trade Agree-
    ment on fragile resources, 142; insuf-
    ficient funds for system, 142–143;
    problems facing system, 145–146
National Register sites, 11, 143
Nature Magazine, 22
Neff, Pat, 19
Ness, Howard, 120
Newbold, Bill, 5
New Deal, 62
Newell, Johnny, 81, 82
New Jersey, 137
New Mexico, 34, 95, 99, 103
Newsome, Carter "Buck," 81–82
New York, 60
New York Times, 6–7
Nobel Peace Prize, 104
North America, xiv
North Rosillos Mountains, 51
Northrup, Jim, 133
Northwestern University, 123

Oak Ridge, Tennessee, 77
ocotillo bushes, *59, 132*
O'Daniel, W. Lee, 39–42, 43, 62
Odessa, Texas, 125
Ohio, 46
Ohio River Valley, 142
Oklahoma, 18, 73
Oklahoma City, *114*
Olympic National Park, 30
Ordoney, Ben, *24*
Organ Pipe Cactus Monument, 103
oyster fossil, *11,* 12

Palo Duro Canyon National Park (pro-
    posed), 18, 19
Pan American Union, 113

Panther Junction, 75–76, 82, 100, 126,
    127, 130, *132,* 138, 145
Parade, 66
Parent Teachers Association, 36
Parque Nacional de la Gran Comba
    (proposed), 116–117
Pearson, Drew, 60
Pecos, Texas, 24
Peregrine Falcon, 11, 95, 96, 118
Perez, Carlos Villas, 117
Persimmon Gap, 50, 126, 145
Phillips, H. M., 90
Pichacho de las Vacas, *112*
Pierce, Richard H., 81
Pinchot, Gifford, 18, 105
Pine Canyon, 14
Pitcock Rosillos Mountain Ranch, 51
pocket gophers, 10
pocket mice, 10
Polvo, Texas, 131
Ponderosa pine, 10
Presidio, Texas, 131
Presidio County, Texas, 60
Presidio County Airport, 5
Presnall, Clifford C., 115–116
prickly poppies, 10
"Project Diablos," 75
pronghorn antelope, 88, 94
pterodactyl, 12

Quevedo, Manuel A. de, 105
quicksilver mine, *59*
Quinn, Frank, 154n.7

raccoons, 10
Rancho Estelle, 11
rattlesnakes, 10, 146
Rayburn, Sam, 35
Record, James, 36, 38
Red River, 18
Red River Improvement Association, 18
Regan, Ken, 24
Regional Marketing Plan for Southwest
    Texas and Adjacent Mexican Border,
    170n.34

Rhode Island, 9

Rio Grande, xiv, xv, 3, 9, *14*, 17, 20, 50, 54, 61, 68, 74, 75, 76, 77, 98, 99, 102, 105, 106, 107, 109, *110*, 111, 116, 118, 119, 131, 133, 136, 146, 148n.9

Rio Grande Electric Cooperative, 127

Rio Grande Village, 81, 82, 125, 127, 130, *134*

River Riders, 98

Roadrunners, 10

Roark, Alf, 34

rock-nettle, 10

Rocky Mountain National Park, 25, 34, 63

Rocky Mountains, 12

Roosevelt, Franklin D., 22, 29, 35, 44, 45, 62, 74, 102, 103, 104, 111–112

Roosevelt, Theodore, 105

Rosita Livestock Company, 117

Ross Maxwell Scenic Drive, 14–15

Rotary International, 68, 167n.3

Salinas de Gortari, Carlos, 118–119, 120

Saltillo, Mexico, 111, 118

San Angelo, Texas, 25, 48, 66

San Angelo Standard Times, 86

San Antonio, Texas, 38, 63, 117

San Antonio Express, 63, 64

San Carlos, Mexico, 107

San Francisco, California, 18

Santa Elena, Mexico, 125

Santa Elena Canyon, xiii, 7, 8, *13*, 20, 25, 46, 54, 55, 57–58, 64, 81, 105, 106, 128, 129

Santa Fe, New Mexico, 128

Santiago Mountains, 14

San Vicente, 127, 136

San Vicente anticline, 12

San Vicente School District, 126

Saturday Evening Post, 66–67

scorpions, 10

Secretaria del Desarrollo Urbano y Ecologia (SEDUE), 118

Secret Service, U.S., 132–133

See America First campaign, 3

Sheep and Goat Raisers Magazine, 86, 90

Shenandoah National Park, 36, 39

Sheppard, George H., 48

Sheppard, Morris, 18, 19, 35, 43; sponsored legislation in Senate, 29; wrote Roosevelt about parks at Big Bend, 29, 103

Shipman, Jimmie, 54

Sholly, George, 126

Sierra Club, 94

Sierra del Carmen Mountains, 7, 12, 22, 102, 113, 117, 118, *119*, *134*

Sierra del Carmen National Park (proposed), 111, 112

Sierra Madre Mountains, 12

Sierra Ponce, 14

Sierra Quemada, 14

Simpich, Frederick, 66

Skaggs, Thomas, 54, 55

Smith, Baylor, 121

Smith, Maggie, xiv, 121–123

Smith, Preston, 81

Smithers, W. D., 23, 25

Snelsen, W. E., 81

Society of American Foresters, 105

Sonora, Mexico, 103, 116–117

Sonora, Texas, 96

Southern Pacific Railroad, 64

South Rim, 57, 106, *108*

Southwestern National Monuments, 123

Spanish daggers (cactus), 66

Sparks, 66

Stark, Luther, 38

State, U.S. Department of, 29, 113, 116, 117, 118

Statement for Management, 137

Stephens, John H., 18

Sterling, Ross, 19

Stevenson, Coke, 24, 33–34, 43–44, 49, 57

Stillwell Crossing, 17

Stinson, Jeff, 42

Story, Isabelle F., 61, 67

sulphur dioxide gas, 141

Sul Ross State University, 23–24, 36–37, 57, 64, 96

Swift, Roy, 64
Swift, W. E., 64

tamarisks, 10
tarantulas, 10
Taylor, Gus, 38
Taylor, Mrs. M. A., 38
Tennessee, 62
Tennessee River Valley, 142
Terlingua, Texas, 59
Terlingua–Alpine road, 127
Terlingua Medics, 124–125
Texarkana, Texas, 18
Texas, University of, xiii, 22, 24, 53, 88, 123
Texas Air Control Board, 163n.29
Texas Big Bend Park Association, 38, 40, 42, 47, 48, 68
Texas Canyons State Park, 23
Texas Centennial celebrations, 34, 61
Texas Club in New York City, 68
Texas Congress of Parents and Teachers, 68
Texas Court of Civil Appeals, 48
Texas Department of Agriculture, 163n.29
Texas Department of Health, 126
Texas Federation of Garden Clubs, 68
Texas Federation of Women's Clubs, 18, 67–68
Texas General Land Office, 23
Texas Gulf Coast, 22
Texas Gulf Sulphur Company, 61
Texas Highway Department, 81, 163n.29
Texas Highways, 15
Texas Hill Country, 22
Texas Historical Commission, 163n.29
Texas Hotel Association, 68
Texas Industrial Commission, 163n.29
Texas Junior Chamber of Commerce, 68
Texas Land Commission, 60
Texas Legislature, 19, 22–24, 28, 31, 38, 50, 62, 83
Texas Livestock Sanitation Commission, 98

Texas National Park (proposed), 19, 20–22
Texas Parks and Wildlife Department, 58, 81, 83, 84
Texas Permanent School Fund, 28, 29, 32, 33, 34, 39, 40
Texas Press Association, 68
Texas Rangers, xiii, xiv, 7–8, 54
Texas Real Estate Club, 68
Texas Sheep and Goat Raisers Association, 89, 91–92
Texas State Attorney General's Office, 33
Texas State Board of Education, 32, 33
Texas State Parks Board, 19, 21, 28, 29, 34, 38, 41, 43, 46, 47, 48, 49, 50, 66, 103, 121, 123
Texas State Planning Commission, 33
Texas State Railroad Commission, 57
Texas State Teachers Association, 32
Texas Supreme Court, 48
Texas Tourist Development Agency, 81, 163n.29
Texas Water Quality Board, 163n.29
Texas Water Rights Commission, 163n.29
Texon, Texas, 64
thistles, 10
Thomason, Ewing, 29, 39, 48, 62
Thompson, E. O., 57
Thompson, Eugene, 47, 48
Thoreau, Henry David, 146
Throckmorton, Texas, 47
Tillotson, Minor, 43, 48, 57, 63, 72, 74, 76, 78, 113
Tisinger, Ben F., 32
Titanic, 55
Toll, Roger, xv, 57; biography, 25–26; with International Park Commission, 106, 107, 109–110, 109, 114, 171n.14; recommended Big Bend for national park, 25
Toll Peak, 129, 171n.14
Tolson, Hillory, 91, 117
Tornillo Creek bridge, 14, 132
Tornillo Flat, 73

Townsend, Everett E., xiv, 33, 46, 47, 54; accompanied Roger Toll, 25, *26;* assists legislative effort for state park, 23, 24–25; discovered water in Chisos Basin, 27; involved with land acquisition, 46, 47; led Governor Allred's party, 31; NPS lobbyist, 43; proposed international park, 27, 103; proposed park, 7–8; *Saturday Evening Post* article about, 67
Trans-Pecos region, 9–10, 62
Turkey Buzzards, 7
Turrentine, Mrs. Richard J., 38
Tuttle, W. B., 38
Tyler, Texas, 38, 63

Udall, Mrs. Stewart, 5, 7
Udall, Stewart, *2,* 3, 5, 7
United Nations Educational, Scientific, and Cultural Organization (UNESCO), 75
U.S. Highway 67 Association, 68
Utah, 63
Uvalde, Texas, 91, 117

Vasquez, Dennis, 144
Villa, Pancho, 109
Virginia, 39
Vogt, William, 113
Volunteers-in-Parks (VIPs), 144–145

Wagstaff, R. M.: leads legislative effort to establish Big Bend State Park, 22–25
Walden Pond, 146
Walker, Ronald H., 102
Walker, T. H., 23
Washington, D. C., 46
Waterton-Glacier International Peace Park, 58, 74, 103, 167n.3

Wauer, Roland, 94–95
Webb, Walter Prescott, xiv, xv, *56,* 61, 88; accompanied Texas Rangers, xiii; consultant for NPS, 53–57; first visit to Big Bend Country, xiii; float trip through Santa Elena Canyon, 54–57
Wegemann, Carroll, 57
Western Union, 148n.2
West-Tex Ambulance Service, 125
West Texas Historical and Scientific Society, 87
White-throated Swifts, 7
Wichita Falls, Texas, 18
Wichita Mountains Game Preserve, 73
Wilbur, Ray Lyman, 19
Williams, Ray, 91
Wilson, Homer, ranch site, 11
Wilson, Woodrow, 104
Winfield, H. L., 33, 34, 40, 50
Wirth, Conrad, 7, 29, 38, 76, 79, 105, 106, 109
wolf, Mexican (gray), 83, 85, 87, 88, 93, 94, 95
Wood, Major, 33
Woodul, Walter, 32–33
Woodville (Texas) *Booster,* 57
World War I, 17, 70, 87
World War II, 45, 47, 60, 68, 74, 85, 111
Wright, George, 109, 111, *114*
Wychgel, Adrian, 39
Wyoming, 63

Yellowstone National Park, xiv, xv, 17, 18, 25, 57, 63, 94, 100, *114*
Yosemite National Park, 18, 63

Zion National Park, 63
Zonta Club, 68